# NATIVE AMERICAN ANARCHISM

*A Study of Left-Wing American Individualism*

A Da Capo Press Reprint Series

# THE AMERICAN SCENE
*Comments and Commentators*

GENERAL EDITOR: WALLACE D. FARNHAM
*University of Illinois*

# NATIVE AMERICAN ANARCHISM

*A Study of Left-Wing American Individualism*

*By*

EUNICE MINETTE SCHUSTER

DA CAPO PRESS · NEW YORK · 1970

A Da Capo Press Reprint Edition

This Da Capo Press edition of *Native American Anarchism* is an
unabridged republication of the first edition published in 1932 as
Volume XVII, Numbers 1-4 in the *Smith College Studies in
History*.

HX 843.S35 1970

*Library of Congress Catalog Card Number 79-98688*

SBN 306-71838-3

Published by Da Capo Press
A Division of Plenum Publishing Corporation
227 West 17th Street
New York, N. Y. 10011
All Rights Reserved

Manufactured in the United States of America

# NATIVE AMERICAN ANARCHISM

## A Study of Left-Wing American
## Individualism

*by*

EUNICE MINETTE SCHUSTER

# CONTENTS

# PREFACE

The writer has attempted in the following study to delineate the character and form of native American anarchism and to suggest what the conditions were which promoted its growth, and wherein lay its significance for American history. The writer is aware, however, that other aspects and problems are equally important and necessary to a proper understanding of anarchism. The limited time has necessarily set limits to research. The problem which presents itself in the study of any idea appears vital to an appreciation of the influence of anarchism in the United States, that is, to what extent did it influence thought and modify action, in spite of the fact that it met with no wide acceptance at any period? Suggestions have been made in the text, therefore, concerning the point of departure for the study of this problem.

A second aspect of anarchism which has only been touched upon, but which merits detailed study and analysis, is the technique of propaganda. This should be correlated with a study of the temperament, the personal experiences, and general environmental conditions of the particular individuals who are the agents of propaganda. Such an investigation would lead the investigator to a third question of significance, that is, what are the factors in the making of an anarchist? To what extent are personality and temperament determining factors? The research which the writer has already done in the biographies of the leading anarchists (which unfortunately cannot be set down in this study) seems to indicate that here is one key to an understanding of the psychology of the anarchist. The life of an anarchist for whom there is abundant biographical material, as for example Emma Goldman, would be the proper subject for investigation of this problem. Cesare Lombroso and Monsieur A. Hamon have contributed something to this subject, but the former has limited himself almost exclusively to the study of the anarchist attentäter who, as we shall see, is not a *typical* offspring of anarchism.

A fourth question of importance is to what extent is anarchism an "escape" from reality. The subject of anarchism has rich unexplored fields for the philosopher, the psychologist, and the historian. To be definitive, however, studies would have to be based upon the four richest collections of anarchist material in the United States—at the University of Michigan (the Labadie Collection), the University of Wisconsin, the New York Public Library, and Columbia University.

Shortly after this study was first completed, a number of materials such as, Emma Goldman's *Living My Life* and Clarence Darrow's *The Story of My Life* were published. In order to bring this work up to date, therefore, the writer has included in the main text and in the footnotes such evidence from these books as seemed pertinent.

The following study could not have been completed without the materials contributed by Mr. Walter Starrett, editor of *The Road to Freedom,* and by Miss Emma Goldman. The writer wishes to thank them for their generous assistance. Recognition is also due to Doctor Max Nettlau of Vienna, Austria, Miss Agnes Inglis, cataloguer of and contributor to the Labadie Collection, Mr. Hippolyte Havel, anarchist writer, and Mr. Jacob Baker of the Vanguard Press, for their helpful suggestions. To Professor Merle Eugene Curti who has patiently guided me in the preparation of this thesis and rendered me invaluable assistance, I wish to express my sincere appreciation.

# INTRODUCTION

Anarchism is a philosophy, a way of life. Its positive concept is freedom unrestricted by man-made law—freedom for the Individual. The Individual for the anarchist is the only social reality. Society has no existence, *per se,* as distinct from the individuals who compose it. As life and activity have become differentiated, so has the conception of the Individual. We would expect to find, therefore, and we do find in anarchism, an expansion and clarification of the idea of what the individual is and how his freedom can be limited legitimately without destroying the essential condition of growth and progress. Social progress or even social change the anarchist maintains is realized through the diversity of individual character just as the evolution of the plant and animal species is effected largely through its "sports." Society, therefore, must be flexible to permit this development. Diversity in unity, unity in diversity is the ideal. Proudhon has most adequately expressed this idea in his well-known words, "Liberty is the Mother not the Daughter of Order." This principle cannot be over-emphasized because it is central to the philosophy of anarchism. Its corollaries are its opposition to church, to state, to society, to everything which restrains the free development of the Individual and the free coöperation of individuals. It is the source of its negative doctrine—life *without* authority (the Greek word anarchy άν—and άρχή means "without authority"). Freedom is attained by Justice. Justice has been variously interpreted by anarchist philosophers—by the Individualists as a recognition of "mine and thine"; by the Anarchist-Communists as a recognition of my right and your right as an individual to the satisfaction of physical need and the rendering of service according to ability.

When they visualize the establishment of society on the principles which guided man in the state of nature, the anarchists are in agreement with Rousseau, and with him they propose not a return to that state but rather a recognition of those principles. They deny the social contract and the theory of natural rights as he conceived them. They say that a surrender of rights is not only unnecessary but impossible. In the struggle for existence the individual will protect himself. A state is not necessary. Nor will this result in a "war of all against all," as Hobbes believed, or in a ruthless struggle in which the fittest, the strongest alone survive. By studying science they found (chiefly Peter Kropotkin, Russian scientist and anarchist) that another law, the law of "Mutual Aid," functioned to restrain the ruthlessness of the law of the survival of the fittest. The protection of the weak followed as a natural consequence. The natural rights which they assume are not rights in the old sense—they are not rights inherited or arbitrarily bestowed upon the Individual. They are rights to which he is entitled by virtue of his existence as a human being. The growth of the idea of anarchism, as we shall see, was indebted to the development in science as much as it was to the evolution of the industrial system.

Anarchism, therefore, has both a positive and a negative aspect. Its positive character is revealed in its demand for liberty for the Individual, its negative character in its demand that society destroy all authority. In its positive aspect its critics have declared it to be impractical—assuming, as it does, that human nature if left uncorrupted by social institutions is naturally good. In its negative aspect it is declared to be destructive of peace and harmony—hence the connotation and use of the word "anarchy" as chaos, disorder, confusion. The emphasis which anarchists of different periods have placed upon the negative or positive, constructive or destructive aspects of anarchism has been determined largely by the character of the anarchists themselves and by the nature of the authority which they attacked—whether they were men of thought or of action, whether the authority was oppressive or merely stimulating. The anarchist today says (and he has formulated what the earlier one implied) that the struggle for "bread" is the cause of selfishness, bloodshed. If the bread which is in the world (and they say that there is enough for everyone) be distributed so that everyone has enough to live comfortably, so that each man can work for a few hours in a day in the production of this bread, he can satisfy his wants and enjoy leisure. We know, therefore, that under such a condition he ought not to kill, steal, or do what we consider now the *raison d'être* for police, judge, and president. If he does, he is a patient for a hospital, not a prison. We can see here the influence of the scientific approach to crime which looks upon crime and perversion as a disease of inheritance and environment, and less as a lapse of morality. Human nature, the anarchist says, is neither good nor bad, it *is*. And as it *is* and as he sees that it has been, it can and will create its own restraints—but only in a condition of freedom. By analogy, he says, we strengthen a weak ankle not by bracing it, but by exercising it. The desire to work, to live, and to help one another is regulative desire. In short, he would return society to a point where its institutions or whatever it creates is spontaneous. He opposes the process in social evolution which is known as the tendency for ideas and customs to become institutionalized, for conduct to become patterned—in short, the tendency to become fixed, static. Anarchists have in a sense, therefore, coöperated with those forces of social evolution which break up the static and which are the elements of social change.

Such a treatment is of necessity general and indefinite, for this is the character of anarchism itself. Postulating, as we have seen, the principle that the Individual must be free and that all restraint must come spontaneously from within that Individual, anarchism, however, has specifically opposed government, law, organized religion, accepted social custom and the industrial system as we know it. From this fact it derives its just reputation of being anti-State, anti-law, anti-society, and anti-religion. For external government it would substitute self-government.

The attacks and the positive program of individual anarchists have been as varied as their personalities. A general classification can be made, however, for the purpose of convenience, but we must remember that such classifications are largely arbitrary. In general there is Individualist Anarchism, Christian Anarchism, Mutualist Anarchism, Anarcho-Syndicalism, and Communist-Anarchism. They agree on the essential position which we have already described. The chief source of difference between them is to be found in their economic systems and their conception of the Individual.

The Individualist-Anarchist has been generally philosophical, practical, yet slightly removed from reality by virtue of his philosophical tendency, and at the same time highly self-conscious (in the sense which Professor Fite uses the word[1]). His philosophy stresses the isolation of the individual—his right to his own tools, his mind, his body, and to the products of his labor. To the artist who embraces this philosophy it is "aesthetic" anarchism, to the reformer, ethical anarchism, to the independent mechanic, economic anarchism. The former is concerned with philosophy, the latter with practical demonstration. The economic anarchist is concerned with constructing a society on the basis of anarchism. Economically he sees no harm whatever in the private possession of what the individual produces by his own labor, but only so much and no more. The aesthetic and ethical type found expression in the Transcendentalism, Humanitarianism, and Romanticism of the first part of the nineteenth century, the economic type in the pioneer life of the West during the same period, but more favorably after the Civil War.

Christian Anarchism is closely akin to Individualist Anarchism. It is just as "selfish" but it would realize the "self" in the service of others, in a mystical "God-self." For the law of natural consequence of the Individualists, it substitutes the law of God and especially the Golden Rule. It was slightly less isolated. In its purest form it would not recognize formalism in religion. In the earliest days of American history it appeared in the Antinomian heresy and Quakerism, but not in a complete form until the time of Adin Ballou. Neither the Individualist Anarchist nor the Christian Anarchist, however, could realize their objectives, as we shall see, for reasons inherent in their very doctrines. The former could not establish a society ordered by the law of Individual Sovereignty or the latter by Christian Law because they had to use force to do so. But to use force in the first case was to

[1] Warren Fite, *Individualism. Four Lectures on the Significance of Consciousness for Social Relations* (London, Bombay, and Calcutta, 1911).

violate this fundamental principle—the right of every individual to his own opinion and life—in the second case to wield an instrument outlawed by Christian Law. Both groups, therefore, gave their thought to constructing ideal social systems rather than to destroying the existing social order. This we shall find to be a persistent dilemma in all varieties of anarchism, one which the anarchist cannot successfully meet and continue to be a consistent anarchist. It is one which makes our problem of estimating the importance of anarchism as a practical theory a difficult one. We shall find, therefore, that it is not in the realization of these ends, but in the struggle to attain them, that anarchism is of service to society.

Beyond these varieties of Anarchism and into Mutualism, Anarcho-Syndicalism, and Anarchist-Communism, as we should expect from the names, anarchism becomes concerned more with the economic problem—that is, in trying to protect the individual who is being submerged in the industrial system. It has broadened, however, to include art, literature and drama as its proper fields. Mutualism is closely allied to the Individualist Anarchism of the economic type in its conception of labor and in its proposals for labor-exchange. Its emphasis, however, is more on coöperation in a Bank of Exchange which would eventually take the place of the political state. Proudhon in France, William B. Greene, and to a certain extent Benjamin R. Tucker in the United States, are the leading exponents of this doctrine. While their interest is in the labor problem, they see no objection to the wage system, to the relationship of employed and employer. Such objectionable features they believe would be absorbed and obliterated in a proper system of exchange. But the Anarcho-Syndicalist is concerned more directly and is more intimately acquainted with the problem of the property-less wage earner, the proletariat, the disinherited. The Anarcho-Syndicalist in the United States formed the left wing of the Industrial Workers of the World after 1905. He advocated the social revolution or the General Strike, sabotage, and the solidarity of Labor in Industrial Unions rather than trade unions. Harry Kelly, Hippolyte Havel and a few others of the anarchists were active in this group.

The difference between the Anarcho-Syndicalist and Anarcho-Communist was not very distinct. The former was interested in existing labor problems and their immediate solution, the latter in the solution of the same problems but only in relation to a future ideal society. The one was native, the other foreign in origin. The Anarchist-Communist was trying to prepare the proletariat for the social revolution. This revolution would realize first, federative industrial production made efficient by voluntary coöperation between groups; second, the division of labor according to ability, and of products according to need. Emma Goldman and Alexander Berkman were concerned in the late nineteenth and early twentieth centuries in awakening the laborer to his power, to the "rottenness" of the present system, and educating him to a point where he himself could take over industry and government, not to relegate it, as Socialism would, to the State, or as "Moscow Communism" would to the "Soviet." While their emphasis was chiefly on the education of the proletariat to anarchism in its broadest sense, they were also interested in the education of the general public, as we shall see. Properly speaking, this type of anarchism is not "native American." The distinction between the native American anarchism and the type introduced by the foreigner is important, first, as a convenient limitation to the present study, and second, as an explanation of why Anarchist-Communism was rejected and forcibly ejected by the authorities and by the general public. But anarchism, finally, is best understood by examining its various manifestations and the conditions in which it germinated. We shall study native American anarchism, therefore, from its conception in the earliest colonial days to its maturity in the late nineteenth century, and its disillusion in the early twentieth century.

# I

## ANARCHISM CONCEIVED—INDIVIDUALISM IN THE COLONIAL PERIOD

### The Antinomians

The Puritans of the early Massachusetts Commonwealth, in their desperate struggle for existence and self-preservation, built up the first rigid authority in the United States—an authority of Church and State in the form of a Theocracy. Necessity demanded of each individual absolute conformity to a strict code of thought and action—a code immutable, divinely conceived, and ordained of God. Their leaders, both civic and religious, were goaded by an ever-present fear, a fear which bore two aspects.[1] The one was the fear of extermination by the Indians,[2] the other of loss of self-government privileges through Royal decree—that is, through the withdrawal of the Charter by the King of England.[3] Governor Winthrop, twelve times elected Governor of the Commonwealth from 1629 to 1649, refers frequently in his *Journal* to fights with the Indians and to the necessity for constant vigilance. The fear that the colonists would be defeated recurs as

---

[1] The character of the leaders was no doubt another important factor in determining the severity of the government. Professional men of little or no political influence in England, elevated to posts of important responsibility in the Commonwealth, they seem to have become intoxicated with their power. John Winthrop had held an unimportant position in a law court. John Cotton had been the rector of a large provincial parish. James Truslow Adams, *The Founding of New England* (Boston, 1921), 147.

[2] Thomas Hutchinson, *The History of Massachusetts From the Earliest Settlement Thereof in 1628 Until the Year 1750* (Third ed., Boston, 1795), 2 vols., I, 34.

[3] Jared Sparks, "The Life of Anne Hutchinson," *The Library of American Biography* (Boston, 1845), VI, 207. The fear of losing the Charter was well grounded, for a 'judgment' had already been filed in the court of King's Bench in 1637 declaring the Charter vacated. Charles I had in fact publicly declared his intention to appoint Sir Ferdinanda Gorges the Governor-General of New England. And in June, 1637, George 'Cleeves had brought to Governor Winthrop a commission creating a provincial government for New England. *Antinomianism in the Colony of Massachusetts Bay, 1636-1638* (Documents) edited by Charles T. Adams (Boston, 1894), 21-22.

a subdued minor note. But if they dreaded the domestic foe, they trembled even more from the threat of a foreign one, one which was more unpredictable and beyond their immediate control. The Royal Charter had granted them self-government, but only on the condition that they conduct their government in an orderly, peaceful fashion. Accounts of disagreement, rebellion, or heresy, therefore, were not to reach the royal ears. As the Jacobins in France more than a century later were driven to bloody repression by the threat of enemies both from within and from without, so were the Puritans to repressive legislation.

The laws which they passed were rigorous. In order to protect themselves against the Indians, they formulated and enforced rigid laws for military service. Fasts and thanksgiving services were prescribed to insure victory, to prevent defeat, or to render thanks for success. That the government might be efficient, requirements were many and rigid for participation in it, either as an officer or as a voter. Judicial procedure was severe and in some cases arbitrary. *Efficient* management of colonial affairs enabled Governor Winthrop to draw up glowing reports in good conscience and dispatch them to England for His Majesty's perusal. Reassuring letters were also written to relatives in England who might have contemplated settling in the New World.

Not only by the civil authority, however, but also by the religious authority were the lives of the colonists carefully grooved. The restraints which the religious body laid upon the members of the Puritan church were even more intimate and personal than those of the civil order because religion was one of the most vital forces in their lives. In the lives of many of the Puritans it can be said to have been central. It was the source of their ideas, their inspiration, even their diversion, as well as the guide of their moral action. They saw the hand of God in the common events of the day, almost as the Pantheist Spirit God in the wind and trees, less ethereal, no doubt, but certainly as unpredictable, uncontrolable, and absolute. The desire to exercise their religion freely without interference was, in fact, one of the strong motivating forces which brought them originally to America.[4] It was, however, a desire not long satisfied. It soon appeared that the freedom for which they came was a freedom merely to lay down certain theological tenets as the ultimates of truth, truths which they need not and could not question.

The process by which faith came to be determined and measured by orthodoxy of belief and conventionality of religious worship converted the doctrine of Justification by Faith into Justification by Works, the very doctrine which Luther had assailed in the Catholic creed. The Old Testament more often than the New was the source of Puritan inspiration. The God who was all-powerful, remote, austere, and quick to punish sinners, was the God whom they obeyed. And since truth had been discovered for all generations, revelation and understanding were no longer necessary. To question the truth, or to claim the right of immediate revelation was heresy. The ministers, therefore, like the priests in the Catholic Church, became Divine Interpreters and Mediators between God and Man. The Bible became the spiritual constitution of the Puritan community, and the Ministers the guardians and legislators of Biblical Law. Their doctrines finally narrowed down to a strict Calvinism, that is, Predestination, Justification by Works, the Depravity of Man, and the Bondage of the Will—in short, a "legalistic" religion. Puritan religious doctrine became dogma and religious practices fixed in habit and law. To question the necessity for church attendance, for fasts, for prayers, for the mortification of the soul and body was to question God himself.

It can be said, therefore, that the State and Church functioned together as coercive authorities. Their connection was established by the requirement of church membership for the franchise. Elders of the church were frequently magistrates. Furthermore, *all* law was essentially Scriptural and took precedence over common law. The State and the Church were organically bound

[4] For an interesting discussion of the relative importance of the economic and religious motives of the Puritan migration to America see: Samuel Eliot Morison, *Builders of the Bay Colony* (Boston and New York), 1930, Appendix, 339-346.

together. Attack on the Church was conceived as a challenge to the State and as a danger to the whole social structure. Both were called into question by the Antinomians, who were for the most part "new-comers," "aliens." To consider the nature, the extent, and the results of their attack is the purpose of this preliminary study.

This movement was not unique to the colonies. In Europe a similar development had taken place. The Protestant Reformation which was supposed to have brought in a personal religion and the doctrine of the "priesthood of believers"—that is, *individualism* in religion, ended in the formalism of Presbyterianism, Calvinism, and Lutheranism. It was against this development that the Anabaptists in Germany, the Pietists in France, and the Fifth Monarchy men in England had thrown their weight—and with as little success as the Antinomians in Massachusetts. It is true, however, that because of the narrowness of life in the colony and the solidarity of the group life, the heresy of Antinomianism was not allowed to breed as extensively as similar heresies in Europe, and was crushed with far more efficiency and consequently with greater harm to the Commonwealth.

Antinomianism has a three-fold significance, first, as a revolt of the individual against coercive authority which usurps dominion over the mind and the body; second, as the first criticism of American life and institutions by the freedom-loving and disillusioned immigrant; and third, as the first appearance of the delusion, which showed itself in the Alien Act of 1637, that foreign countries are the source and immigrants the carriers of certain dangerous doctrines. The means which the authorities used to root out the heresy of Antinomianism recoiled on the Commonwealth and struck upon it marks which it bears today. The process of banishing the leaders of revolt was in itself a violation of all civil liberty, but the actual forcing out of the colony all those who dissented from the accepted, conventional beliefs, whether right or wrong, reacted to the exclusion of liberalizing influences and checked spontaneity of development for the sake of uniformity. It was not until the first half of the nineteenth century that Massachusetts

felt again the severe pains of stirring individualism, when static
belief was broken up by the disintegrating doctrines of Unitarianism, Perfectionism, Transcendentalism, and Non-Resistance. The
exact nature of this breaking-up process will be considered in the
following section.  Whether or not the results are to be similar
to those which followed from the banishment of Anne Hutchinson
and John Wheelwright, the principle of the deportation of Emma
Goldman and Alexander Berkman in 1919, the leaders of the
anarchist movement in America, was, as we shall see, the same.

Antinomianism was the name applied to the beliefs of a particular religious sect; the Antinomian controversy was a religious
controversy centered chiefly in Boston and lasting from 1636 to
1638, apparently only an unintelligible, casuistical fencing of wits
which even Governor Winthrop said was not understood by the
participants themselves.[5]  It will be shown, however, that its true
significance lay far deeper in political, social, and philosophical
sources.  An understanding of the controversy can be approached
by a consideration of the origin of the word "Antinomianism."
It was originally applied by Martin Luther to the doctrines which
John Agricola upheld in a controversy with him over the interpretation of Law and Gospel during the period 1537-1560.  Luther
interpreted Law as a command accompanied by threats which
forces obedience by fear.  Christ and hence all Christians were not
under the dominion of this law since Christ's supreme act of love
had set men free from the Hebraic God's act of mercy.  Christians,
he maintained, lived virtuous lives not because of fear of punishment, but by love of noble precepts, precepts which were to be
found in the Gospel.  But John Agricola and his followers saw
that the Gospel precepts were fast becoming law in the sense that
Luther conceived it.  They concluded, therefore, that the Elect
predestined to salvation by God were free from and above law,
especially the moral code.  God had written the laws on their heart;
what they did, consequently, was good.  The unregenerate were
free from the moral code, because they *could not* do good.  Both

---

[5] John Winthrop, *The History of New England from 1630 to 1649*, edited
by James Savage (2 vols., Boston, 1825), I, 221.

the elect and the unregenerate were free from law. It is clear, therefore, why the term antinomianism has been applied to libertines and why John Wheelwright exhorted his followers "to have a care that we give not occasion to others to say we are libertines or Antinomians, but Christians."[6]    The antinomianism of John Wheelwright and of Anne Hutchinson laid chief stress on the freedom of the Elect from a "legalistic" moral code. They assailed the formalism already described with the doctrine of the Covenant of Grace as opposed to the Covenant of Works, the "indwelling of the Spirit" as opposed to "Legalism," and revelation as superior to the ministry of the word. They believed that "a condition of true inwardness" was a sufficient guide in life; law, therefore, was not only unnecessary but blighting to the spirit. But they fell short of a true Christian anarchism by limiting this freedom to the Elect alone. Their test of Election was, of course, a saving grace for individualism because they believed it to be in inner consciousness. As with the later Christian anarchists they trusted inner guides as checks to license. Nevertheless, they were branded by their opponents as libertines and as enemies of peace and security. If peace and security meant conformity and obedience and stagnation, Anne Hutchinson was an enemy.

A study of the details of this controversy shows it to contain both political, social, and religious elements. For the purposes of the present survey, the last two elements will be given chief consideration. Roger Williams and Henry Vane caused the first disturbances in the political field. The former for his refusal to conform was disenfranchised and banished from the colony in 1635. The latter, as a rival of Governor Winthrop for the Governorship of the Commonwealth, asserted his independence and attempted to strengthen his position by favoring the antinomian doctrines of Anne Hutchinson and John Wheelwright. It cannot be a mere coincidence that strongest opposition came from those colonists who had arrived after the government had been fairly well established and the religious practices quite generally accepted. John

[6] Charles H. Bell, *John Wheelwright, His Writings, and a Memoir* (Boston, 1876), 175.

Cotton arrived in Boston in 1634, Mrs. Hutchinson in the same year, Henry Vane in 1635, and John Wheelwright in 1636. In a sense they were immigrants, aliens. Filled with the questioning spirit of the time and fired by the belief that perfect freedom was to be enjoyed in the Puritan colony, they landed at Boston only to pass through an "Ellis Island" for doctrinal examination. Their religious beliefs were combed through by austere ministers both for admission to the colony, for church membership, and for the franchise. The courts of elders and magistrates they found arbitrary in their procedure. Even the leading minister of Boston they found cold, unimaginative, and uninspired. Their high expectations were soon disillusioned. But instead of settling down to their respective occupations and accepting conditions as they were, they tried to assert their own individualities. They paid for their efforts, however, with loss of citizenship and banishment.

Most of the dissension centered about Anne Hutchinson, Henry Vane, and John Wheelwright, all three of whom had settled in Boston. Henry Vane was a young and adventurous youth when he arrived in America, in eager sympathy with the most advanced thoughts of his day. His zeal, simplicity, and directness of purpose won all hearts. And as soon as he came to Boston he became active in politics. The faction which had drawn away from Governor Winthrop soon joined the adherents of the "young Sir Harry Vane." Vane allied himself, moreover, with the dissenting religious faction of which Mrs. Hutchinson was the leader. But the course of his rise to the Governorship, his final defeat in the following year, and his departure from America in disgust, are important to this study only in so far as they are directly related to the antinomian controversy. The first real overt act of challenge was the agitation of certain active members in the Boston Church to install the Reverend John Wheelwright by John Cotton's side as an additional teacher in November, 1636. But it is necessary to consider the circumstances which lead up to this demand. The prime mover was Mrs. Anne Hutchinson.

Anne Hutchinson was a young woman of thirty-four or thirty-five years of age when she and her husband followed John Cotton to America in 1634.[7]  John Cotton had been her favorite minister in England.  She was of a fearless temper.  "The fear of man is a snare, why should I be afraid and I will speak freely," she declared.[8]  Already on the ship coming to America she had shown "a secret opposition to things delivered."[9]  She herself testified later in her trial that in England even she had been "much troubled to see the falseness of the constitution of the church of England" and "had like to have turned separatist."[10]  To her worst enemy, Thomas Welde, she appeared as an "American Jezebel" and to Cotton Mather, "a gentlewoman, of an haughty carriage, busie spirit, competent wit, and a voluble tongue.[11]  John Winthrop found her "a woman of a ready wit and bold spirit."[12]  Her boldness, her fearlessness and her magnetic insight drew some of the leading spirits of Boston to her.  Mather contemptuously attests that "it was wonderful to see with what a speedy and spreading fascination these doctrines did bewitch the minds of people, which one would not have imagined capable of being so besotted" (referring, no doubt, to Henry Vane and John Cotton).[13]  By her charm she won over opponents and held them even when they were threatened by persecution.[14]  So great was her personal influence, in fact, that she was suspected of witchcraft by no less a person than Governor Winthrop.[15]  By her gentleness, sympathy,

---

[7] It is said that he came to America against his own desires—his wife's eagerness over-riding his unwillingness.  Perhaps this is the basis of John Winthrop's observation that William Hutchinson was "a man of a very mild temper and weak parts, and wholly guided by his wife."  Winthrop, *op. cit.,* I, 295.

[8] Hutchinson, *op. cit.,* Appendix II, "The Examination of Mrs. Ann Hutchinson at the Court at Newtown," II, 446.

[9] *Ibid.,* II, 430.

[10] *Ibid.,* II, 439.

[11] Winthrop, *op. cit.,* I, 258; Cotton Mather, *Magnalia Christi Americana or The Ecclesiastical History of New England, 1620-1698* (2 vols., Hartford, 1820), II, 446.

[12] Winthrop, *op. cit.,* I, 200.

[13] Mather, *op. cit.,* II, 447.

[14] Governor Winthrop describes how two young men were converted against their wills and apparently without conscious effort on her part when they chanced to meet and converse with her at Portsmouth.  Winthrop, *op. cit.,* II, 9.

[15] *Ibid.,* I, 271; II, 9.

and skill as a practical nurse and mid-wife, she endeared many women of Boston to her—and most particularly Mary Dyer, who remained true to Mrs. Hutchinson until she herself met death at the scaffold. Today she would be called a powerful personality.

Since she was a woman, her natural field of action was her own home. Her "ready wit" drew a select group of friends to her house, where she was accustomed to entertain them with short summaries of the sermons which she had heard in Church on Sundays and Thursdays, "gossipings," as Cotton Mather called them.[16] At first they were innocent enough, but soon they became more than mere summaries. Mrs. Hutchinson began to make the sermon the point of departure for the exposition of her own ideas which were often at variance with those in the sermon. She even went so far as to say that John Wilson was under the Covenant of Works and unfit as a minister of the Gospel, while John Cotton was under the Covenant of Grace.[17] It became clear to the minister in Boston that she was setting herself up as a minister of the Gospel (a woman!) and was usurping the divine function of John Wilson, whose austerity she thoroughly disliked. As many as sixty people were reported to have attended her meetings at one time.[18] Governor Winthrop in a state of alarm said that "all the congregations of Boston except four or five, closed with these opinions, or the most of them."[19]

It was at the height of Anne Hutchinson's personal influence that her brother-in-law, the Reverend John Wheelwright, came to America. Shortly after his arrival, as we have seen, attempts were made to get him appointed assistant to John Wilson and John Cotton in the church at Boston. But it was generally known that he "closed with her doctrines." The request was refused. Wheelwright promptly withdrew from Boston and began to build his own church at the Mount. His friends followed him there. This very act of withdrawal was a challenge to the ecclesiastical author-

[16] Mather, *op. cit.,* II, 447.
[17] Hutchinson, *op. cit.,* II, 429.
[18] *Ibid.,* II, 425.
[19] Winthrop, *op. cit.,* I, 212.

ity, but when he actually preached doctrines contrary to the accepted ones, his conduct was regarded as intolerable. John Cotton, furthermore, was known to sympathize with Wheelwright. Finally when Henry Vane, John Winthrop's rival, showed a leaning toward these dissenting doctrines and with Cotton "did publicly declare their judgments in some of them," the magistracy began to take alarm.[20]

The opportunity came when Wheelwright directly and openly challenged an established religious practice—the observance of Fast Day. In the church of Boston itself he preached a sermon in which he set forth all the reasons why Fasts should not be observed and at the same time expounded antinomian doctrines. The effect was dynamic and yet it can scarcely be appreciated or understood today.[21] Perhaps an exact parallel could be found by comparing it with the effect which the speech of Emma Goldman had on the authorities when she attacked the Conscription Act of 1917, and counselled the citizens not to register. For thus counselling disobedience to federal law she was sentenced to two years in the Penitentiary at Jefferson, Missouri. For thus counselling disobedience to ecclesiastical law, John Wheelwright was banished from the colony.

Since the Fast Day Sermon is one of the few sources of antinomian doctrine, it is necessary to consider briefly the line of argument which Wheelwright followed. The Fast Day, Winthrop wrote, was ordained by the government and kept in all the churches, "the occasion was the miserable state of the churches in Germany; the calamities upon our native country, the bishops making havock in our churches, putting down the faithful ministers, and advancing papish ceremonies and doctrines, the plague raging exceedingly, and famine and sword threatening them; the dangers of those at Connecticut, and of ourselves also, by the Indians; and the dissensions in our churches."[22] It was on Jan-

---

[20] *Ibid.*, I, 206.

[21] The effect of Wheelwright's sermon against Fasting and his refusal to observe it was increased by Henry Vane's and William Coddington's joining him at the Mount on the prescribed day.

[22] *Ibid.*, I, 213.

uary 19, 1637, that John Wheelwright preached his Fast Day Sermon.[22a] In this sermon he opposed fasting chiefly because it was prescribed as a law by the magistracy. True Christians were above strict law because they were guided by an inner light. Obedience to external law he declared to be a sign of weakness or absence of the inner spirit. "Either Christ he is present with his people, or else absent from his people; if he be present with his people then they have no cause to fast:—therefore it must be his absence that is the true cause of fasting, when he is taken away then they must fast."[23]

An inner light or conscience reveals the ways of God and the precepts which every Christian is to follow. In his words: "Therefore if we mean to keep the Lord Jesus Christ, we must keep open this fountain and hold forth this light, if there be a night of darkness, the fear (faith the Spirit of God) is in the night. . . . To keep Christ, we must hold forth this light. . . . The soul cometh to know that it is justified."[24] The soul knows it is justified, that is, saved, by a "new heart," a new spirit, but not in fastings and days of humiliation.[25] In spite of this freedom, however, Wheelwright still held to the idea that men were divided into the "elect" and the unregenerate, for he said, "The saints of God are few" and "the battle is between God's people and those that are not."[26] It remained for the later Romanticists of the early 19th century to extend "election" to all men.

For true Christians, however, Wheelwright was absolutely opposed to law and to this extent he was a Christian anarchist. He opposed law because it kills the Spirit and substantiated his position by a quotation from Scripture: " 'I will forgive your sins, and write my Law in your hearts and inward parts'; if a believer had power in himself to work, it killeth the spirit of God's children, *put any worke of sanctification in a legalle frame and it killeth him, the Law killeth,* but it is the spirit that quickens, that

---

[22a] Bell, *op. cit.,* pp. 20-179.
[23] *Ibid.,* 155.
[24] *Ibid.,* 164, 165, 166.
[25] *Ibid.,* 175.
[26] *Ibid.,* 167, 170.

is the Gospel in which the spirit is conveyed, when God speaketh he speaketh the words of eternal life . . . therefore ought no words of sanctification to be urged upon the servants of God, so as if they had a power to do them, it will kill the soul of a man, and it oppresseth the poor souls of the saints of God."[27]    His conclusion was, therefore, that every good Christian could live a good life by bringing Christ into his heart and hence peace to the church and Commonwealth.[28]

The method of propaganda which he advocated was that of rational conviction which he here described: "They (the children of God) must fight, and fight with spiritual weapons, for the weapons of our warfare are not carnall but spirituall," and later that they must kill the enemies of the Lord with the words of the Lord's truth.[29]

In order to inform the General Court on the "offensive passages" of this sermon, he was brought before the Assembly on March 9th.    Examined by the Court behind closed doors, accused of declaring the clergy to be under the Covenant of Works and of inciting the people to violence especially against the magistrates and ministers, he was convicted of "sedition and contempt of court."[30]

A protest against the injustice of this sentence was drawn up in the form of a petition and signed by approximately sixty people. They held that Wheelwright was a worthy citizen, sincere, upright, and not guilty of inciting them to violence, for they had committed no act of violence.[31]

The petition and general objections increased the anxiety of the magistrates.    Winthrop declared that "every occasion increased the contention, and caused great alienation of minds,"[32] and Mather that the heresy had spread even to condemn the army and the magistracy:

[27] Ibid., 165-166.
[28] Ibid., 178, 179.
[29] Ibid., 160-161, 166.
[30] Bell, op. cit., 13, 14, 15, 17; Winthrop, op. cit., I, 215.
[31] Winthrop, op. cit., Appendix I, 401-403.
[32] Ibid., I, 213.

"The contention spread itself even into families, and all private and similar societies, who were to be accounted under a Covenant of Works, and so enemies unto the Lord Jesus Christ. . . . The disturbance proceeded from thence into all the general affairs of the public: the *expedition* against the *Pequah Indians was most shamefully discouraged, because the army was too much under the Covenant of Works; and the magistrates began to be contemned* as being of a legal spirit, and have therewithal a tang of Antichrist in them."[33]

Conquered by their fear the magistrates proceeded to adopt any measures which would stop the spread of heresy which threatened to break up the solidarity of the Commonwealth. They began by cutting off what they considered to be one of the chief sources—the alien. In May of the year 1637 they passed the first Alien Act in the history of America. This Act was the "spiritual relative" to the Alien Act of 1903. The Act of 1637 forbade the entrance of immigrants "who might be dangerous to the Commonwealth,"[34] that of 1903, of those who professed to be anarchists. Although the Act merely provided that "no towne or person shall receive any stranger resorting hither with intent to reside in this jurisdiction, nor shall allow any lot or habitation to any, or entertain any such above three weeks except such person shall have allowance under the hands of some one of the Council, or of two of the magistrates,"[35] it worked to the exclusion of those who professed antinomianism, because the magistracy belonged almost exclusively to the majority party. The Law itself had been drawn up specifically with the coming of certain friends and relations of Mrs. Hutchinson in mind,[36] and when they did arrive in Boston, they were given only a four month dispensation to remain, at the end of which time they were separated from their friends and forced to leave the Commonwealth.[37] So much

[33] Mather, *op. cit.,* II, 441.
[34] *Ibid.,* I, 224.
[35] A fine of 100 £ was levied against every violation of this act. Charles F. Adams, *Three Episodes of Massachusetts History* (2 vols., Boston and New York, 1893), I, 459-460.
[36] Winthrop, *op. cit.,* I, 224.
[37] *Ibid.,* I, 232, 233.

feeling was aroused in Boston by this arbitrary procedure, that the four sergeants who customarily attended Governor Winthrop when he came to Boston, refused to do so, forcing Winthrop to use two of his own servants.[38]

The magistrates of Massachusetts might well have feared the importation of radical ideas from abroad for a similar intellectual opposition to authoritarian religion and government had manifested itself in England first in the 16th century and again in the 20's of the 17th century.[39] During and after the crisis of 1640 in England the program of the Millenarians or Fifth Monarchy men, the Antinomians, the Anabaptists, and the Levellers assumed a definite anarchistic character. The Antinomians, commonly associated with the Anabaptists, declared themselves not under the Law but under Grace, and opposed civil authority.[40] The ideas and opposition of these sects, half-formed but not objectified crystallized into pure Christian Anarchism in Millenarianism.

The Fifth Monarchy, the future ideal society, the Millenarians visualized as a reign of saints, shortly to be realized, but only by the removal of priests, lawyers, nobility, and magistrates. The future society was to have no law or government in the worldly sense. Church organization, therefore, was also dispensed with. As strict non-resistants they could not exercise any compulsion over the thought or action of another. Their cry was "to make way for Christ's monarchy on earth."[41] Increasing in strength, power, and intensity of conviction, the Fifth Monarchy men attracted the notice of the government. Their meetings were broken up; their leaders were arrested.[42] One member of the sect was reported to have declared at his trial that God would de-

[38] *Ibid.,* I, 224, 225.

[39] Although the Anabaptist uprising at Munster (Holland) had been suppressed in 1536, for about a century and a half afterwards it was referred to as a conclusive object lesson, and made the pretext and excuse for a policy of rigid suppression in all acute cases of religious difference. *Antinomianism in the Colony of Massachusetts Bay,* note, p. 179.

[40] G. P. Gooch and H. J. Laski, *English Democratic Ideas in the Seventeenth Century* (Second edition, Cambridge, 1927), 109.

[41] *Ibid.,* 222.

[42] *Ibid.,* 224.

stroy not only unlawful but lawful government, not only the abuse but the use of it.[43] Attacked by civil authority, they deserted their doctrines of non-resistance and resorted to force for the defense and realization of their ideas. It was reported that they had even drawn up a list of names of individuals whom they had marked for destruction.[44] Their following grew smaller, but they were never reconciled to the accession of King Charles, and with one dramatic act they withdrew from English life.[45] After the Restoration Millenarianism was quickly suppressed. But more than a century and a half later it appeared in New England, reincarnated in Non-Resistance.

Millenarianism differed from New England Antinomianism in two respects; first, it was more political in character, and second, it was more concrete, definite, and hence more extreme. A partial explanation for this difference lies in the "milieu" where each developed. Conditions were unsettled, almost chaotic during the Commonwealth period in England. Millenarianism was at first "lost" in the general dissension which was rife. During the early days of the Commonwealth in New England, however, one dissenting voice sounded like a shout in a hushed, crowded hall. Under such a condition the possessor of the voice was easily discovered. In England the sect was left undisturbed until it became violent and attracted public notice. It, therefore, developed more definite ideas of the Fifth Monarchy. It was more political in character because it felt the iron hand of government in the realm of politics, whereas the colonists of Massachusetts felt it in religion. It may be said, therefore, that although Millenarianism reached its final development several years after the Antinomian controversy had been forgotten in Massachusetts, the germs of dissension had existed in 1637 and were no doubt carried to New England by the newer colonists. To prevent the strengthening

[43] *Idem.*
[44] *Ibid.*, 225.
[45] A short time after the return of Charles II, a small group of Millenarians is reported to have broken into St. Paul's and demanded of the first person they met whom he was for and receiving the reply "for King Charles," they shot and killed him shouting, "We are for King Jesus." *Ibid.*, 273-274.

of this dissension, therefore, the General Court passed the Alien Act in May, 1637.

The second step was to proceed to the destruction of those germs which were already there and multiplying. The method they adopted was banishment. The General Court agreed that "two so opposite parties could not contain in the same body without apparent hazard of ruin to the whole" and therefore decided "to send away some of the principal."[46] When in August, 1637, after having been defeated in the election by Winthrop, Henry Vane sailed for England in disgust, never to return, the chief protection of the minority was taken away. The General Court proceeded to "wholesale" banishment. In the last of August a Synod met at Newtowne (now Cambridge) to draw up a list of doctrines which it branded as heretical. It was further agreed that "a set assembly (as was then in practice at Boston), where sixty or more did meet every week, and one woman (in a prophetical way, by resolving questions of doctrine, and expounding scripture) took upon her the whole exercise, was disorderly and without rule."[47] On November 2 the General Court summoned John Wheelwright, disenfranchised and banished him.[48] In the same month Winthrop wrote to Coddington, Coggeshall, and Colburn, the chief signatories of the petition submitted in defense of John Wheelwright, accusing them of "unwarranted and seditious delinquency, because in that," he continued, "you affirm, that all the acts of that major part of that court are void, whereby you go about to overthrow the foundation of our Commonwealth and the peace thereof, by turning all our magistrates out of office and by nullifying our laws, . . . because you invite the body of the people to join you in your seditious attempt against the court and the authority here established. . . ."[49] Because they challenged the authority of the State and the Church, they and some seventeen others were disarmed, dismissed, and disenfranchised.[50]

[46] Winthrop, *op. cit.,* I, 245.
[47] *Ibid.,* I, 240.
[48] *Ibid.,* I, 246.
[49] *Ibid.,* Appendix, I, 403-404.
[50] This group formed the nucleus of the colony at Aquiday (Rhode Island). *Ibid.,* 245, 246.

The Court then went on to get rid of the cause and root of all their trouble, Mrs. Hutchinson. She was summoned before the Court at Cambridge on the 7th of November (now the 17th), 1637, examined and cross-examined for two days without a counsel by the magistrates, her judges, made to give evidence against herself, badgered and insulted. They showed her no leniency, although it was apparent to all that she was soon to give birth to a child. She was convicted and sentenced to be banished. The trial of Mrs. Hutchinson is classic as a trial for an idea.[51] She was sentenced not for anything she had done but for what her words might have inspired a weaker person to do. The parallel between this trial and that of Emma Goldman in 1919 is most striking.

At the opening of the trial Governor Winthrop, the presiding judge, designated Mrs. Hutchinson as "one of those who have troubled the peace of the Commonwealth and the churches" and expressed the hope that she would change her opinions in order that she might become "a profitable member here among us."[52] This same implication, that only conforming individuals are "profitable citizens," is to be found in the Goldman-Berkman trial, when Judge Mayer said: "The defendants have shown remarkable ability, an ability which might have been utilized for the great benefit of this country had they seen fit to employ themselves in behalf of this country rather than against it."[53] Both Governor Winthrop and Judge Mayer further implied that liberty had already been sought and won, in the case of the former when the Pilgrims had settled at Plymouth, in the case of the latter when the Revolutionists had freed the colonists from British dominion. "American liberty," Judge Mayer declared, "was won by the forefathers, it was maintained by the Civil War."[54] Anne Hutchinson and Emma Goldman believed, however, that liberty was never *won*, that every citizen must be ever vigilant for his freedom.

Anne Hutchinson was then charged not with sedition for sign-

[51] Account of trial—Hutchinson, *op. cit.,* Appendix II, 423-447.
[52] Hutchinson, *op. cit.,* Appendix II, 423.
[53] *Mother Earth,* XII (July, 1917), No. 5, 162.
[54] *Idem.*

ing the petition in defense of John Wheelwright, because she had not signed it, but with harboring and countenancing this act. Her objection to the charge on the grounds that it was a "matter of conscience," was answered by Governor Winthrop with this astounding doctrine: "If you countenance those that are transgressors of the law, you are in the same fact."[55] Not only had she countenanced disobedience, but what was far more serious, she had "seduced" many honest persons in her meetings, "so that now they are flown from magistrates and ministers," a course which was "greatly prejudicial to the State."[56] On the same grounds a charge was laid against Emma Goldman. In the language of the 20th century it reads: "In this country of ours, we regard as our enemies those who counsel disobedience of our laws by those of minds less strong."[57]

Fundamentally, Anne Hutchinson's gravest offense was the assertion of her own right as an individual to express her own ideas even when they ran counter to those accepted by the ministry. She gave voice to her opinions because she was an individual, she attracted followers because she was charming and because her doctrines satisfied a spiritual need which certain of the colonists felt. By doing this "she hath traduced the magistrates and the ministers of their jurisdiction," and had defied the law that no one "should have authority to set up any other exercises besides what authority hath set up."[58] She had even declared that the ministers were not able ministers of the New Testament, that John Wilson did not have the zeal of the Spirit, and "she spake plump that we (the ministers) were not sealed."[59] Her individualism was uncovered in her "devilish delusion" of immediate revelation, "the immediate revelation of the Spirit, and not by the ministry of the word." Excited and over-wrought, she gave to the court a description of her own spiritual development. She told them that in England she had "like to have turned separatist,"

[55] Hutchinson, op. cit., II, 424.
[56] Ibid., II, 426.
[57] Mother Earth, XII, No. 5, 162.
[58] Hutchinson, op. cit., II, 426, 435.
[59] Ibid., II, 438.

because of the wickedness of the church, but that she had been saved from denying Christ by direct communion with him. She had been led by God to distinguish between "the voice of her beloved and the voice of Moses." Astonished, the Deputy Governor asked, "How do you know that was the Spirit?" Mrs. Hutchinson replied, "How did Abraham know that it was God that bid him offer his Son, being a breach of the sixth commandment?" Deputy Governor: "By an immediate voice." Mrs. Hutchinson: "So to me by an immediate revelation." Deputy Governor: *"How! An immediate revelation?"* Mrs. Hutchinson: *"By the voice of his own Spirit to my soul."*[60] Where then would be the need for the clergy? And this conclusion they feared. This Governor Winthrop declared to have been "the ground of all these tumults and troubles, and I would that those were all cut off from us that trouble us, *for this is the thing that hath been the root of all the mischief."*[61]

Mrs. Hutchinson had convicted herself, only the sentence remained. It was delivered to her in these words:

"The Court hath already declared themselves satisfied concerning the things you hear, and concerning the troublesomeness of her spirit and the danger of her course amongst us, which is not to be suffered. . . . Mrs. Hutchinson, the sentence of the court you hear is, that you are banished from out of our jurisdiction as being a woman not fit for our society, and are to be imprisoned until the court shall send you away."

Mrs. Hutchinson: "I desire to know wherefore I am banished?"

Governor: "Say no more, the Court knows wherefore, and is satisfied."[62]

Only two men, Coddington and Colburn, voted against the sentence.

Judge Mayer sentenced Alexander Berkman and Emma Goldman with these words:

"For such people as these, who would destroy our Government and nullify its laws, we have no place in our country. In

[60] *Ibid.,* II, 439.
[61] *Ibid.,* II, 443.
[62] *Ibid.,* II, 447.

the United States law is an imperishable thing, and in a case such
as this I can but inflict the maximum sentence which is permitted
by our laws."[63]

In accordance with the sentence, Mrs. Hutchinson was sent to
Roxbury, where she was imprisoned in the house of Thomas
Welde, and in March, 1638, formally excommunicated and cast
out of the church by the Synod. John Wilson read her out of
the church. As she passed down the aisle, Mary Dyer left her
place in the audience to walk by the side of Mrs. Hutchinson.
They both moved out together.[64]

When the news of this procedure reached England, it aroused
considerable comment and criticism from liberal people. Sir
George Downing wrote from England that "the law of banishing
for conscience . . . makes us stinke everywhere."[65] Reverend
John White wrote to Governor Winthrop, "to have an eye to one
thinge, that you fall not into that evill abroad, which you labored
to avoyd at home, to binde all men to the same tenets and practice."[66] Already America had its critics abroad.

Whether or not the Antinomians actually approached Christian Anarchist doctrines could be tested by the type of society
which they established on the island of Aquiday or Aquidneck,
now Rhode Island, where the banished Antinomians and their
friends settled.[67] The Rhode Island Colony Records describe the
early governments established on the Island as democracies. But

[63] *Mother Earth,* XII, No. 5, 162.

[64] Mary Dyer, early a disciple of Mrs. Hutchinson, was converted to
Quakerism on a visit to England; returned to the Commonwealth as a
Quaker, was sentenced to be executed on October 27, 1659, but was saved by
a reprisal. Finally because of her return to Boston and especially because of
her efforts to effect a repeal of laws against the Quakers, she was executed
in May, 1660. Winthrop, *op. cit.,* I, 261. Rufus M. Jones, *The Quakers in
the American Colonies* (London, 1911), 84, 87.

[65] James T. Adams, *op. cit.,* 173.

[66] *Ibid.,* 172.

[67] Nineteen of the disenfranchised under the leadership of John Coddington and John Clarke settled at Aquidneck and on January 7, 1638, formed
an association, in January, 1639, remodelled their government, and in April,
1639, certain of them "swarmed" and settled at the other end of the Island,
at Newport, under Coddington. In March, 1640, Portsmouth and Newport
united under one government and in 1641 formed a "Democracie." Winthrop, *op. cit.,* I, 258-259; II, 2-25; Jones, *op. cit.,* 22-23.

there is some evidence which suggests that Mrs. Hutchinson and certain of her closest friends actually dispensed with magistrates and laws. Governor Winthrop recorded in his Journal in 1638 that "At Aquiday, also, Mrs. Hutchinson exercised publicly, and she and her party (some three or four families) *would have no magistracy.*"[68] And again in 1641:

"Mrs. Hutchinson and those of Aquiday island breached new heresies every year. Divers of them turned professed Anabaptists, and *would not wear any arms,* and *denied all magistracy among Christians,* and maintained that there were no churches since those founded by the Apostles and evangelists, nor could any be, nor any pastors ordained, nor seals administered but by such, and that the church was to want these all the time she continued in the wilderness, as yet she was."[69]

This would, of course, be the consistent application of her doctrines, but whether or not she did apply them cannot be established by such slight evidence, particularly since it came from her chief prosecutor. It is a fact, however, that Rhode Island was a haven for the persecuted, particularly the Quakers, and that "none be accounted a delinquent for doctrine" became a traditional principle there. It is possible that the Antinomians and their sympathizers were, therefore, a liberalizing influence in Rhode Island.

From the point of view of Colonial history, the Antinomian controversy may be interpreted as an unsuccessful attempt of the individual to break up the repressive system of authority in religious dogma and action as prescribed by a civil code, a system which was fast becoming rigid. In a half-conscious manner certain ones of them had tried to establish a line beyond which the State or Church should not go. They supported their claims with a doctrine of inner revelation, one which made the spiritual life of the individual spontaneous and personal and all law, which, as we have said, was essentially Scriptural and took precedence over common law, not only unnecessary but harmful. Whether or not they actually demanded the *destruction* of all magistrates and ministers, as the Fifth Monarchy Men did, cannot be affirmed on

[68] Winthrop, *op. cit.,* I, 293.
[69] *Ibid.,* II, 38.

documentary evidence. It can be said, however, that they challenged and even denied the control of magistrates or minister over their religious life, but that their doctrines were torn out of the colony before they could thoroughly crystallize. It is also possible that certain ones of them actually established a small Christian Anarchist community at Portsmouth, Rhode Island.

The struggle of the Antinomians in Massachusetts is typical of those which followed in American history, the struggle of a minority to maintain its own identity and to give to the majority group principles which it believed would elevate group life. But at this time, as well as later (the parallel was drawn especially between the years 1637 and 1917), they were regarded not as friends of society but as enemies. This belief reacted on colonial policy to the exclusion of those aliens who might have brought in dissenting and dangerous doctrines. In 1637 certain aliens were turned away from Massachusetts because of their doctrines. In 1904 the same belief appeared, under different circumstances of course, when immigrants were turned away from the United States because they professed to be anarchists. Both acts mere motivated by fear. The denial of the right of asylum was maintained as a principle in both cases. It reacted in the second place, on colonial policy, to the banishment of those people who propagated doctrines which ran counter to accepted beliefs, which were the sustaining supports of church and state. In 1637 twenty-one dissenters were banished from the Commonwealth. In 1919 two hundred and forty-two anarchists and their sympathizers were deported from the United States. The banishment of Anne Hutchinson from the colony was followed by even more repressive laws. The courts appointed "a committee of some magistrates, some ministers, and some others, to compile a body of fundamental laws."[70] While this policy once embarked upon in the Commonwealth, brought in its train rigidity, conformity, solidarity, it cannot as yet be established what a similar policy will bring to the United States in the Twentieth Century. Except for the attempts of the Quakers, who directly followed the Antinomians in Massa-

[70] Winthrop, op. cit., I, 257.

chusetts, the authority established in the Colonial Period was virtually unchallenged for two hundred years. It was then due to many varied forces, that a breaking-up process had begun. Seeds similar to Antinomianism were sown, took root and flourished for short periods of time. It is necessary before discussing this later development, however, to consider briefly what the Quakers contributed or attempted to contribute to the general movement of anti-authoritarianism.

### The Quakers.

The Quakers came to America in about the year 1655.[71] America to them was a new, free country where everything and anything might be tried and perhaps realized. Their deep purpose was to make a fresh experiment in spiritual religion. Experiments in government were not their primary aim. They did believe, however, that they had discovered a new principle which would revolutionize life, society, civil government and religion.[72] This principle was the presence of a Divine Light in man, a radiation from the central light of God, and if followed, the Kingdom of God could be established on earth. This is in the soul of every man—life to follow and obey; death to disobey. God speaks directly to *every* human spirit without the intercession or interpretation of a minister.[73] Here is the priesthood of believers in its purest form.

This Light which the founders of Quaker doctrine described as the "guide of life" was a real light. It was a "new law written within, on the table of the heart," and "not properly a law written."[74] Hence, "the Spirit and not the Scriptures, is the rule."[75] This Spirit is within and makes harmful, even unnecessary external law. The law or letter, which is without us, kills, but the

[71] George Fox (1624-1691), the founder of Quakerism, began his preaching tour of England in 1647. In 1650 Justice Geroose Bennett hurled the epithet of "Quaker" at the followers of Fox, a name which has clung to them.

[72] Rufus M. Jones, *The Quakers in the American Colonies,* xvi-xvii.

[73] Robert Barclay, *An Apology for the True Christian Divinity* (14th Edition, Glasgow, 1886. First English Edition, 1678), 35.

[74] *Ibid.,* 34.

[75] *Ibid.,* 50.

gospel, which is the inward spiritual law, gives life; for it consists not so much in words as in virtue.[76] And for this reason "the principle rule of Christians under the gospel is not an outward letter, nor law outwardly written and delivered, but an inward spiritual law, engraven in the heart and in the mouth."[77]

These principles dispense with and condemn *all* authority, law, or precept in religion. Had they been consistently applied to all society as originally intended, they would have served as the basis of an anarchistic society. But the Quakers failed to apply their doctrines universally, first, because of their belief in a duality of human nature, a strict separation and almost antipathy of the spiritual and the physical, and second, because they were actually forced from their position in order to preserve a few of their beliefs from the attack of society. Faith in the natural goodness of man and the belief in his unity, as well as the favorable "spiritual climate" of the early nineteenth century, carried the Perfectionists and Non-Resistants into a true Christian Anarchism. How this came about we shall consider in the following chapter.

But since in the creative stage of Quakerism, the leaders of the movement were inspired by the ideal of establishing a complete society on their basic principles, they are worthy of consideration. When the Quakers met opposition, as well as a refusal to incorporate and accept their ideas, they turned to defend and preserve the truth which they believed they held.[78] As their world vision faded, they began to focus their attention on Quakerism as such. The "truth" became definite and static; their forms of worship became fixed and almost unalterable. Silence was accepted as the proper form of worship. Even their freedom in social customs

[76] *Idem.*

[77] *Ibid.,* 51.

[78] Cotton Mather voiced the opinion of the Puritans in general when he called Quakerism "the sink of all heresies." (*Magnalia,* II, 451.) Massachusetts was particularly vigilant in burning Quaker books and pamphlets. In 1656 it passed the first law against Quakers setting (1) fines for reading of Quaker books, (2) banishment for those harboring Quakers, (3) execution for those professing Quakerism (see above, note 64). Jones, *op. cit.,* 36, 37. During the Revolutionary War and all subsequent wars, the Quakers suffered persecution for refusing to fight. Leon Whipple, *The Story of Civil Liberty in the United States* (New York, 1927), 7, 8-9.

ended in conventionality of dress and speech.[79] The things against which their conscience revolted became traditional, such as the bearing of arms, the taking of an oath, and in some cases, voting. Their doctrines, by a very natural process, as well as their customs, became rigid. A Quaker became a well-marked individual.

In order that they might keep their religious ideas and practices, they adopted a passive attitude toward government. William Penn, an ardent Quaker and founder of Pennsylvania, declared that the Quakers were not enemies of the government, and even defined government as "an external order of justice, or the right and prudent disciplining of any society by just laws, either in the relaxation or execution of them."[80] But he would create a religious preserve beyond which the government could not go, a dominion of God which no earthly law could invade. "Force, in matters relating to conscience, carries a plain contradiction to Government, in the Nature, Execution, and End of it."[81]

Robert Barclay, an English Quaker, in one of the most systematic formulations of Quaker doctrine extant, held virtually the same opinion. "No man," he maintained, "by virtue of any power or principality he hath in the government of this world, hath power over the conscience of men . . . because the conscience of man is the seat and throne of God in him, of which God is the alone proper and infallible judge."[82] And conscience he had defined as "that persuasion of the mind which arises from the understanding being possessed with the belief of the truth or falsity of anything."[83] In other matters the magistate may use his authority.[84]

Laws, Penn divided into two kinds, first, "fundamental laws," which are "indispensible and immutable," second, "superficial laws" which are temporary and alterable.[85] The law of conscience

[79] Jones, *op. cit.,* xxiii-xxiv.
[80] William Penn, *Select Works of William Penn* (London, 1771), 185, 191.
[81] *Ibid.,* 191.
[82] Robert Barclay, *op. cit.,* 351.
[83] *Ibid.,* 349.
[84] *Ibid.,* 350.
[85] William Penn, *op. cit.,* 192.

is a law of the first order. In the matters of conscience, therefore, the Quakers were as obedient as they were to civil laws which did not touch their consciences.[86] When the government commanded them to bear arms, they disobeyed the command and suffered the consequences. But outside of that limit they accepted government. In Pennsylvania, Rhode Island, North Carolina, and New Jersey, Quakers took an active part in government, in spite of William Penn's "advice to His children," "Meddle not with Government, never speak of it; let others say or do as they please. But read such Books of Law as relate to the office of a Justice. . . . Meddle not with the Publick, neither Business nor Money; but understand how to avoid it, and defend yourselves upon occasion against it."[87]

In conclusion it may be said, therefore, that both the Antinomians and the Quakers revolted against the invasion of the sovereignty of their religious life. In this they were partial anarchists. The Quakers, moreover, went even further in defining the exact limits beyond which government or law could not intrude on the individual. Law and authority in this preserve they held to be not only unnecessary but harmful. They were unnecessary because the inner sense of good—the Light—guided men in their conduct. It is for subsequent philosophic anarchists to attempt to define the exact nature of that Light, and to objectify it in laws of nature— the laws of individual sovereignty and voluntary coöperation. The Antinomians and the Quakers touched upon the belief of the "innate goodness of man," but mostly for the Christian man.

While this limitation in doctrine may have prevented the Antinomians from applying their principles of no government and no law to a particular society, the most serious check they felt was their banishment from the colony before their ideas had fully matured. They may even have incorporated such principles in their colony at Portsmouth, but it is not certain. With the Quakers it was quite otherwise. Beginning with the ideal of establishing a society based upon their religious principles, they were forced

---

[86] Jones, *op. cit.*, 459.
[87] William Penn, *op. cit.*, 853.

to cast off all those positive, aggressive aims in order to prevent the complete destruction of their whole sect. They kept only those principles with which they could comfortably and peaceably live within society. Although they still refuse to bear arms or to take oaths, they are essentially law-abiding citizens. They are, in a sense, "disillusioned radicals." Like all groups of this class they were forced to choose between three courses of action—to submit to majority pressure in order to live peacefully in society, to leave the country in disgust, or to refuse to compromise even in the face of banishment or death. The course which they accept depends partly on the solidarity of the society in which they are agitating and partly on their own individual temperament. The Quakers chose, for the most part, the former of these three courses.

As will be seen in the following chapter, two conditions made possible the rebirth of Antinomian and Millenarian ideas in the early part of the nineteenth century—first, the breaking up of the rigid and static condition of society (which was achieved by many forces to be considered later), and second, the general dissemination of a belief, a faith in the innate goodness of human nature (which was the central faith of Romanticism). In such conditions Anarchism flourished. It died when society again became more rigid. The seeds of Anarchist Communism were sown later in a barren, stiff soil, flourished for a time in the conditions of economic unrest and uncertainty, and died when society again became relatively adjusted and static. The periodic appearance of these ideas is the subject of the subsequent study, as well as the expanding field of individualism.

## II

## ANARCHISM ADOLESCENT—INDIVIDUALISM IN THE
## ROMANTIC PERIOD (1812-1860)

Ideas enjoy a kind of immortality. They fade and die in one epoch; they spring up in the next, perhaps in a new form, but from the same seed. That they are healthier, more vigorous in one period than in another is true, for the soil of one age is often more suitable for them than that of another. The idea of anti-authoritarianism or no-government, no law, no coercion of the individual is no exception to this rule. What appeared in the seventeenth and early eighteenth centuries as a feeble, under-nourished plant, sprang up and blossomed in all its glory in the first half of the nineteenth century. What were the common ingredients of the soil for these two periods and what new fertilizing elements were added? Who were the carriers of the seed and what were the full-blown blossoms?

The soil of the early colonial days in New England, out of which Antinomianism grew, was one of rigid authoritarianism. Its elements were obedience, conformity, the depravity of man, the bondage of the will. Into this new elements such as the Priesthood of Believers, immediate revelation, Spirit not Law the Light and Guide of Life were introduced by certain rebellious colonists. But the plant which it yielded, Antinomianism, was under-nourished and was quickly uprooted as a pesky weed. Quakerism was soon cultivated into a prim garden variety of plant and lost most of its weed-like, crowding propensities. Thus it remained until the beginning of the nineteenth century. Those elements which were so small and weak in the seventeenth century were strengthened; the whole character of the soil changed. Individualism flourished in hundreds of different species and varieties. A study of the soil in which it grew, therefore, will reveal a clearer perception of its character, at the same time as it yields a better understanding of the conditions necessary for its growth.

America in the first half of the nineteenth century was shifting, restless, youthfully optimistic, eager to explore and to better itself. In the last years of the eighteenth century it had come out of its first struggle for national self-assertion, having freed itself from the restraints on industry and on trade which the Mother Country had placed upon it. It was proud of its independence from England. With new economic realms to conquer, the imagination visioned worlds with undreamed of potentialities. The period from 1812 to 1860 was one of expansion into the West and of the opening up of new industries in the East.

The New England States were exploring and increasing all the possibilities of manufacturing with the multiplication of new industries, machinery and factories. The rights of unrestrained individual enterprise set up areas into which government by state or national law was not to intrude. A certain one-sided individualism of laissez-faire was the rationalization of common practice. The Southern States were settling down to agriculture on a large scale, with slave labor as the characteristic means of production. There also one type of individualism was crystallizing into an agrarian philosophy, of which Thomas Jefferson was the most able exponent. But in both cases it was an individualism which asked the government to interfere only when it was to the advantage of the particular group for it to do so. It was one-sided in the sense that it demanded the right to act without interference but not to give and defend that right for *everyone*—it was particular, not universal, egoistic, not altruistic. The "idealistic" individualism of this period, which will be considered later, was one of *universal* application, and based on the assumption that the individual was free only in so far as he did not injure someone else or in so far as he acted on the natural good impulses which were within him. Although the "popular" individualism was egoistic and not anarchistic, it had attempted to delimit both law and government. Although the individualism of the reformers of this period for the most part fell upon unfriendly ears, it was not as startling as it might have been had public opinion approved absolutism in government. The complete anarchism of certain groups did shock and startle the general public because it over-leaped those low outposts which the accepted individualism had established for government, and there proceeded to build up a society free from *all* restraints except moral ones.

The period under consideration was a period of westward expansion. Only a small portion of the country had even been observed by white men. To the West lay land to be had for the taking of it. The West was still a haven of escape. If conditions became unbearable, or business failed, it was still possible for a courageous, adventurous family to assemble its worldly goods and try its fortune in the West. If they survived the attacks of the Indians, the rigors of the climate, crop failures, and all the trials of pioneer life, they did so by good fortune and their own physical strength. In general they did not want the government to interfere with them. The government had not assisted them in their struggle. They asked only complete personal sovereignty. And although practice tended to build up fairly rigid codes of social behavior, an individualism which broached no organized or governmental force was the natural product of pioneer life.

The period from 1812 to 1860 was one of intensive and extensive economic activity. This very activity contributed to an unsettled condition, to an atmosphere of breaking-up, searching, exploration. Out of this social and economic environment came social and moral philosophies which were not dissimilar. Their general character was optimistic, idealistic, even utopian, daring, and romantic. Their field was the world, man, and his whole cultural environment. Their common bases were first, the belief in the inviolability of human life, and second, an unbounded faith in the natural goodness and infinite perfectibility of human nature. While the general physical condition of the country made such creeds possible, certain philosophies had invigorated them and had given them expression. Rousseauean Romanticism and Hegelian idealism influenced moral philosophy, English Utilitarianism economic philosophy. Rousseau's *Discours sur l'Originie de l'Inegalité* and *Émile* nourished a faith in the naturally good instincts of *every man* and in the possibility of maintaining that virtue by the proper environment. Hegelian idealism, as well as that of

Schelling and Fichte, as it came to America by the course of Coleridge-Carlyle-Emerson, was a common glorification of the ideal of individualism. The Platonic ideal of "Know Thyself" and of the necessity as well as the possibility of living by rational ideas, was accepted. With this as an ideal any corruption of human nature, any maltreatment of mankind became particularly intolerable.

This early self-consciousness and sensitivity were reflected in the attitude of reformers toward evils which before had not been observed. At this time there was scarcely an evil which was not poked at and pried out. They attacked Calvinism for its authority over the human mind and will. They opposed the inequality of the sexes, capital punishment, intemperance, war and slavery, both white and black.

In 1809 William Ellery Channing made one of the most able attacks on Calvinism that had as yet been heard. He soon became the leader of the Unitarian movement. David Low Dodge in 1812 published the first pamphlet in America directed expressly against the war system of nations.[1] The first temperance periodical in the world was established in 1826 with William Lloyd Garrison as editor.[2] The cause of equal rights for women found one of its earliest champions in Frances Wright, who lectured throughout the country from 1828 to 1830. As early as 1829 she advocated birth control. And through her interest in women's rights she approached one phase of anarchism in marriage—that is, in advocating moral obligation rather than legal authority as the sanction for marriage.[3] The year 1831 saw the publication of the most influential abolitionist magazine, *The Liberator,* and 1839 the foundation of the *New England Non-Resistance Society.* Through their interest in slavery and the abolition of war, some of these

---

[1] *War Inconsistent with the Religion of Jesus Christ.*

[2] W. P. Garrison and F. J. Garrison, *William Lloyd Garrison, The Story of His Life Told by His Children* (4 vols., New York, 1885), I, 79-80.

[3] William Randall Waterman, "Frances Wright," *Studies in History, Economics, and Public Law,* edited by Columbia University, Volume CXV, No. 1 (New York, 1924), 158, 159-160; see below, Chapter III, for her temporary economic anarchism.

reformers approached anarchism. Their creed was the sacredness of human life, the right of each individual to control his own life, and the supreme value of freedom. It was to be realized by some in destructive agitation within society, by others in constructive withdrawal from society. To select certain individuals who through their enthusiasm for and faith in human nature arrived at a social and moral anarchism, and to describe the process by which they arrived there, is the purpose of the following study. Since the non-resistants of New England constructed the most positive philosophy of Christian Anarchism, and since they seemed to have carried the ideas of the Antinomians and Quakers to their logical extreme, the major interest lies in them.

The religious idols of the Puritan New Englanders were destroyed by William Ellery Channing (1780-1842) who set up in their place three favorite doctrines of the period—the goodness of God, the essential virtue and perfectibility of man, and the freedom of the will with subsequent responsibility for action. In 1809 Channing delivered his epoch-making sermon, *The Moral Argument Against Calvinism,*[4] and showed himself the spiritual successor to Anne Hutchinson. "Calvinism," he said, "owes its perpetuity to the influence of fear in paralyzing the moral nature. Men's minds and consciences are subdued by terror, . . . and, by thus smothering their just abhorrence, they gradually extinguish it, and even come to vindicate in God what would disgrace his creatures." To attribute a cruel, tyrannical character to God as well as to his mandates, he held to be a false interpretation of Christianity and Christian doctrine. In such misinterpretation the belief in the bondage of the will, the evil nature of man, and predestination took its origin. These beliefs he counteracted with a positive individualism. "It is an important truth," he said, "which we apprehend has not been sufficiently developed, that the ultimate reliance of a human being is and must be on his own mind. For the goodness of human nature he argues, "In affirming the existence and perfections of God we suppose and affirm the

---

[4] *The Works of William E. Channing,* new and complete edition, American Unitarian Association (Boston, 1875), 459-468.

existence in ourselves of faculties which correspond to these sublime objects, and which are fitted to discern them. . . . *Nothing is gained to piety by degrading human nature."*

In fact, he believed that individuals have innate and natural, rational and moral powers. Any moral weakness a man may have is a natural weakness, one which he can work to improve, for the possibilities of self-improvement are limitless. In order to do this, God has given men a conscience, "a sense of right and wrong," "of justice and injustice." God's spirit of "love, charity, and benevolence" inspires men "to love and imitate him." And in closing he expressed the conviction that "Calvinism . . . is giving place to better views," that "it has passed its meridian, and is sinking to rise no more." Its foes are "the progress of the human mind" and the "progress of the spirit of the gospel." His optimism inspired him to the belief that "Society is going forward in intelligence and charity."[5]

The doctrine and the faith expressed here is essentially Rousseauean Romanticism combined with English Deism and Rationalism applied to religion. Voltaire, Rousseau, and Paine were the idols of the students in 1794 at Yale;[6] Rousseau, associated with them, captured Harvard in 1809 in the form of Unitarianism.[7] From this time on Channing became the champion of Unitarianism, assisting in 1825 in the founding of the Unitarian Association.

It is important to note, however, that although his principles were a logical foundation for no-government ideas, as they were later developed by the non-resistants, Channing's conservatism checked him on the verge of such a conclusion. He, as many others of the time, believed, however, that government was only a negative good—that is, in repressing injustice and crime. Nevertheless, and in spite of his belief that the individual should be allowed "free exercise of human powers," he held that the solemn

[5] *Ibid.*, 459-468.
[6] *Religious Experience of John Humphrey Noyes*, compiled and edited by George Wallingford Noyes (New York, 1923), 32.
[7] Vernon Louis Parrington, *The Romantic Revolution, 1800-1860 (Main Currents in American Thought Series, An Interpretation of American Literature from the Beginnings to 1920.* 3 vols., New York, 1927), 322.

duty of a citizen was to respect civil government. Since government had lifted society from savagery, the duty of the citizen was submission to it.[8] Essentially, of course, this is the conclusion of *Le Contrat Social*. His chief contribution, therefore, lies in pointing out the religious implications of a doctrine which others took as a point of departure into other fields.

Henry David Thoreau (1817-1862) makes this his point of departure and actually reaches thereby aesthetic anarchism which is anarchism in its purest form. For this reason he has been selected from that group of individualists which flourished in New England under the name of Transcendentalists.[9] He was not only an anarchist in thought, but also in action. Rather than pay taxes, he went to jail.[10] From 1845-1847 he lived at Walden, where he had built his own house and provided for his own food, proving to himself and to his friends that he could live by the work of his own hands. In 1859 he made an ardent defense of John Brown and his method of direct action, an act which was also lauded as that of a "militant libertarian" by the French Anarchist-Communist, Joseph Déjacque, who lived in America from 1855 to 1861.[11]

Thoreau's underlying assumptions agreed with those of Channing—the right of an individual to his own life and property, the goodness and perfectibility of human nature. The law which for him had supreme validity was the law of equal justice. From this he deduced the right of the individual to do what he thought was right. On this ground he defended the right of the minority against the majority. In his conception action should be based

---

[8] *The Works of Channing*, 680. Although a few suggestions are set forth subsequently, the problem of why one individual, saturated with the same ideas of the period, and exposed to similar conditions, as another, does not arrive at anarchism and another does ought to be studied in more detail.

[9] Ralph Waldo Emerson, Orestes A. Brownson, Nathaniel Hawthorne, George Ripley, Margaret Fuller, were prominent members of this group.

[10] "Civil Disobedience" (first edition, 1864), *The Writings of Henry David Thoreau* (20 vols., Boston and N. Y., 1906), IV, 356-387, 375.

[11] Max Nettlau, *Der Vorfrühling der Anarchie, Ihre Historische Entwicklung von der Anfängen bis zum Jahre 1864* (Berlin, 1925), 219.

upon well thought-out and intensely perceived principles, but not necessarily upon rigid doctrines or schemes which checked spontaneous action. An inner conviction, therefore, will lead the honest individual to break any law which he believes to be wrong or unjust. Furthermore, it is his *duty* to disobey under those circumstances. The Quaker doctrine of obedience to the conscience appears here in a new form. Revolution or direct action he finds infinitely superior to political action because it is more expeditious and hence more effective. Freedom, not reform, was his goal. Thus along the line of his own faith and belief in individualism, Thoreau arrived at anarchism.

Thoreau proceeded with the other reformers of his time to this point. But when he affirms that "that government is best which governs not at all. And when men are prepared for it, that will be the kind of government which they will have," he departs from accepted thought and enters a realm of an ideal anarchist future.[12] He rests his faith on what has gone before, that which has been done before has been done by the American people and not by the government. He concludes, therefore, that it is not talk about "no government" that is needed but action for better government, which can be realized only by the reform of the individual. In his own words: "I think we must be men first and subjects afterward. It is not desirable to cultivate a respect for the law, so much as for the right." And for this reason he opposes the rule of the majority. "A government in which the majority rule in all cases cannot be based on justice, since it decides by expediency and not by conscience." He concludes that "the only obligation which I have a right to assume is to do at any time what I think right." Enlightened individual conscience is the guiding light of life.

In the same vein he continues, finding law no proper guide to action, for "Law never made men a whit more just; and, by means of their respect for it, even the well-disposed are daily made the agents of injustice." Not only does law itself render injustice, but

[12] "Civil Disobedience," 356.

undue respect for it makes men machine-like.  It kills their spontaneity and conscience—an argument which the Antinomians drew
forth to destroy the jurisdiction of law.  The representatives of
the law—soldiers, jailers, constables, and policemen, as well as
politicians, lawyers, ministers, and office holders forcing others to
obedience, themselves become machines.  They are regarded as
the friends of society.  But "heroes, patriots, martyrs, reformers,
in the great sense, and *men*—serve the state with their consciences
also, and so necessarily resist it for the most part; and they are
commonly treated as enemies by it."

Thoreau, therefore, belongs to that small group of intellectuals
of his time who carried their individualism to its logical limits.  If
the government violates the equal right of every individual to his
own life, it should be resisted.  Slavery, he held, was a violation
of this right.  For this reason a man "cannot without disgrace be
associated with it."  He personally cannot for an instant recognize
the political organization as his own government which is the
slave's government also.  Of the two possible attitudes which an
individual can assume toward the government—resignation or
active criticism—the latter is infinitely preferable.  The masses of
men will resign themselves to the evils but "there is little virtue
in the action of the masses of men."  Two means are open to the
individual—political action and direct action or peaceful revolution.
Political action, he opposes, on the ground that it takes too long
and is often ineffective.  The refusal to participate in the government on the part of every individual who disapproved of its
action would bring a peaceful revolution.  This type of resistance
to the government, he defends with precedent and with the Declaration of Independence.  He, therefore, urges the minority, and
he assumes that it is a minority, to refuse to vote, to pay taxes, or
to participate in any way in the government, and if necessary to
go to prison because "under a government which imprisons any
unjustly, the true place for a just man is also a prison."

Contrary to the spirit of democracy he builds up a case for
the minority.  Instead of urging people to conform for the "general good," he urges them to disobey. Furthermore, these minorities

should be cherished because they alone act on principle and advance the good of society. They, on the contrary, are often persecuted by the powerful majority. He asks, "Why does it (the government) not cherish its minority. . . . Why does it always crucify Christ and excommunicate Copernicus and Luther and pronounce Washington and Franklin rebels?" When to conform is to become an agent of injustice to another, it is necessary to "break the law." Majority rule is the rule of the strong arm not of honesty. In this light Thoreau saw the government when he reflected in jail. When he came out he said, "I saw the State was half-witted, that it was timid as a lone woman with her silver spoons and that it did not know its friends from its foes, and I lost all my remaining respect for it."[13] Just as others, he felt an aversion for the conduct of government, but unlike others he counselled disobedience to it and obedience to that inner conviction of honor and justice.

A further elaboration of Thoreau's ideas of direct action may be found in his essays defending John Brown's raid.[14] At the same time as he defends John Brown personally, he defends generally the acts of solitary individuals motivated by a law higher than the Constitution. His defense was a powerful one, and particularly courageous when it is remembered that the majority of the people of the time—even ardent abolitionists—condemned it as an insane act. Joseph Déjacque, the French Anarchist-Communist referred to above, wrote from New York to his friend Pierre Vésinier on February 20, 1861, commenting on this fact:

"Es gibt wohl, wie auf dem alten Kontinent, revolutionäre Elemente, aber in latentem und teilweisem (parcellaire) Zustand. Männer von militanten Libertarismus sind in der ungeheuren Minderzahl. John Brown, eine dieser mutigen Ausnahmen, wurde, wie Sie wissen, unter dem Applaus der Sklavenhalter und, was noch trauriger ist, von der grossen Mehrzahl der als abolitionistisch geltenden Partei verleugnet."[15]

[13] *Ibid.*, 357-376.
[14] "A Plea for Captain John Brown" (1859), IV, 409-440; "The Last Days of John Brown" (1860), 441-450; and "After the Death of John Brown" (1860), 451-454.
[15] Nettlau, *op. cit.*, 219.

Thoreau defended John Brown for his courage, his self-sacrifice, his magnanimity. John Brown's motives he held to be too high for the comprehension of his accusers. His inspiration had moved him to act without fear of government. "He did not set up even a political graven image between him and his God."[16] Such conduct is admirable, even inspiring. "When a man stands up serenely against the condemnation and vengeance of mankind, rising above them literally by a whole body, . . . the spectacle is a sublime one . . . and we become criminals in comparison." Materially its results were barren, spiritually it was fertile for "when you plant, or bury a hero in his field, a crop of heroes is sure to spring up." As a method, this act was preferable to indifference. Thoreau said, "I speak for the slave when I say that I prefer the philanthropy of Captain Brown to that philanthropy which neither shoots me nor liberates me." It was an act of love, for "no one loved his fellow-men so well" as John Brown.

Thoreau took one more bold step. He declared that the government had placed itself in the class of tyrannical governments by executing John Brown, one of its best citizens. It had shown itself to represent injustice, not justice, and the ignoble, not the noble faculties of the mind and the whole heart.[17] And he finally concluded that the future of America lay not in its government but in its individuals. It is they who are the guides. "Look not to legislatures and churches for your guidance, nor to any soulless *incorporated* bodies, but to inspirited or inspired ones."[18]

Since this is true, Thoreau declared that "there will never be a really free and enlightened State until the State comes to recognize the individual as a higher and independent power, from which all its own power and authority are derived and treats him accordingly."[19] Was it not then inevitable that individualism of this type should lead to anarchism? Thoreau reveals that it was in his own visionary words he describes a theoretical anarchist society.

[16] "A Plea for Captain John Brown," IV, 419.
[17] *Ibid.,* 425-430.
[18] "The Last Days of John Brown," 446.
[19] "Civil Disobedience," 387.

"I please myself with imagining a State at last which can afford to be just to all men, and to treat the individual with respect as a neighbor; which even would not think it inconsistent with its own repose *if a few were to live aloof from it,* not meddling with it, nor embraced by it, *who fulfilled all the duties of neighbors and fellow-men. A State which bore this kind of fruit, and suffered it to drop off as fast as it ripened, would prepare the way for a still more perfect and glorious State, which also I have imagined, but not yet anywhere seen."* [20]

Thoreau was an anarchist in the sense that he believed in the sovereignty of the individual and voluntary coöperation. He held the individual supreme and free to live and act by his best impulses, which were both rational and emotional, restraining himself only that he might be a "good neighbor." Freedom and justice are the highest values. Moral values, therefore, would not take the form of doctrine or dogma. An aesthetic sense of proportion would present individualism from becoming license. Thoreau represented that type of intellectual of the Romantic period, which arrived at anarchism by aesthetic experience. Others, however, came to similar conclusions by religious experience, and still others by practical life experience.

*Perfectionism*

Of that group which was inspired to sweep away all earthly authority by its religious faith, John Humphrey Noyes was the best representative. The religious philosophy of Perfectionism which he built up took as its starting point, as did Thoreau's, the accepted faith of the time and ended at spiritual anarchism. Although Perfectionism was essentially a religious philosophy, it exerted an important influence on the social reformers Henry C. Wright, Edmund Quincy, the Grimké sisters, and William Lloyd Garrison, who came to a certain type of anarchism through their personal experience and their particular interests in reform.

John Humphrey Noyes (1811-1886) reached conclusions similar to those of Thoreau and the non-resistants through revelation and Scriptural inspiration. His spiritual development was that of

[20] *Idem.*

a Fifth Monarchy Man, and his conclusions similar. As with Channing and Thoreau, whose environment had influenced their philosophy, so with Noyes. This was a period of religious revivalism, as well as of reform. Conversion was the fashion. In 1831 Noyes was "converted to religion," and abruptly gave up the study of law for theology, studying first at Dartmouth and then at Yale.[21] After much pondering of the problems of religion, he came to the belief in 1833 that the second coming of Christ had been realized with the foundation of the Christian Church. This idea was the key to his theology and to his anarchism as well.

Two years before, in 1831, William Miller had seized upon the belief in the second coming of Christ, which was not to be realized until the year 1842. He began prophesying and lecturing throughout New England and New York.[22] For him it was a haven of escape, preferring as he did the heaven and hell of the Scriptures to the denial of a future existence which he had met with in his former deism.[23] Millerism became almost a religious hysteria, spreading rapidly particularly among the farming classes. The Second Adventists, however, were too much taken up with praying and preparing their earthly goods for the ascent or descent in 1842 to concern themselves with their spiritual regeneration.

Noyes seems to have conceived the second coming as a spiritual advent, that is, the destruction of all earthly law and government, all authority except that of God. By examining the Scriptures, he discovered that this had already been realized by the disciples in the foundation of the Christian Church. The apostolic church then passed from the outer world to the inner world, marking the end of the Jewish era and the beginning of a new age.[24] It was necessary, therefore, that all men realize that they had been saved. Noyes at once began to proselyte among his friends.

If he was to believe the Scriptures, he would believe that the complete salvation from sin had already been realized, for it was

---

[21] *Religious Experience of John Humphrey Noyes,* 34.

[22] Clara Endicott Sears, *Days of Delusion, a Strange Bit of History* (Boston and New York, 1924), 32.

[23] *Ibid.,* 27.

[24] Noyes, *op. cit.,* 69-88.

promised that all men would become perfect just preceding Christ's coming. Consequently he cast aside the old Calvinistic belief in the depravity of man, as Channing had done in 1809. But this was not the end of his religious revelations. He himself on February 20, 1834 came to the momentous realization that he, Noyes, had been saved from sin and being perfect was free from law, government, and all earthly authority.[25] His mission was at once clear to him. He was to withdraw from society and build the perfect kingdom which Christ had begun at his second coming. This kingdom was to be without law, guided only by love.

The conviction that he and all those whom he converted were set free from law by salvation from sin, deepened with his realization that law interfered between God and man. The study of the New Testament and especially of Paul's words, "Ye are not under the law, but under grace" brought him to the conclusion in May, 1834, that "union with Christ gave complete freedom from law.[26] On November 20, 1834, he further elaborated this point when he wrote in the *Perfectionist:*

"The new covenant gives liberty from external law. . . . Under the old covenant the law was written on tables of stone. Under the new it is written in the heart. . . . *External law of necessity supposes human depravity.*"[27]

Under such a condition it is just as natural and inevitable to do good as it is to eat or sleep. Law under such circumstances is unnecessary. God's rule is "Do as you please for I promise that your pleasure shall be mine."[28] Through the study of the Scriptures, therefore, he came to a belief, a faith in the natural goodness of human nature, and in its infinite capacity for perfectibility. In the same way, he came to a belief in the sovereignty of the indi-

[25] *Ibid.,* 112.
[26] *Ibid.,* 183.
[27] *Ibid.,* 184. *The Perfectionist,* a monthly for the new doctrine of Perfectionism, appeared for the first time on August 20, 1834, *ibid.,* 115. Although its circulation was not very large, it exercised an influence out of all proportion to its size. Garrison had read it; the Beechers were familiar with and had expressed their satisfaction with it. *Ibid.,* 336-337; Garrison, *op. cit.,* II, 114, 145.
[28] *Ibid.,* 184.

vidual. In a letter to his mother, September 9, 1835, he said: "I have learned that the love of God, self-love, and the love of mankind are all one; that perfect, that is, enlightened self-love is and ought to be the mainspring of the human machine; that in blessing and perfecting myself I glorify God, and bless mankind."[29] And like Thoreau he had decided to strive for perfect self-knowledge and perfect self-control before teaching others.[30]

For these reasons he emphatically denounced all government and law and most particularly the government of the United States. He went even farther than that—he declared it was the duty of a Christian man who believed in God's laws either to resist the government by a refusal to take part in it or actually to withdraw from it. Government in general was bad, but its worst crime was the sanction of human slavery. By its conduct it had violated Christian law which for Noyes was supreme, but which according to his interpretation, was essentially the same as Thoreau's aesthetically perceived law. Noyes' most forceful denunciation appears in a letter which he wrote to William Lloyd Garrison on March 22, 1837, a momentous letter from the point of view of Garrison's personal development.[31] In this letter Noyes described the government of the United States as "a bloated, swaggering libertine, trampling on the Bible—its own constitution—its treaties with the Indians—the petitions of its citizens: with one hand whipping a negro tied to a liberty-pole, and with the other dashing an emaciated Indian to the ground."[32] On one side he pictured "the despots of Europe, laughing and mocking at the boasted liberty of their neighbor," and on the other "the Devil, saying, 'Esto perpetua'."

Since the government had always violated liberty and Christian law and would continue to do so he was willing that all men should know he had subscribed his name to an instrument similar to the Declaration of 1776, renouncing all allegiance to the government

[29] *Ibid.*, 234.
[30] *Ibid.*, 235.
[31] Garrison, *op. cit.*, II, 145-148.
[32] *Ibid.*, II, 145-146.

of the United States and asserting the title of Jesus Christ to the throne of the world.[33] But he had thought still further. He decided that it was the duty of a Christian either to go out of the world or to find some way to live "without being a hypocrite or a partaker in the sins of the nation."[34] Just as Thoreau held that the place for an honest man was in jail when a government violated the right of equal liberty, so Noyes thought the rôle of an honest man was that of a rebel within the government, or a perfect Christian outside of it. Criticism, petition, and reform he deemed useless because they only aggravated tyranny. It was, therefore, necessary to declare war on tyranny "by a declaration of independence and other weapons suitable to the character of a son of God."[35]

Noyes' hope of the millenium began, as he said, "at the overthrow of this nation."[36] He aimed to be an agent of destruction. He believed that the territory of the United States belonged to God, was promised to Christ and his followers, that the nations had to be dashed to pieces before the Kingdom of God could be established, that existing governments were only "preparatory forms of discipline, fitted to the childhood of the race," and finally that God had especially ordained this hypocritical nation for destruction.[37] At the destruction of this nation, which was to come shortly ("The country is ripe for a convulsion like that of France"), his spiritual anarchist kingdom would be realized. Christ "will ascend the throne of the world and then the world will be free and the convulsion which is coming will be, not the struggle of death, but the travail of childbirth—*the birth of a ransomed world*."[38] He nominated "Jesus Christ for the Presidency not only of the United States, but of the world," and exhorted the Abolitionists to do likewise, "to abandon a government whose

[33] *Ibid.*, II, 145.
[34] *Ibid.*, II, 146.
[35] *Idem.*
[36] *Ibid.*, II, 147.
[37] *Ibid.*, II, 146-147.
[38] *Ibid.*, II, 147.

President had declared war upon them." In order to prepare for withdrawal, however, it was necessary to be emancipated from sin.

Since he conceived the rule of God, the love of God as self-rule and self-love, and since he believed that in order to become good, men were to live on the assumption of perfection *without braces* and *without weakening supports,* Noyes was a true anarchist. Men, he believed, could not become good men by living evil lives, or attain self-government by being governed. This is essentially the position of a true anarchist. Absolute denial of all external government or force is the only way to prepare men for self-government, which is the goal of life.

This was his central theme. The years after 1837 he spent in applying it to actual life. One of the first difficulties which he met was misinterpretation. Some of his followers interpreted his doctrine of freedom from law as license. Some of them indulged in sexual promiscuity,[39] others of them in the denial of all restraints. The New York Perfectionists under James Latourette and Theophilus R. Gates, and especially the latter, leaned toward the belief that the Christian stood in a direct spiritual relation with God and needed no human leader or teacher.[40] Noyes believed that at the present time even Christians required *voluntary* leadership. At the same time he disapproved of some of the applications of his doctrine of Perfectionism, especially that of the non-resistants, whom he called "ultraists" and their conduct "acts of sedition against God.[41] Noyes' opposition is difficult to explain. He certainly objected to their extreme pacifism and they to his communal marriage,[42] but they agreed on the essentials, that is, that love, faith, and Christian law as affirmed by Paul, were to take the place of civil law and force. Perhaps misunderstanding and rivalry would partially explain this lack of sympathy.

Between 1840 and 1848, when he founded the community at Oneida, New York, Noyes injected into his philosophy two practical restraints to license, that is, voluntary subjection to enlight-

[39] Noyes, *op. cit.,* 197-199.
[40] *Ibid.,* 203, 204.
[41] Garrison, *op. cit.,* III, 11.
[42] *Idem.*

ened leadership and mutual instruction. He came to believe more strongly that righteousness was a condition for freedom from law. In January, 1840, he said: "The idea of the law's coming to an end is frightful only when disjoined from that which Paul constantly connects with it, namely righteousness."[43] Love he substituted for Law. Law abolished, there was still the necessity of acting on moral principle. By way of illustration, he said that the abolition of legislatures and courts would not leave men free from conscience or the necessity for virtuous conduct, but it would take away force and authority. This is an answer to the objection so often brought against anarchism that the absence of authority would bring chaos and immorality. God, he said, would become a father instead of a law-giver and would put love and truth in their hearts. "Absolute personal liberty is essential to holiness. That is Paul's doctrine. But in Paul's doctrine as a whole there are a thousand safeguards against antinomianism which the liberty maniac knows nothing about."[44] Exhortation, persuasion, and example would take the place of formal obligation.[45] The antinomians, the Quakers, and such men as Thoreau substituted "conscience" for law, Noyes' love for law.

The fact that Noyes resorted to the use of force by approving leadership may signify one of two things—that pure anarchism is impossible or impractical, or that Noyes was afraid of losing his preëminent position. The fact remains that the community which he established prospered and was a striking success. But whether it succeeded because it had a sound economic basis, or because it had a true social and moral foundation is a debatable question. It is true that practical experience demanded that he reconcile religious individualism with communal life. The product in the community was Anarchist-Communism.

Aside from this question, however, Noyes' Perfectionism remains an excellent illustration of the type of anarchism which was born of a union of the devout religious faith with the extreme

[43] Noyes, op. cit., 369.
[44] Ibid., 369.
[45] Ibid., 371.

individualism of the Romantic period. Still other leaders of the day, however, were drawn to a similar type of anarchism through their absorbing interests in social reform causes, such as peace, slavery, capital punishment, temperance, and women's rights. The majority of the social reformers avoided extreme views of anarchism, because they feared public censure. A small minority, however, "landed into" an extreme radicalism which amounted to anarchism. The Non-Resistants were the finest representatives of this minority.

### Non-Resistance

The belief in the inviolability of human life and the infinite perfectibility of man was the basis of most of the social philosophies during the Romantic period. The nervous systems of the leading reformers were delicately sensitive to all violations of these principles. They attacked war because it resulted in the destruction of human life. The more devoutly religious of them came to anarchism through this channel, for in attempting to live a life ordered by Christian law, they found condemnation of war in the principle "Resist not Evil." Since the government was the chief prosecutor of this war principle, they denounced it. David Low Dodge, Henry C. Wright and Adin Ballou belonged to this class. They attacked capital punishment because it deprived men of their lives. They assailed slavery because it was a violation of liberty, of the right of every human being to control his own life. William Lloyd Garrison was the most ardent and uncompromising assailant of slavery. Even the right of woman to her own life and property was defended. Finally, the supreme agent and guarantor of these violations was the government, a realization to which they came gradually and largely through the government's use of violence against them in their reform activity. The force with which they attacked government and law varied with the individual. It depended upon the strength of his convictions, upon the center of his interest, and upon his personal experience as an agitator. Upon similar factors depended his consistency or inconsistency. On the general principles, as stated above, their anarchism rested.   It is necessary, therefore, to consider their philosophy and their spiritual development in detail.

It is not difficult to understand how the philosophy of the extreme pacifists led to anarchism.   It is, however, an involved problem to determine *why,* from among all the individuals who were interested in peace, they, the extremists, should have built up such a philosophy.   While this problem lies more in the realm of psychology than of history, a systematic and unprejudiced study of it would help the student of history to a better understanding of radical philosophies.   The Non-Resistants appeared to be men with an intense emotional life who felt deeply and personally social evils and suffering, and toned to a clear and simple perception of the remedies, almost too clear, they were impatient of compromise and gradual reformation.   Their intellectual and moral courage steeled them against opposition.   Freeing themselves from conventionality of thought and of action, they pushed to a goal, an ideal goal, with a singleness of purpose.

They were certainly men of their time, for the question of peace was one which interested reformers as early as the beginning of the nineteenth century.   One of the first, if not the first, peace society in the world was formed in August, 1815, in New York, with David Low Dodge as president.[46]   The organization of the Massachusetts Peace Society on the initiative of Noah Worcester followed on December 28, 1815, and of a London peace society in June, 1816.[47]   The large circulation of peace books and tracts indicates that the peace cause had won considerable attention. Nearly a thousand copies of Dodge's *The Mediator's Kingdom not of this World* were sold within two weeks in 1809.[48]   Noah Worcester's *Solemn Review of the Custom of War* passed through five editions in fifteen months from the date of its first appearance on December 25, 1814, and by 1846 it was reprinted in the United

---

[46] David Low Lodge, *War Inconsistent with the Religion of Jesus Christ.* Introduction by Edwin D. Mead, Boston, 1905 (reprinted from 1812 edition), vii.

[47] *Ibid.,* vii; Merle Eugene Curti, *The American Peace Crusade, 1815-1860* (Durham, North Carolina, 1929), 11, 12, 14.

[48] Dodge, *op. cit.,* xix.

States more than a dozen times.[49]  A similar interest existed in England, as evidenced by the organization of peace societies and the publication of peace tracts.[50]

While the majority of the peace advocates conservatively condemned only offensive war, a small minority as early as 1809,[51] opposed *all* war, defensive and offensive, and even the use of any force by an individual as well as by the nation.  One of the first to express these opinions was David Low Dodge.[52]  He proclaimed it unlawful for a Christian to take part in war or to approve capital punishment on such grounds.  With the Quakers, however, he objected only to the government's use of force to execute its laws, laws which he felt were so often contrary to the laws of Christ (to them he gave his sole allegiance).[53]  In matters of conscience he believed that an individual should refuse to sacrifice his principles.  But all laws which were not contrary to the laws of the gospel, the true Christian should obey.[54]  Dodge did vision a time, however, when the earthly kingdoms would fall and God would reign.[55]  He, himself, would neither vote nor hold office.[56]

The American Peace Society on its foundation in 1828 and its incorporation of the New York Peace Society in the same year, took a moderate position specifically condemning only offensive war.[57]  Within the society a forceful minority agitated for the adoption of the principles of true non-resistance.  Already in 1833 Henry C. Wright was urging this policy on the President of the Society, William Ladd.[58]  On March 11, 1837, he suggested the

[49] Curti, *The American Peace Crusade,* 11.

[50] *Ibid.,* 5, 6.

[51] The Quakers, of course, had more or less consistently opposed war and the use of force much earlier.

[52] In his books: *The Mediator's Kingdom not of this world* and *War Inconsistent with the Religion of Jesus Christ.*

[53] Dodge, *op. cit.,* xvi.

[54] *Ibid.,* 105.

[55] *Idem.*

[56] *Ibid.,* xvi.

[57] Curti, *The American Peace Crusade,* 43, 46.

[58] *Ibid.,* 69.

formation of a peace society based entirely on non-resistance.[59] Out of this suggestion and immediately out of Wright's motion in the Peace Society meeting for the calling of a convention, grew the New England Non-Resistance Society. Henry C. Wright, William Lloyd Garrison, Amasa Walker, Edmund Quincy, and Maria Chapman were its staunchest supporters. Adin Ballou joined them later. As a society they took the final step which Dodge had hesitated to take, when they denounced all law and all government as inconsistent with Christianity. While this complete acceptance of non-resistance should have brought them logically to this point (Dodge, however, had not arrived there through logic), the threats of the government against their anti-slavery agitation and especially the identification of the government with slavery made them take the final step to Christian Anarchism. This situation intensified Wright's convictions because he almost alone had been forced to this point by his religious faith. With Garrison and the others, however, it was a decisive influence. Since the cause of anti-slavery bore such an important relation to the no-government theories of the Non-Resistants, it is necessary to consider what that relationship was and how it was established. A survey of Garrison's development is particularly revealing.

It is certain that in 1826 William Lloyd Garrison held no anti-government notions, for at that time he was an ardent Federalist, as well as a very patriotic citizen. The motto of the paper, the *Free Press,* which he edited from March to September, 1826, was, "Our Country, Our Whole Country, and Nothing But Our Country."[59a] Although in 1827 he was listening to the sermons of Lyman Beecher and William Ellery Channing, he disagreed with them, admiring only their intellectual power.[60] By 1828 he had already shown an interest in reform by appealing to Christian influence to sponsor the causes of peace, temperance, the abolition of vice, and the enlistment of women in the Temperance Move-

[59] *Ibid.,* 75.

[59a] Garrison, *op. cit.,* I, 60. A large proportion of this *Life of Garrison* is primary source material. Wherever it is possible it is this, rather than the secondary material which is cited as evidence.

[60] *Ibid.,* I, 78.

ment.[61] It was at this time that he edited the Temperance paper, *The National Philanthropist.*

His active interest in slavery was first stimulated by his contact with Benjamin Lundy and by his early experiences in Baltimore, Maryland. Benjamin Lundy, a Quaker and active in forming anti-slavery societies in Ohio and Tennessee, had considerably advanced the cause of abolitionism through the *Genius of Universal Emancipation,* a periodical which he had begun publishing in 1821.[62] It was in the early part of the year 1828 that he met Garrison in Boston, and by his fiery enthusiasm and ardor converted Garrison to active participation in the cause of abolition. After that Garrison arranged public meetings in Boston, where Lundy spoke. He appreciated for the first time the full force of the indifference of the majority and the opposition of the minority to abolitionism.[63] His faith in political action, and conservative political action at that, however, as a means to the end was still strong. He actually supported John Quincy Adams against Andrew Jackson in the Presidential campaign of 1828. He even consented to publish a paper, the *Journal of the Times,* for Adam's party agents, reserving the right at the same time, of propagandizing for the cause of Abolitionism, Temperance, Peace, and Moral Reform. Nor can it be said that his nationalism had cooled when he is found to approve "national aggrandizement" by industrial improvement, as he did at this time.[64]

Garrison's experience in Baltimore, however, effected an important change in his attitude. He became more uncompromising and more violent in his attacks on slavery men and the whole institution of slavery. It was there that he decided to devote his life to the overthrow of the three greatest evils that cursed the human race—war, intemperance, and slavery.[65] In August, 1829, he went to Baltimore to become the Associate Editor of the *Genius of Universal Emancipation.* One of his most telling experiences was his

[61] *Ibid.,* I, 84, 85-86.
[62] *Ibid.,* I, 88.
[63] *Ibid.,* I, 94.
[64] *Ibid.,* I, 101-109.
[65] *Ibid.,* I, 142.

arrest and imprisonment. For his attack on Frances Todd, a slave trader, in the columns of the *Genius,* he was indicted by the Grand Jury for gross and malicious libel, and on April 17, 1830, fined and placed in jail, where he remained for seven weeks. Prison experience does not necessarily moderate men's ideas; it often intensifies their convictions. Garrison's experience made him reflect on the nature of law and conclude that the one by which he had been convicted was "abhorrent and atrocious" and illustrative of his quotation: " 'of all injustice, that is the greatest which goes by the name of Law; and of all sorts of tyranny, the forcing of the letter of the Law against the equity is the most insupportable'."66 He found it also a violation of the freedom of the press. And as with people who feel themselves convicted by an abridgment of fundamental rights, he used the accounts of his trial as propaganda material. In this respect he was a typical radical.

During this same period in Baltimore, Garrison came to a more poignant realization of what slavery meant. He saw slaves beaten until they bled, he heard their cries—and this for the first time.67

It is not surprising, therefore, in view of this early experience, that in 1831 Garrison definitely renounced political action as a means to the abolition of slavery. He renounced as a general policy petitioning the government or working to elect an abolitionist to the presidency. He renounced it only to take up a new method, a direct method—the propagation of harsh uncompromising truth, truth based on the fundamental principle of freedom, the only effective weapon. This he proclaimed in the first issue of the *Liberator,* January 1, 1831:

"I will be as harsh as truth, and as uncompromising as justice. On this subject, I do not wish to think, or speak, or write with moderation. No! No! . . . I am in earnest—I will not equivocate —I will not excuse—I will not retreat a single inch—and I will be heard."68

66 *Ibid.,* I, 165-178.
67 *Ibid.,* I, 150.
68 *Ibid.,* I, 225.

And later in more positive terms, "We are out of the arena of politics, and we mean to keep out of it."[69]

His renunciation of political action as ineffective, a waste of time, and a wrong was only one step removed from the denunciation of government as a wrong in itself. He took this last step in 1837. The ideas which before he had felt but vaguely were crystallized by the fire of experience. At this crucial point John Humphrey Noyes appeared and completed Garrison's development. At the same time his new experiences were to be a school of preparation.

In the first place, he met obstacles to the cause of abolition which had become so important to him. It is possible, therefore, that he adopted a method of spiritual violence in order to waken the apathetic from indifference, and to startle the vituperous from opposition. In the *Liberator* of January 11, 1831, he wrote:

"In New England I found contempt more bitter, opposition more active, detraction more relentless, prejudice more stubborn and apathy more frozen, than among the slave-owners themselves. . . . The apathy of the people is enough to make every statue leap from its pedestal, and to hasten the resurrection of the dead."[70]

And that this was one of the purposes of his method he himself implied: "My language is exactly such as suits me, it will displease many, I know—to displease them is my intention."[71]

In the second place, Garrison was driven to his extreme position as a reaction against the violence which was used to attack him and his abolitionist friends. In a sense, it was a natural psychological reaction. Churches were shut against him.[72] Threatening letters were addressed to him. The newspapers incited mobs to violence, calling him an "incendiary" and a "mad man."[73] A New York mob threatened to tar and feather him, who had slandered America in Europe as a country of renegades and thieves, and who

[69] *Ibid.*, I, 226.
[70] *Ibid.*, I, 224, 225.
[71] *Ibid.*, I, 227.
[72] *Ibid.*, I, 208, 475.
[73] *Ibid.*, I, 238.

would take away well-earned property.[74]   Then again he was burnt in effigy in Charlestown and even in Boston a gallows was erected in front of his house.[75]   But these were mere gestures compared with the direct physical attack made upon him by a Boston mob on October 21, 1836.[76]   The mayor, powerless before the crowd, had Garrison put in jail for protection.   The contrast between the action of the mob and that of the early revolutionists, martyrs for the liberty of all, was revolting to him.[77]   In the next year he suggested that he had been fortified by their opposition when he said:

"The pressure upon me was like an avalanche, and nothing but the power of God sustained me.   The clergy was against me—the nation was against me.   But God and his truth, the rights of men, and the promise of the Holy Scriptures were with me."[78]

Through the same channel Adin Ballou, a prominent non-resistant, came to condemn government and to approve withdrawal from it.   Ballou attested to the fact that before he was waked up by the violence used against the abolitionists, he had not thought much about abolition.   He was a "born Democrat" and the wrongs and outrages of slavery were out of his sight and so out of his mind.[79]   He declared that "a thick veil of reverent patriotism" had shut out of his vision many things which he saw afterwards. Brought up to idolize his country, its constitution, laws, and to reverence the national union, he was disturbed by the outcry of the abolitionists that slavery was a national sin of which all participants were guilty.   And when they attacked the ark of the national covenant, he said, "my blind patriotism was shocked and deplored the agitation that had been raised."[80]   But when violence was used against the leaders, prices were put on their heads, and their lec-

[74] *Ibid.*, I, 382-385.
[75] *Ibid.*, I, 485, 519.
[76] *Ibid.*, I, 12-29.
[77] *Ibid.*, II, 21.
[78] *Ibid.*, II, 155.
[79] *Autobiography of Adin Ballou (1803-1890),* edited by William S. Heywood (Lowell, Mass., 1896), 277.
[80] *Ibid.*, 278.

tures broken up, it became impossible for him as an honest, conscientious person not to reflect on the question. When he reflected he could not be neutral. He concluded after reflection that slavery was the "sum of all villainies," that the constitution protected slavery by its support of slave power. Church and State were controlled by slavery. This required every honest, conscientious opponent of slavery to withdraw from both State and Church which attacked abolitionists as "pestilent fellows."[81] He expressed surprise that he had not come to these conclusions before, especially since all the principles involved were to be found in the Bible. Light came to him in 1837.[82] Adin Ballou was not the first citizen to be interested in and converted to anarchism by the government's use of violence.[83]

In the third place, Garrison, like a few other abolitionists, came to the final conviction that the government of the United States was identified with and defended his most deadly foe—slavery. In the beginning Garrison and others believed that they could bring about the abolition of slavery by political action. He had supported John Quincy Adams with this expectation and had petitioned him to work for the abolition of slavery in the District of Columbia. Adams refused firmly,[84] and Garrison lost faith. The political situation of 1834 had destroyed whatever hope for governmental action he might have had, when the party choice lay between Jacksonianism, which he hated in principal and practice, and Whiggism, which had disappointed him.[85] Furthermore, both parties had campaigned vigorously against extreme abolitionism.

[81] *Ibid.*, 279.

[82] *Ibid.*, 281.

[83] Adin Ballou in 1838 became interested in non-resistance, concluded after studying it that its principles had a basis in Scripture and that consistency demanded the withdrawal from all governmental society constitutionally committed to force in slavery, war, and capital punishment, that Christ did not ordain civil government. With religious conviction he became a confirmed non-resistant. *Ibid.*, 306-308. Voltairine de Cleyre and Emma Goldman, the two most prominent anarchist women of the late nineteenth and early twentieth centuries, were converted to anarchism by the execution of the Chicago Haymarket rioters in 1887.

[84] Garrison, *op. cit.*, I, 264.

[85] *Ibid.*, I, 456.

In the year 1836, therefore, Garrison went so far as to warn abolitionists against voting for any presidential candidate.[86]

Not only had the government failed to emancipate the slaves as Garrison demanded, but it also defended slavery by declaring it constitutional. Governor McDuffie of South Carolina declaimed that "Domestic slavery . . . , instead of being a political evil, is the cornerstone of our republican edifice." Interference like that of the abolitionists, he declared, should be punishable "by death without benefit of clergy."[87] For this reason Garrison could not regard the constitution as a sacred compact. It was in his mind "the most bloody and heaven-daring arrangement ever made by men for the continuance and protection of a system of the most atrocious villainy ever exhibited on earth." And therefore, "let the superstructure crumble into dust—if it must be upheld by robbery and oppression."[88] The full effect of the government's position was evident in a letter which he wrote to Thomas Shipley on December 17, 1835. He quoted Governor McDuffie's statement that slavery was the cornerstone of the republican edifice and that called upon the forceful opposition and threats of both state and church combined to secure the passage of laws to deprive abolitionists of their liberty of speech and of the press. He concluded that 'all good men and true' . . . will rally under a common standard, adopt common measures, and cherish common principles."[89] True abolitionists should unite to resist a government which supported slavery. He recalled that it also supported war and capital punishment. He had developed a sound case against government. He was ripe for the influence of John Humphrey Noyes.

On March 20, 1837, Noyes called at the Anti-Slavery office in Boston, where he found Garrison, Stanton, Whittier, and others engaged in a warm discussion about political matters. Noyes wrote:

[86] *Ibid.,* II, 81.
[87] *Ibid.,* II, note 62.
[88] *Ibid.,* II, 307-308 ; 309.
[89] *Ibid.,* II, 64-65.

"I heard them quietly, and when the meeting broke up I introduced myself to Garrison. He spoke with great interest of *The Perfectionist*,[90] said his mind was heaving on the subject of holiness and the kingdom of heaven, and he would devote himself to them as soon as he could get anti-slavery off his hands. *I spoke to him especially on the subject of government, and found him, as I expected, ripe for the loyalty of heaven.*"[91]

Following up this interview, Noyes wrote a long letter to Garrison on March 22, 1837, setting forth his doctrines of the Second Coming of Christ, Salvation from Sin, which demanded withdrawal from the government and even the overthrow of all civil government in preparation for the new kingdom—without government and without law.[92] In closing he counselled Garrison to set his face toward *perfect* holiness for "if you plant the standard of perfect holiness where you stand, many will see and flow to it."[93] Eleven days before this Henry C. Wright had suggested the formation of a peace society based solely on the principles of non-resistance.[94]

The full effect of these influences was most apparent in a letter which Garrison wrote to Henry C. Wright on April 16th of the same year, in which he spoke of his faith in non-resistance as a means of breaking down "the heart of an adversary" and of a society without human law and human government as the ideal future state.

"Human governments will remain in violent existence as long as men are resolved not to bear the cross of Christ, and to be crucified unto the world. But in the kingdom of God's dear Son, holiness and law are the only magistracy. It has no swords, for they are beaten into ploughshares—no spears, for they are changed into pruning hooks—no military academy, for the saints cannot learn war any more—no gibbet, for life is regarded as inviolate— no chains, for all are free. And that kingdom is to be established upon the earth, for the time is predicted when the kingdoms of

[90] It is not impossible that Garrison had read *The Perfectionist* from the beginning. He had read it certainly by 1836. *Ibid.*, II, note 145, 114.

[91] Noyes, *op. cit.*, 328.

[92] See above, 54-56.

[93] Garrison, *op. cit.*, II, 148.

[94] See above, 60-61.

this world will become the kingdoms of our Lord and of his Christ."[95]

More and more frequently Garrison's thoughts recurred to this idea. In the *Liberator* of June 23, 1837, he denounced human government as "the result of human disobedience to the requirements of heaven" and "better than anarchy just as a hail-storm is preferable to an earthquake, or the small-pox to the Asiatic cholera," and proclaimed that "the kingdom which Christ has established on earth is ultimately to swallow up or radically to subvert all other kingdoms."[96] Here is John Humphrey Noyes' Christian anarchist society. The chief obstacles of human governments he found to be a lack of faith in the possibility of society without authority, the desire for power or authority over others, the spirit of retaliation, the belief that constables, sheriffs, judges, and lawgivers could direct other men righteously.[97] They were obstacles but they could and should be destroyed by Christians. He asked, "Shall we as Christians, applaud and do homage to human government? Or shall we not rather lay the axe at the root of the tree, and attempt to destroy both cause and effect together?"[98] Later, on July 4, 1837, in an address before the Anti-Slavery society, Garrison acknowledged that Noyes' belief and hope for the overthrow of the nation had deeply affected his mind.[99] He was convinced that both State and Church would be dismembered because of their support of slavery. And in August, 1837, Garrison gave notice that he would part company with the American peace society unless it changed its course.[100] He and his adherents did so in September, 1838, when they formed the New England Non-Resistance Society.

By this devious course, the non-resistants, who before had formed merely a dissenting minority within the peace movement had now achieved a separate organization. As an independent

[95] *Ibid.*, II, 148-151.
[96] *Ibid.*, II, 150.
[97] *Ibid.*, II, 150-151.
[98] *Ibid.*, II, 151.
[99] *Ibid.*, II, 151-152.
[100] *Ibid.*, II, 222.

body, they proceeded to apply non-resistance to all the social evils of the day—to slavery, to capital punishment, to war, to intemperance, to the inequality of the sexes—on the basis that life and freedom were the highest values. They fortified their universal individualism with the Christian doctrine that Love was more powerful than force. Force which was used to destroy life or freedom was, therefore, to be eliminated from society. Government and law consequently, as the embodiment of force and the chief obstacles to the realization of the ideal would be swept away. The philosophy of the Society was virtually Christian Anarchism. Its organ of expression was the *Non-Resistant,* a semi-monthly periodical, its agent of propaganda, Henry C. Wright, and its practical application (as Adin Ballou interpreted it), the Hopedale Community.

The Non-Resistant Society was formally established at the peace convention held at Boston from the eighteenth to the twentieth of September, 1838.[101] Garrison, as chairman of a committee of nine, assisted in drawing up a constitution and himself wrote the Declaration of Sentiments.[102] By a vote of twenty-six to five the assembled group adopted the resolutions on September 20th.[103] On January 1 of the following year *The Non-Resistant* appeared for the first time, published thereafter on the first and third Saturday of every month until June 29, 1842. The editorial staff was made up of Garrison, Maria Chapman, and Edmund Quincy. The Society itself existed until 1849, when it held its last meeting.[104] The philosophy which the Society evolved, however, is more significant for this particular study than its physical birth and death.

The philosophy of Non-Resistance as it was developed in the first half of the nineteenth century was anarchistic in the sense that it visualized the destruction of all human law and government as well as all human authority and the construction of a new order

---

[101] *The Non-Resistant,* Boston, January, 1839-June 29, 1842; January 1, 1839.

[102] Garrison, *op. cit.,* II, 228.

[103] *Idem.*

[104] *Ibid.,* III, note 419.

in which the individual enjoyed absolute freedom, was "inspired" by the Love of God and was guided only by the Golden Rule. While the "individualist anarchists," Josiah Warren, William B. Greene, Lysander Spooner, and Benjamin Tucker would supplant existing law by the laws of nature, the non-resistants would substitute the laws of God as simply set forth by the Golden Rule and by Christ in the Sermon on the Mount—a difference only in name.

The original position of the Non-Resistants was set forth in the Declaration of Sentiments,[105] where they declared, "We cannot acknowledge allegiance to any human government" recognizing as they did only one Lawgiver, one King, and bound as they were by "laws of a kingdom which is not of this world." They could not, therefore, either hold office or vote. Believing as they did that Evil was to be resisted by Law, they denounced capital punishment and warfare, both defensive and offensive. Love, they declared, was not only omniscient, but omnipresent. The Brotherhood of Man was a reality, and Internationalism, not Nationalism its embodiment. Hence they "can allow no appeal to patriotism, to revenge any national insult or injury." Their end, peace, their means were to be peaceful. Their instruments of propaganda, therefore, included lectures, conversation and correspondence, the circulation of tracts and circulars, and the organization of auxiliary societies.[106] In many communities, however, they met forceful opposition to their activity. But as a minority they anticipated and even welcomed it, regarding it a "privilege to be a martyr to the truth." This, in general, was their position in 1838. Time, experience, and momentum, however, clarified, expanded and crystallized their philosophy.

The absolute inviolability of human life was the creed which

---

[105] *The Non-Resistant*, January, 1839.

[106] Some of the non-resistants, Parker Pillsbury and a number of his friends, adopted a plan of propaganda about 1839, a plan of "creating moral power." It was to go into churches at the time of the regular services and to lecture the congregations without leave until they were put out by force, sometimes even roughly. William Birney, *James G. Birney and His Times*, 325.

they all accepted.[107]    It justified their refusal to acknowledge allegiance to any government which claimed the power of taking life in any case.   To most of them, moreover, "human government" was "a wrong in itself because its very essence was violence and an assumption of power of man over man."   In the words of Henry C. Wright, the most forceful critic of all government:

"The powers assumed by all human governments are essential to their existence and execution, have been proved to be wrong; and the practices of such governments, without which they cannot exist, have been proved to be hostile to the spirit and positive commands of Christianity.   Therefore, human government is a wrong in itself."[108]

The past of government, furthermore, he declared to be just as black as its present, for

"There is not a crime in the catalogue of crimes which has not been committed by human government; and that, too, in the appropriate and necessary use of the powers which are essential in its existence. . . . Men, as a government over men, in the legitimate use of their governmental powers have trampled under foot the moral government of God."

The history of human government was a dismal one but he asked,

"What else can be expected of it than theft, robbery, and injustice. . . . Human government has made the earth a slaughter house of the human race for 6,000 years."

Government not only persecuted the weak, it corrupted the strong in the use of government, for it was impossible to be invested with power and not abuse it.   By these words he earned the title of a Christian Anarchist:

"I look at human government as it is; I analyze it as it is; I denounce it as it is; and as it is I pronounce it a system of legalized warfare upon the prerogative of Duty. . . . No human government can be approved of God, whose existence is his dethronement. No human government can be approved of God, which plants one

[107] The main body of these conclusions are to be found in an editorial written by Edmund Quincy in *The Non-Resistant*, March 23, 1842.

[108] *Non-Resistant*, February 26, 1840.

heel upon his Eternal Throne and tramples his image in the dust with the other."

"We call, then, for an immediate abolition of dominion of man over man, of all government of human will and human slaughter, as in itself wrong and only wrong."

"To God alone belongs dominion over man. . . . Man to hold dominion over Beasts and Things. God to rule over man. In this there is found the lost hope of bleeding humanity."[109]

Although Henry C. Wright represented the most extreme of the non-resistants, they agreed generally in this position. On the basis of this principle, therefore, they refused to hold office, to vote, or to resort to courts for redress of injury. On minor questions they differed as to whether or not they should take oaths, pay taxes or hold land. Others of them differed over procedure. One group believed that society would be good if the evil cornerstones on which it rested were removed. The other group believed, however, that a complete remodelling of the social system was necessary to get rid of the evils which were in the very inner core. Edmund Quincy suggested that perhaps a "complete triumph cannot be attained until men are ready to seek a new arrangement of the social system." The adoption of such a principle would mean a peaceful revolution in details as well as in the groundwork of society.

Non-resistants agreed on their central position but differed in the matter of specific details. Each carried it out "according to the 'light given to him'." The belief in the sacredness of the Life of Man they arrived at by three different routes—through Christianity or faith in God, through Individualism or faith in their own souls, and through Nature or faith in the law of nature. In the first case, it was revealed as the will of God in the Scriptures, and especially as the authority of Jesus Christ. In the second case, it was heard as a Divine voice uttering the truth in their own souls. In the third case, it was accepted as the result of right reason and the nature of things. In all three ways, therefore, the individual was free and had absolute control over his own life, but *only* over *his own* life. The law which was equally binding

[109] *Idem.*

upon all lives and without which there could not be peace or security, was the observance of the Golden Rule and the Sermon on the Mount. Do good for evil, resist not evil, love your enemies, do unto others as you would be done by, were the *general* injunctions. "Love" would be substituted for force, "divine government" for human government.

Faith in these principles inspired a belief that they would be realized in a new "kingdom,"

"The kingdom which is the theater of our conflict and the scene of our triumphs is within us. It is an eternal kingdom, which can never be destroyed, though it may be laid in ruins. . . . His Laws are written upon the tables of the heart. . . . To expound and enforce these venerable laws, the Lawgiver has erected a solemn tribunal, where he sits in judgment in the person of his minister Conscience . . . and having learned the laws of the Kingdom of God within us, perfect obedience to which will make a heaven within us, and a paradise on earth, let us strive to govern ourselves by them—to bring all mankind to that submission to their behests which is perfect freedom."[110]

When men submit to these laws, therefore, they will realize a new society.

This was the philosophy of New England Non-Resistance in its mature form. From its very inception it was violently assailed —and with the same arguments that have been brought against anarchists in every age. It was branded as "incendiary," "anarchistic," "unChristian," "destructive," "fanatical," "monstrous and absurd," and "impractical." The advocates of non-resistance were cried down as "fanatics," "mad-men," and the "enemies of the human race," "anti-God, anti-Bible, anti-everything that is good." Their opponents defended the existing order on the grounds that any other was impossible. Civil law and civil government were not only divine but necessary. They were afraid to trust human nature, even if it was "perfectible," to live by the Golden Rule. Others feared non-resistance, because the absence of government to them meant chaos, disorder, bloodshed, and the

[110] *Non-Resistant,* January 1, 1840.

destruction of the family.[111]   Even the Quakers attacked them.
Charles Marriott, a well-known Quaker, wrote that he and the
majority of the Friends were not opposed to law and government
*per se,* but only to those laws which violated Christian principles.[112]

The authorities in education and government, even a large
number of abolitionists, peace men, and reformers in general disapproved of their extreme principles.   The American Education
Society, a student-loan foundation, ruled that it would not aid
students who embraced radicalism as professed by the New England Non-Resistant Society.   The President of Dartmouth sanctioned this ruling.[113]   Because of such action, J. E. Hood, a
student at Dartmouth, wrote to the Association and declined the
aid it gave him, saying, "I can never give the shadow of a sanction, however trivial, to any attempt to abridge freedom of inquiry
or liberty of conscience in any of my brethren."[114]   He was not a
non-resistant; he was a champion of the freedom of conscience.

Echoes of opposition were to be heard in the Houses of Legislature.   A resolution introduced in the House of Representatives
in Massachusetts granting compensation for property destroyed
in riots was amended so as not to give compensation to persons
professing to be non-resistants because they objected to receiving
aid from the strong arm of government as well as to giving it.
Although the bill was shelved it was regarded by the non-resistants
not only as a commentary on government but also as an invitation
to the people to attack them and their property.[115]

Even the conservatives of the abolition and peace causes
mingled their voices with the crowd to cry down the non-resistants.
The American Peace Society denied all relations with the Non-
Resistant Society, condemned its stand on capital punishment,
civil government, and its program of "universal reformation" particularly in its application to all existing civil, political, legal, and
ecclesiastical institutions.   This Society restated its conservative

[111] *Non-Resistant,* February 16, 1839.
[112] *Non-Resistant,* February 2, 1839.
[113] *Non-Resistant,* July 22, 1840.
[114] *Idem.*
[115] *Non-Resistant,* February 16, 1839.

position as recognizing "the existence and powers of civil governments as ordained of God."[116]　But the New York Peace Society in even more positive tones denounced the Non-Resistant Society, when it adopted the following resolution at one of its meetings January, 1839:

"Resolved, that the non-government principle recently adopted by an association in New England is, in the opinion of this Society, unscriptural and impracticable; that instead of being a Peace principle *it would, if reduced to practice, involve the world in Anarchy and Bloodshed,* and resolve Society back to its original elements, by compelling the defenseless to fly from the presence of the monsters of human depravity, to the dens and caverns of the earth, . . . and that it is the imperative duty of the friends of peace and order everywhere publicly to disclaim such a sentiment."[117]

The Abolitionist Societies split over the question of political action and direct action, over the maintenance or destruction of government.[118]　On May 27, 1839, the Massachusetts Abolition Society was organized in Boston affirming "the duty of upholding civil government" and abolishing slavery at the polls.[119]　On May 7, 1839, "the duty of political action" was affirmed by a vote of 84-77 in the American Anti-Slavery Society.[120]　Two years before that Henry C. Wright had been recalled from his position on the Executive Committee of this Society because of his no-government professions.[121]　As the labor leaders of the late nineteenth century feared that the anarchists would bring discredit to their cause, so the abolitionists feared the non-resistants.

It is more difficult to determine the extent to which non-resistance was accepted or to mark off the sphere of its influence. Certainly its staunchest supporters made up only a small minority. The actual membership of the Non-Resistance Society never ex-

[116] *Non-Resistant,* January 19, 1839.
[117] *Idem.*
[118] William Goodell, *Slavery and Anti-Slavery* (Third Edition, New York, 1855), 449.
[119] *Ibid.,* 461.
[120] *Ibid.,* 463.
[121] Garrison, *op. cit.,* II, 159.

ceeded two hundred.[122] But the size of the subscription list of the *Non-Resistant* would seem to indicate that its sphere of influence was considerably larger. The editors reported at the Second Annual Meeting of the Society on September 23, 1840, that the paper had paid for itself that year, that it had a subscription list of one thousand names, and that 1,148 copies of the paper had been sent gratus to Theological Seminaries, Colleges, and prominent individuals.[123] Furthermore, Henry C. Wright had scattered the ideas of non-resistance quite generally throughout New England, New York, Pennsylvania, and Ohio by his debates, lectures, conversations, etc. Through his efforts and those of a few other non-resistants auxiliary branches had been established in Indiana, Michigan, and particularly Ohio. One especially prominent group was formed at Oberlin Collegiate Institute, Oberlin, Ohio, on June 18, 1840. Its membership was no larger than thirty students and townspeople. In spite of the opposition of the greater part of the Faculty and student body, a "protest and disclaimer" was sent to the Faculty setting forth the principles of non-resistance.[124] The students were *not* expelled from the College.

Through the intensive activity of the advocates of non-resistance, the principles of the Society were made generally known to the people of the time. Emerson regarded the non-resistants as the successors to the Antinomians of the Puritan days.[125] Their principles struck a sympathetic note in him. He recorded in his Journal on October 27, 1839, his impressions of a lecture on Non-Resistance which he had heard Garrison give the night before. He wrote,

"But to the principle of non-resistance again, Trust it. Give up the government, without too solicitously inquiring whether roads

[122] Goodell, *op. cit.*, 462; Merle E. Curti, "Non-Resistance in New England," *The New England Quarterly*, II (January, 1929), No. 1, 54.

[123] *Non-Resistant*, October 14, 1840.

[124] *Non-Resistant*, September 9, 1840.

[125] Ralph Waldo Emerson, *Essays* (Everyman Edition, London and New York, 1906), 338, 339.

can be still built, letters carried, and title deeds secured when the government of force is at an end."[126]

Thoreau was familiar with their doctrines but did not agree with them.[127] Their philosophy and inconsistencies interested even the following generation of reformers and especially the Individualist Anarchists, William B. Greene and Ezra Heywood.[128]

The Non-Resistant Society existed scarcely more than eleven years, the *Non-Resistant* less than three and a half years. Virtually all of the Non-Resistants, with one outstanding exception, acted contrary to their earlier principles and rejected Non-Resistance as a way of life. Ballou was the exception. Garrison and Wright abandoned it, but the latter returned to his earlier faith after the Civil War. The explanation of the decline of the Society and of the inconsistency of its members lies in a complicated mesh of circumstances and ultimately in the very character of Non-Resistance.

Most obviously the society ceased to exist because the *Liberator* and the cause of abolition required all of Garrison's time and energy, because Henry C. Wright, the most energetic propagandist, was in England part of the time, and because after 1848 its staunchest exponent, Adin Ballou, was occupied with a practical experiment in non-resistance at the Hopedale Community. The society was "without an organ, without funds, without agents, without publications."[129] Furthermore, the almost universal opposition and rejection with which their principles had met, made them reflect and even doubt whether the "complete reformation" which they demanded could be realized in as short a time as they had anticipated. They concluded that non-resistance was a "temper of mind" with which to approach reform rather than a distinct "enterprise."[130] Moreover, the sustained enthusiasm which support of such an extreme cause required was almost an

---

[126] *Journals of Ralph Waldo Emerson,* edited by E. W. Emerson and W. E. Forbes (Boston and New York, 1909-14, 10 volumes), V, 302-3.

[127] "Civil Disobedience," 357.

[128] See below, note 134.

[129] Garrison, *op. cit.,* III, note 80.

[130] *Idem.*

emotional impossibility.  Not only did the general rejection of the principles of Non-Resistance discourage its advocates, it also made the practical realization of Non-Resistance impossible.  The efficacy and success of non-resistance as a practical principle depends largely on its general acceptance, as illustrated in India today by the Mahatma Gandhi.

After 1842 the slavery cause pushed more and more into the foreground.  Garrison's whole life interest became the emancipation of the slaves, almost to the exclusion of peace, temperance, and capital punishment.  His tendency to subordinate the principle to the "cause" which was apparent from the beginning, became at this time a marked characteristic.  Up to 1862, he grew even more violent in his denunciation of government.  On July 4, 1854, flourishing a copy of the constitution, damning it as a "covenant with death and an agreement with Hell," he burnt it to ashes on the spot exclaiming, "so perish all compromise with tyranny."[131]  Furthermore it was easier for Garrison to hate a government which supported and approved of such an atrocious crime as human slavery than in time of peace to hate a government for its war-power, just as it was easier for an anarchist laborer to hate capitalism and government when he was underpaid or without work, than when his dinner pail was full.  It was, in short, easier to be anti-government when the government approved slavery in 1838, than when it emancipated the slave in 1863.  Garrison burned the constitution in 1854, but in 1862 he withdrew the "Covenant with Death" motto from the head of the *Liberator*.  At the same time he declared that he had no idea that he should live to see "death and hell secede" and from then on was "with the government."[132]  At the same time he approved of the war, of the emancipation of the slaves on the grounds of military necessity, denied the right of the Southern States to secede, and supported the reëlection of Lincoln.[133]  He thereby violated every principle of non-resistance—the sacredness of

[131] *Ibid.*, III, 412.
[132] *Ibid.*, IV, 40-41.
[133] *Ibid.*, IV, 21, 22, 143; 26; 104.

human life, resist not evil by force, the right of the individual to his own life and property (which was denied to the southern slave owners).[134] Garrison was swept away from his position of non-resistance by his singleness of purpose and by practical necessity. Non-resistance a means to the end, the end realized, the complete reformation of society was forgotten. The labor question which had assumed importance by 1875 left him cold.[135]

Certain other Non-Resistants, however, and particularly those whose beliefs were based on religious convictions were the last to compromise their principles. Adin Ballou never did. His non-resistance was part of his inner religious experience. It became his religion. Unlike Garrison, his principles assumed greater importance than the reform issues themselves. Furthermore, he was not in the thick of the reform battle after 1848. From that time until 1856 he was attempting to establish a community which lived by the principles of Non-Resistance. Ballou's gravest error lay, however, in prescribing for those who were members of the community certain rules of conduct—as abstinence from intoxicating liquors, denial of divorce, in short all the *specific* exhortations of Christ's Sermon on the Mount. And although no member entered the community unless he accepted these principles, yet the very requirement was a resort to coercion, although it was moral.[136] It was Tolstoy who later in the century professed complete Non-Resistance. This Ballou believed was carrying the doctrine to absurd conclusions.[137] Certainly, Ballou was consistent with the principles which he had laid down. He opposed Conscription for the Civil War,[138] and even the war itself.[139] He

[134] The individualist anarchists, William B. Greene and Ezra Heywood, appreciated this inconsistency keenly. Heywood declared that Garrison, in condemning secession, crushed "the cardinal principle of self-government, the pivotal force and philosophical method of peaceful evolution." *The Radical Review*, I (November 1877), 566-567, in William B. Green's *Socialistic, Communistic, Mutalistic, and Financial Fragments* (Boston, 1875), 169-174.

[135] Garrison, *op. cit.*, IV, 248-249.

[136] See Constitution and By-Laws of Community, Appendix A: Adin Ballou, *History of the Hopedale Community* (Lowell, Mass., 1897), 368-396.

[137] *Autobiography*, 509.

[138] *Ibid.*, 449.

[139] *Ibid.*, 422, 462.

lost faith in the causes of Labor and Women's Rights when they resorted to the ballot and political action.[140]   Aloof from the main flow of action and devoutly wedded to his principles, Ballou lived and died a Non-Resistant.

As to the principle of Non-Resistance itself—it presents an unavoidable dilemma to its advocates.  Presumably an individual must either remain in society or withdraw from it.  If he remains in society, he must compromise his principles, for, as he himself realizes, present society is based on resistance to evil.  If he accepts the protection of government, or in any way participates in government, he violates his principles.  The Antinomians were spared this dilemma by forcible ejection from the community.  The Quakers, however, submitted to the situation and were only partial non-resistants as a result.  The very fact that the most devout non-resistant, Adin Ballou, found it necessary to withdraw from society, in order to practice complete non-resistance, is significant evidence of this weakness.  Tolstoy found it necessary as well as personally satisfying for him to retire from the rush of civilization to the quiet of the rural district, Yasnaya Polyana.  The very success of Non-Resistance seems to depend upon its general acceptance.  When it was not widely accepted and its exponents remained in society, it proved to be "impractical," "too extreme," "too idealistic," and "impossible."  The most noteworthy exception to this rule is Non-Resistance in India today as it is professed by the Mahatma Gandhi.  What appears to be the success of Non-Resistance as a philosophy, however, may be rather the triumph of Nationalism, the result of a special technique effectively adapted to a unique political situation.  Perhaps Non-Resistance as a technique of propaganda rather than as a complete social philosophy will be the "prosperous relation" in the future of Non-Resistance in the Romantic period.  Time alone will give us the answer.

In the late nineteenth and early twentieth centuries, Count Leo Tolstoy and the Mahatma Gandhi became the new prophets of

[140] *Ibid.,* 463.

Non-Resistance.[141]   It was Tolstoy's writings rather than those of Adin Ballou, moreover, that won converts to Non-Resistance in America.   There has been, to be sure, a close connection between these two strains.   Although Tolstoy arrived at Non-Resistance independently through his own interpretation of the Sermon on the Mount,[142] he was inspired by the discovery that Garrison and Ballou had not only recognized and proclaimed Non-Resistance, but had also used it as the basis of their practical activity in freeing the slaves.[143]   Tolstoy actually acknowledged that two of Ballou's tracts which had been translated into Russian had greatly encouraged and strengthened him.[144]   He wrote to the Reverend Lewis G. Wilson in 1889, "Tell him (Ballou) that I deeply respect and love him, and that his work did great good to my soul."[145]

Tolstoy's doctrine of Non-Resistance and philosophy of love appealed to many classes of people in the United States—judges, lawyers, ministers,[146] social reformers, and dilettantes.   Tolstoy clubs and colonies were established in many places throughout the country.[147]   The most outstanding exponents of the doctrine in the United States were Ernest Crosby and for a time Clarence Darrow and Jane Addams.   Ernest Crosby was a well-to-do American living in Alexandria, Egypt, as Judge of the Interna-

[141] Tolstoy's doctrine of Non-Resistance is most systematically set forth in his book, *My Religion.*   Translated from the French by Huntingdon Smith (New York, 1885).

[142] *Ibid.,* especially 7-12.

[143] Leo Tolstoy, "Garrison and Non-Resistance," *The Independent,* Vol. 56 (1904), 881.

[144] The Reverend Lewis G. Wilson, "The Christian Doctrine of Non-Resistance," *The Arena,* Vol. XIII (1890), 1 ff.

[145] *Idem.*

[146] The Reverend R. Heber Newton of All Saint's Protestant Episcopal Church, New York, startled his hearers on October 20, 1901, by his endorsement of Tolstoyan Anarchism.   Political Science Pamphlets, 1901, No. 15.

[147] Interesting account of a Tolstoy Club in *The Century,* Vol. 21 (1891-92) 761-772, "Our Tolstoy Club," by Dorothy Prescott.   Jane Addams refers to colonies in Southern States which she visited, one particularly at *Commonwealth.*   She also refers to the Dukhobors in Manitoba, Canada, who accepted Tolstoy's doctrines literally.   Tolstoy sent one-half of the proceeds from *Resurrection* to this colony.   Jane Addams, *Twenty-Five Years at Hull House* (New York, 1912), 277-280.

tional Court, when a chance book of Tolstoy came into his hands.[148] This book and a growing disinclination to sit in "judgment" upon any man, brought him to a new spiritual experience. He threw up his position in Alexandria, made a pilgrimage to Tolstoy in Russia, and then returned to the United States to devote his life to a crusade in behalf of his ideals.[149] He believed that Anarchism was a noble ideal and that it would conquer, but was himself identified with no particular party. Many causes won his support. He wrote a letter in 1898 to Andrew Carnegie in behalf of Alexander Berkman, an anarchist-communist imprisoned for his assault on Henry C. Frick, steel magnate, because he did not believe in prisons. For the same reason he tried to secure the release of John Turner, an English Anarchist, imprisoned and deported in 1904.[150] By his lectures he tried to win an acceptance of non-resistance. But he also left no appreciable impress on the intellectual life of the nation.

Clarence Darrow, a prominent American criminal lawyer, has left one book, *Resist Not Evil,* in which he proclaims his "intellectual" acceptance of the doctrine of Non-Resistance in his early life. His book, he said, was not original, but inspired directly by the writings of Tolstoy who was the first and only author in his opinion, who had placed the doctrine of Non-Resistance upon a substantial basis.[151] His main argument was essentially that all government, law, and law courts were based on force and violence, that government originated in force, had been maintained by the strongest for the benefit of the few to keep "the patient, suffering millions from any portion of the common bounties of the world." "Even in democratic countries . . . the nature of the government

[148] Leonard D. Abbott, "Some Reminiscences of Ernest Crosby," *Mother Earth,* I, 12-27 (February, 1907).

[149] Crosby was one of the most outstanding interpreters of Tolstoy to the American public. See his articles especially, "Count Tolstoy's Philosophy of Life," *The Arena* XV (1895-96), 279-295; "Count Tolstoy and Non-Resistance," *The Outlook,* Vol. 54 (1896), 52-53. For reference to liberal activities see Emma Goldman, *Living My Life* (2 vols., New York, 1931), I, 233, 320, 335, 362. Emma Goldman found Crosby "understanding and sympathetic even where he did not entirely agree." *Ibid.,* I, 233.

[150] Abbott, *op. cit.,* 22; Goldman, *op. cit.,* I, 349.

[151] Clarence S. Darrow, *Resist Not Evil* (Chicago, 1903), 7.

is the same."[152] In every case, the real rulers have been and are the strong. The state is used by them to perpetuate their power and to serve their avarice and greed. Through his book and his lectures Darrow disseminated the ideas of Tolstoy. Through one of his lectures Voltairine de Cleyre, poet-anarchist, was lead to the study of "radicalisms."[153]

It seems that Darrow's philosophy of non-resistance was put to a severe test in the War of 1914. Along with many other liberals he discarded pacifism as "a good doctrine in time of peace, but of no value in war time."[154] When he saw what he thought was Germany's guilt, he recovered from his pacifism "in the twinkling of an eye."[155] Nevertheless the repression, the hysterical patriotism, the rush for money and all the evils which resulted from the war seemed to him deplorable. But as much as he hated war, he tended to regard it as inevitable. Although Darrow found non-resistance "impractical," he is still an individualist. He says in his autobiography: "Instinctively I lean toward the integrity of the individual unit, and am impatient with any interference with personal freedom."[156] Law, he thinks, has little to do with conduct or virtue, justice or equality.[157] At the same time he admits that he was always friendly towards the ideals and aims of anarchism as taught by Kropotkin and Tolstoy but that he came to regard it as "a vision of heaven held by the elect, a far-off dream that had no relation to life."[158] From this it is clear that Darrow has modified his ideas as he has met life in its practical aspects. But even with these modified ideas he has vitally influenced American life. It was he who drew up a brief for Turner in 1903, the first to be deported under the Anarchy

[152] *Ibid.*, 17.

[153] Until 1911 when she became a "Direct-Actionist" Voltairine de Cleyre was a firm believer in non-resistance. Through D. D. Lum, secretary to Samuel Gompers and anarchist-communist, she was led to anarchism. *Selected Works of Voltairine de Cleyre* (New York, 1914), 12; 220.

[154] Clarence Darrow: *The Story of My Life* (New York, 1932), 210.

[155] *Idem.*

[156] *Ibid.*, 55.

[157] *Ibid.*, 344-5.

[158] *Ibid.*, 53-54.

law.[159]   It was he who among others strongly urged Governor Altgeld to pardon the Chicago anarchists involved in the Haymarket affair.[160]   Such evidence suggests that perhaps it is more valuable that men modify their ideals in action than that they should preserve the purity of their convictions in metaphysical contemplation.

Jane Addams had similar experiences in another sphere. Since her graduation from college, she had been interested in social reform.   In about the year 1885 a copy of Tolstoy's *My Religion* came into her hands and influenced her ideas on social reform, so much so that in 1895-96, when she went to Europe she made a pilgrimage to Tolstoy hoping to find some clue "to tangled affairs of city poverty."[161]   She came away from Tolstoy with the conviction that she would bake her own bread in order to lose her sense of isolation from the workers whom she was trying to help from her settlement at Hull House.   She directly read everything of Tolstoy's writings which had been translated.   But upon her return to Hull House the practical difficulties of applying Tolstoy's theories became unsurmountable.   Her interest, however, seems to have remained, for she later made a visit to a Tolstoy colony in the South.[162]   Although not an anarchist herself, she defended them against injustice.[163]   While extreme doctrines are not and cannot be completely and immediately accepted, they may, as in these instances, serve as liberalizing influences in establishing the limits between the individual, society, and government.

Although we cannot say that Antinomianism and Quakerism in the colonial days, and Transcendentalism, Perfectionism, and Non-Resistance in the pre-Civil War days were causally connected, we can affirm that they were spiritually related.   Their common parent was oppressive authority—religious and social.

[159] Whipple, *op. cit.*, 304.

[160] *Ibid.*, 100.

[161] Jane Addams, *op. cit.*, 261, 262.   Account of interview, 267-274.

[162] *Ibid.*, 277-280.

[163] In 1901, when Jacob Isaac, editor of *Free Society*, was imprisoned without counsel, Jane Addams tried to secure a lawyer for him. *Ibid.*, 403-407.   In 1899 Prince Kropotkin, Russian anarchist-communist, stayed and lectured at Hull House. *Ibid.*, 402.

As rebellious children, they tried to defend their own individual integrity and sovereignty—their right to control and direct their own lives. They appreciated the importance of society as a whole, but society for them existed only as the corporate mass of single atoms, the individuals. And the preservation of each individual and his individuality was their chief concern. In their moral conduct they were guided by an inner consciousness of goodness. Their general preceptor was, for the most part, Christ. Their precepts were those of the Sermon on the Mount. But they went further than this. They declared that since they were guided by inner consciousness, they were not subject to the laws, to government, or to any coercive authority in this world. Some of them even constructed and prepared for a new world where men would live peacefully without any external authority over their intellectual, social, or moral life. Their speculations and aspirations for the most part lay in the ethical and social field. Within this area they definitely built up a philosophy of Christian Anarchism.

## ANARCHISM MATURED

Moral and social reform was, as we have seen, an essential part of the Romantic period in America—the first half of the nineteenth century. But economic reform claims almost equal rank in reform activity. It yielded the socialism of Robert Owen, and the Fourierism of Arthur Brisbane and Horace Greeley. Nor were the philosophies of Lasalle and Cabet without their American disciples. Association and coöperation became a frequent answer to the economic problem. But just as an "Adolescent" anarchism grew out of the speculation in the moral and social spheres, so did a type of anarchism evolve from the speculation in the economic sphere. It sprang from the same parent—coercive authority. It was an authority, however, which interfered with one of the most essential activities of life—the gaining of a livelihood. For this reason it reached a maturity which ethical anarchism was not able to attain. It combined economic freedom with ethical and social freedom. The Individualist Anarchists, as they were called, were practical, scientific, unemotional, but at the same time speculative men. They were swayed by no Platonic idealism, but by a faith in demonstrating the practicability of their theories, and in cultivating a sentiment against government which would eventually overthrow all government. The process would be one of organic evolution. Their methods were peaceful—practical demonstration and rational conviction. Their economics, adapted as it was to the existing economic conditions, accepted private property—that is, "possession" of it, not exclusive "ownership." This, as we shall see, was a compromise between communism and individualism. As a rule, the Individualist anarchists formed an extreme left wing of similar philosophies—Josiah Warren of the Labor Exchange group in the thirties and forties, William B. Greene of the Greenbackers and Single Taxers of the seventies, eighties, and nineties. They were neither wage-conscious nor class-conscious—the source both of their strength and of their weakness.

The Individualist Anarchists, as we shall see, crystallized the traditional individualism and lawlessness of America into a universally applicable, systematic philosophy. And they were conscious of their heritage. Almost without exception they were the descendants of old New England families, particularly of Massachusetts, and in some cases of Revolutionary War heroes. Ezra Heywood, a Massachusetts anarchist of this native American school in the seventies, acknowledged his inheritance when he wrote that anarchism was not a foreign product but a product of American soil. "It (anarchism) is really only a new assertion of the ideas of self-rule and self-support which Jefferson put 'into the Declaration of 1776,' which suggested the doctrines of 'Cost the limit of Price' and 'Individual Sovereignty proclaimed by Josiah Warren from New Harmony, Indiana, in 1830.' "[1] Benjamin Tucker admitted that he was nothing more than an "unterrified Jeffersonian Democrat." American tradition was their inheritance and European philosophies reënforced their convictions, particularly those of John Locke, Adam Smith, William Godwin, Jeremy Bentham, Proudhon, John Stuart Mill, Max Stirner and Herbert Spencer.

American tradition treasured in its historic documents the freedom of the individual. The Declaration of Independence guaranteed to *all* men certain inalienable rights—the right of "life, liberty, and the pursuit of happiness." It declared *all* men equal and entitled to equal opportunity. The *right* and *duty* of revolution, when the government became destructive of liberty and the fundamental rights of the individual, were specifically affirmed. The constitution established justice and liberty as the ends of government. Liberty, it defined further as the freedom of religion, of speech, of press, of assembly, and the right of private property. The "Bill of Rights" has been interpreted historically in three ways—conservatively as applicable only to the Revolu-

---

[1] *Radical Review,* Quarterly, May, 1877-February, 1878, 573-4. Voltairine de Cleyre, first an Individualist Anarchist and then an Anarchist-Communist, treats most ably the American Anarchist tradition in an essay entitled, "Anarchism and American Traditions." *Selected Works of Voltairine de Cleyre* (New York, 1914), 118-135.

tionary period, practically, as necessary instruments of self-government and a protection against new tyranny, and finally philosophically as an ideal of spiritual and intellectual freedom looking toward the future.[2]

The first political parties in the new United States vigorously defended the rights of the "individual" as against those of numbers. The Federalists proclaimed and fought for the *national* government which represented the capitalistic and aristocratic minority.[3] Of no government at all and of complete and universal individual autonomy they were no more desirous than the Jeffersonian Democrats.[4] The Democrats defended the rights of the farmers against the Eastern capitalists. They opposed protective tariffs, the United States banking system, and high taxes as discriminating against the farmer for the benefit of the capitalist.[5] The sentiment of both agrarian and capitalist was for *less* government and no state interference, *except* where it was to their own advantage. The captains of industry, particularly, still favor freedom of enterprise and applaud President Hoover's "rugged individualism." They still favor, for the most part, only social and industrial legislation beneficial to themselves.[6]

The freedom which the capitalists would reserve for their class and the large land-owners for theirs, the Individualist Anarchists would extend to *all classes*. As such their philosophy was a distinctive product of American soil. It was nevertheless strengthened by European philosophy and science. The progress of the physical sciences disseminated a belief in the universality, inviolability, and non-moral character of the laws of science. It was only necessary to incorporate these laws, which were discoverable by the human mind, into the social organism to realize a

[2] Leon Whipple, *The Story of Civil Liberty in the United States* (New York, 1927), 11.

[3] Charles Edward Merriam, *A History of American Political Theories* (New York, 1903), 253.

[4] Both the Federalists and Democrats proclaimed the absolute necessity for government protection—favorable class legislation particularly.

[5] Charles A. Beard, *Economic Origins of Jeffersonian Democracy* (New York, 1915), 322-352; 415-467.

[6] Merriam, *op. cit.,* 310-342.

virtually perfect adjustment. The laws of nature supplanted the laws of God. The perfection which John Humphrey Noyes would achieve by the observance of God's laws, Josiah Warren, like other reformers of his time, would effect by obedience to the laws of science. Of all the European philosophies, that of Adam Smith was the most enduring in its influence on the early American Individualists. It sprang from the same root of individualism which brought forth French Romanticism. And yet it flourished in an economic system that denied the aspirations of the French school. It assumed the common instinct of acquisitiveness as the motivating force of life. It conceived the free play of economic forces where government restrictions were taken away and the individual was free to buy and sell in the open market. It made labor the only true measure of value. Moral arguments against government and coercive authority over the individual were contributed by William Godwin's *Enquiry Concerning Political Justice and Its Influence on Morals and Happiness,* published by a Philadelphia firm in 1796. Later the American type of Proudhonian anarchism was given an impetus by Proudhon's writings.[7] His ideas of property, labor exchange, and of the dissolution of governments in the economic organism were brought to the United States by American travellers in France and by the French and German radicals of the late forties and fifties. Max Stirner's formulation of a pure individualism was a potent influence, as well as John Stuart Mill's and Herbert Spencer's philosophical attempts to establish the limits between the individual, society, and the State. We shall, therefore, in discussing Individualist Anarchism, consider first the philosophy of Josiah Warren and his disciple, Stephen Pearl Andrews, as the anticipation of Proudhonian Mutualism; second, the pure Proudhonianism unmixed with the American variety, namely that of William B. Greene;

[7] A kind of mutualism was arrived at independently and contemporaneously in England, by John Gray, in America by Josiah Warren, and in France by Pierre Proudhon. Max Nettlau, *Der Vorfrühling,* 90-92. Peter Kropotkin, "Anarchism," *Encyclopaedia Britannica,* 14th edition (New York and London, 1929), I, 875.

and third, the fusion of the two strains in the philosophy of Benjamin R. Tucker and his followers.

The practical efforts of Josiah Warren were among the first attempts to solve the problems which were beginning to disturb the economic order. The year 1827 was virtually the beginning of the labor movement. In that year members of more than one trade united in striking for a ten-hour day and thereafter formed the Mechanics Union of Trade Associations.[8] *The Mechanics' Free Press* was its organ. This marked the beginning of those innumerable trade associations, unions, and other measures, the object of which was to give to the mechanic in the early period shorter hours, better and more secure wages. Robert Owen held out his paternalistic schemes of labor-capital coöperation to the worker. Josiah Warren held out a scheme of individual enterprise and voluntary coöperation. It was a scheme which he demonstrated in a small way would solve the labor problem—would secure *coöperation without sacrifice* of individual sovereignty. The principles which he set forth in 1830 were perpetuated, elaborated, and systematized, and even propagated among the American people until the year 1908. Josiah Warren, Stephen Pearl Andrews, William B. Greene, and Benjamin Tucker are the fathers of Individualist Anarchism, or as they called it, "scientific anarchism." They all agreed essentially that liberty for the individual was the highest good. Liberty meant the recognition of the equal rights of *every* individual to his own life, conscience, and property—a right to his labor, but *only* to so much as he actually produced. The Individual had a right to his tools, his mind, his body. Society as such did not exist. *But* since *nothing* could be produced without the coöperation of individuals, association was necessary, but only *voluntary* association. The selfish interest of every individual, moreover, would be a sufficient check to the exploitation of any one particular individual. Cause and effect, the "law of natural consequence," would maintain the proper balance of individual interest. But complete liberty was a primary condition, *not*

[8] *A Documentary History of American Industrial Society,* edited by J. R. Commons and Associates (Cleveland, Ohio, 1910. 10 volumes), V, 75.

a *result,* or as Proudhon said, "Liberty the Mother, not the Daughter of Order." As a weak member of the body grows strong from exercise, free from supports and braces, so do individuals become self-reliant. They learn to live peacefully with one another only in an environment which outlaws authority and government. The principle involved in this line of reasoning is essentially that which inspires the modern progressive school.

Since the Individualist Anarchists upheld the equal rights of every individual, they could not use force to attain one of their chief. ends—the equitable distribution of wealth according to each man's ability. Direct action was impossible, was destructive of the very end they sought. Rational conviction was their only instrument. For nearly a century they experimented before they were disillusioned in even this method. We shall now consider the philosophy of Individualist Anarchism—this mature and complete American individualism as it evolved, as well as the success or failure which it met.

### The American Proudhon and his followers

Josiah Warren has been called the first American anarchist. In the sense that he was the first to evolve a complete anarchism, economic as well as spiritual and moral, he deserves this title. For this reason he is important. Anarchism, just as authority, has steadily expanded into all the fields of life. Anarchism "ist Leben, das Leben selbst in seiner ganzen Vielseitigkeit, befreit von der Krankheit der Autorität und den Staats-Eigentums—, Religions—, Nationalitäts— und anderes Parasiten, den parasitischen Ausbeutern, welche die Autorität zuchtet."[9] But Josiah Warren is also important for his economic program. In his labor theories he anticipated Proudhon; in his land theories he anticipated Henry George. Through Robert Owen he influenced the British Labor Movement; through Frances Wright the cause of women's rights in the United States. He published the first Anarchist paper, the *Peaceful Revolutionist,* and founded the first anarchist colonies, *Utopia* and *Modern Times.*

[9] Max Nettlau, *op. cit.,* 132.

His philosophy and his achievements were so intimately bound up with his life, that it is necessary to consider them together. It was no mere accident of fate that Josiah Warren came upon a philosophy of Individualism, or as he said, "Individual Sovereigntyism." Within himself he bore many of the powers which make up a self-sufficient individual. He was a musician, a printer, an inventor, and, in general, a very practical man. Josiah Warren was born in Boston in 1798 of famous Puritan stock.[10] His father, General Joseph Warren, was a distinguished Revolutionary War General, a "hero of American liberty." Little is known of his early life except that he early showed a talent for music and married at the age of twenty. Wishing to try his fortune, he went west to Cincinnati, Ohio. During the first years of his sojourn there, in 1823, he invented, patented, and manufactured much more cheaply than the old tallow lamps, a new lamp which burned from lard. But in 1824 Robert Owen came to Cincinnati to lecture. Josiah Warren heard him speak on his ideal society and was so taken with the idea of founding an ideal community which would eventually embrace all mankind, that he sold his lamp factory and moved his young family to New Harmony, Indiana.

If New Harmony were not sufficiently noteworthy as one of the first socialistic experiments in the United States and for its large assemblage of famous scientists and educators, it would be worthy of mention because it produced an anarchist. Warren's experiences at New Harmony were determining influences. His first acquaintance with the new science and the philosophy of Robert Owen made an indelible impression upon him. There from 1825 until 1827 he lived with some of the most advanced thinkers of his day. He met Thomas Say, a zoölogist, Charles A. Lesueur, famous ichthyologist, Sir Charles Lyell, Gerard Troost, minerologist,[11] and William MacClure, "father of American Geology."[12]

[10] For his biography—William Bailie, *Josiah Warren, The First American Anarchist* (Boston, 1906).

[11] See particularly Gustav Koerner's, *Das Deutsche Element in den Vereinigten Staaten von Nord Amerika* (Cincinnati, 1890), 354-356.

[12] George B. Lockwood, *The New Harmony Movement*, 1818-1848 (New York, 1905), 4.

At New Harmony he met with the latest European educational methods, those particularly of Pestalozzi. Through William Mac-Clure, Robert Owen, and Joseph Neef, Pestalozzi's pupil and the author of the first American works on the science of teaching, the Pestalozzian system of education was first successfully transplanted in this country.[13]   The manual training school at New Harmony was the first of its kind in the United States.   There the theory of the equal educational privileges of the sexes was put in practice for the first time.[14]   In this same period he met Frances Wright and Robert Dale Owen, whom he seems to have influenced.[15]   Warren's contact with these scientists emphasized his own questioning tendencies, challenging authority in every form. It gave him the belief that human conduct and human society, just as those of animals, could be investigated for the purpose of discovering laws which, when applied successfully, would make life peaceful and harmonious.   While more learned men lost faith in utopias and in human nature when the New Harmony experiment failed, Warren became more trusting than before in man's intelligence and perfectibility.   But, strangely enough, he was not led, as might have been expected, to a vague generalization of likeness in human nature.   Although he seemed to see laws in society, it was the *differences* which attracted him.   "Infinite diversity," he said, "is the universal law."   In a sense he anticipated the very trend science itself was to take long after he was dead.

Although in certain essentials Josiah Warren's philosophy was a reaction against the beliefs he found at New Harmony, he nevertheless carried with him three important ideas which he had derived from Robert Owen.[16]   With Owen, he believed first, that

[13] *Ibid.*, 3.

[14] *Ibid.*, 3-4.

[15] Robert Dale Owen tells in his autobiography that he enjoyed particularly the weekly concerts at New Harmony because they were so ably led by Josiah Warren. *Threading My Way. Twenty-Five Years of Autobiography* (London, 1874), 245.   For Warren's influence on Frances Wright, see below, 114-115.

[16] For Owen's philosophy—*A New View of Society* (London, 1818). Robert Dale Owen, *op. cit.*, 174 and *passim.*   Owen's cardinal principles

the "emancipation of man" was possible and human happiness only a question of suitable social adjustment to be secured by the incorporation of true principles. Second, utility was the true measure of virtue and happiness the true end of life. Third, in a more specific matter, he learned of labor notes, which Owen, however, had never used as a medium between organized communities.[17]

Warren in his turn influenced Owen. It has been claimed by credible authorities that Owen derived from Warren the central idea of the great labor coöperative societies of Great Britain, which constitute one of the most successful movements of the last century in that country.[18] It is certainly true that in 1832 (Warren had already established his "Time Store" in 1827) Owen was enthusiastically engaged in an enterprise called "Equitable Banks of Labor Exchange." His purpose was to carry out the idea that "the quantity of average human labor contained in a commodity determines the value of such a commodity, hence if all commodities be valued and exchanged by the producer according to that standard, the capitalist will have no room in industry or commerce or the worker will retain the full product of his labor."[19] At Owen's Labor Exchange in London every producer of a useful article could bring the same to a "bazaar" connected with the bank and receive for it notes issued by the bank and representing a number of labor hours equivalent to those contained in his article. With these notes the holder could purchase other articles contained in the bazaar and likewise valued according to the quantity of labor consumed by its production. Adam Smith had, of course, as early as 1776, in his *Wealth of Nations,* declared that labor

were: (1) man is the product of environment, is not responsible for his character, "man is not a fit subject of praise or blame." (2) "Utility is the best and measure of virtue." (3) "Enlightened selfishness is the most trustworthy basis of elevated morality." The "sensationalism" of Locke, the "selfishness" of Malthus and Bentham, the "utilitarianism" of James Mill, were his guides. Robert Dale Owen, *op. cit.,* 165.

[17] Josiah Warren, *Practical Details in Equitable Commerce* (New York, 1852), 15.

[18] Lockwood, *op. cit.,* 5.

[19] Morris Hillquit, *History of Socialism in the United States* (New York and London, 1906), 58.

alone was the ultimate and real standard by which the value of all commodities could be estimated. But Warren was the first to apply this principle in a Bank of Exchange, the purpose of which was to displace *all* currency with Labor Notes based on time *and* intensity or "repugnance." Owen used time only as a basis of evaluation. A. J. Macdonald, a Scotchman, a disciple of Robert Owen and historian of American socialistic experiments, declared that Warren had communicated his plans of Labor Exchange to Owen, "who endeavored to practice them in London upon a large scale."[20] The bank failed, however, but largely because it accepted all products indiscriminately, regardless of whether or not they were in demand.[21] Warren believed that it failed because it did not carry out the principles of individuality.[22]

At this point, however, the contact is broken. Josiah Warren reacted violently against the socialism of Owen. The failure of New Harmony in 1827 did not disillusion him; it intensified his conviction that the true basis of society was the freedom of the individual. Freedom was the right of an individual to dispose of his own property, time, and reputation, *but* "at his own cost." From this period of reaction came his conviction that paternal authority as well as that of the majority rule could not solve the problem of government. The suppression of individuality, the lack of initiative, and the absence of personal responsibility were in his mind the chief causes of failure. When everything was decided by authority, or by the will of the majority, each laid the responsibility on his neighbor. These defects Warren believed were inseparable from any social scheme based upon government and community goods. Private "possession" of property, he concluded, must be accepted for any practical social scheme. He, therefore, constructed his own system for remodelling society. The practical application of his theories is to be found in his "Time Stores" and later in his colonies, theoretically in his *Prac-*

[20] John Humphrey Noyes, *History of American Socialism* (Philadelphia, 1870), 95. Noyes incorporates much of Macdonald's material and in many cases quotes verbatim from him.

[21] Robert Dale Owen, *op. cit.,* 261. Hillquit, *op. cit.,* 58-59.

[22] Noyes, *op. cit.,* 95.

*tical Details in Equitable Commerce* and his *True Civilization,* but most adequately and systematically in the book, *The Science of Society,* written by his disciple, Stephen Pearl Andrews.

Warren returned to Cincinnati determined, with his practical and optimistic idealism, to try his own scheme. He therefore opened on May 18, 1827, the first so-called "Time Store" on Fifth and Elm Streets. From 1827 until 1829 he successfully operated this store on principles which we shall consider subsequently. Again from 1842 until the year 1844 he carried out the same experiment at New Harmony, Indiana, adding what he called "repugnance" or intensity to "time" as a basis of evaluating labor. In practical results his experiment reduced the prices of the competing merchants, prospered for several years because prices were lower, but finally collapsed because of too little patronage and "the want of common honesty."[23] Out of this experiment in dry goods stores grew Warren's interest in applying his business principles to group life, chiefly to colonies. From August, 1830, until March, 1831, he tried to found a village of "Equity" at Spring Hill, Massilon, Ohio. His chief interest was to teach young men trades in a short time in order to eliminate the long apprenticeship. His school here was a precursor of the modern manual training school and the technical trade school. At the same time he set himself to learn the practical arts of wagon-building, wood and metal working, printing and type founding. In 1833 he published the first anarchist periodical in America, the *Peaceful Revolutionist,* a four page weekly, propagating the principles of Equity.[24] He himself cast his own plates, invented his own print-

[23] John Humphrey Noyes sought out Josiah Warren at New Harmony in 1842. He has left an interesting account of a purchase which he made at the "Time Store" and declares that Warren complained of "want of common honesty." Noyes, *American Socialism,* 95-97.

[24] Unfortunately Warren did not continue the publication of this weekly beyond a few months. In 1840, experimenting along the same lines, Warren invented a cylinder press. It was the first press that was ever used to print newspapers from a roll. Lockwood, *op. cit.,* 298. He subsequently discovered a new kind of typographical plate which was made of siliceous earth—smoother, cheaper, and as solid as metal. The importance of this invention was appreciated even in Scotland, where an editor of *Chamber's Edinburgh Journal* declared it was much talked of, that printing had

ing press, made his own type moulds, and wrote his own articles. Was this not a paper of an Individualist? In fact, all of Warren's efforts appear somewhat as a solitary individual's attempt to stave off in his own life and by his own hands the inevitable advance of machine and mass production.

Undeterred by his earlier failures, Warren founded colonies at Tuscarawas County, Ohio (1835-37), at Clermont, Ohio— "Utopia" (1847-51),[25] and at Brentwood, Long Island—"Modern Times" (1850-62?). "Modern Times" was Warren's most successful experiment. It attracted considerable attention both in the United States and in England chiefly because of the economic principle of laissez faire which he worked out there. The basic moral principle observed was expressed in the phrase, "mind your own business." Exchange of products was facilitated by the use of labor notes. Socially Warren's "Modern Times" was an Abbe Thelème with its motto "Fay ce que vouldras." The inhabitants, supporting themselves by farming and by industry on a small scale, lived peacefully and harmoniously.[26] Warren himself visited

already been done with it in Washington and that the Smithsonian Institution was adopting it for its great catalogue of American libraries. "Trialville and Modern Times," *Chamber's Edinburgh Journal,* Vol. XVIII (December 18, 1852), 396-7.

[25] The colony at Tuscarawas was made up of six families with the total of four hundred acres of land which was malarial and totally unsuited for habitation. The colony at Clermont was built up from the six families remaining after the breaking up of the Fourier Phalanx there sponsored by Horace Greeley, Albert Brisbane, and William H. Channing. One of the members writing in the *Harbinger* (Fourierest Magazine) on October 2, 1847, spoke of Warren as a "man of no ordinary talents" and declared that his "character to do instead of say" gave them confidence in him as a man. Noyes, *American Socialism,* 366-374; 374-375.

[26] Warren's account: *Practical Details in Equitable Commerce,* New York, 1852, vii-viii. The chief obstacle at "Modern Times" was *lack of capital.* It actually amounted to scarcely more than an agricultural colony of Individualists! The "Christian Anarchists," chiefly Adin Ballou, who had founded a colony at Hopedale, Mass., in 1842, found "Modern Times" totally unChristian because it was not guided by the laws of God. Certain ones of the Hopedale colonists withdrew to live at "Modern Times." Adin Ballou, *History of the Hopedale Community,* From its Inception to its Virtual Submergence in the Hopedale Parish (Lowell, Mass., 1897), 241-242. Noyes believed that "Modern Times" was an impracticable experiment because it was unChristian. Account: Noyes, *American Socialism,* 99-101. British account: Williame Pare (?) "Trialville and Modern

"Modern Times" for the last time in 1860. After that he devoted himself to writing and to elaborating an original scheme of musical notation, which he called "Mathematical Notation."[27] The perpetuation of his ideas was assured by the conversion of Stephen Pearl Andrews in 1850, and of Benjamin R. Tucker in 1872. Tucker in that year recognized Warren as the originator of American Anarchism.[28] Warren's work was ended. In 1873 he went to live with Mr. and Mrs. Heywood of Princeton, Massachusetts, and then with his friend Edward Lenton in Boston, where he died on April 14, 1874.

At a time when the fashion was Associationism and laissez faire or unrestricted competition was the practice, Josiah Warren proclaimed a doctrine of absolute individual sovereignty and voluntary coöperation. His philosophy was the product of his own strong self-consciousness and of the infinite possibilities for self-expression which still appeared to be open to all in America.[29] His solution was one of the many brought forth to improve the conditions which were fast developing in an industrial society. It was a manifestation of that enthusiasm for economic reform which Robert Owen stimulated in 1825. But Warren's solution differed from all others in that it was an open denial of the validity of the democratic system and a protest *against* the integrative process of modern industrial development. We can best appreciate the char-

Times," *Chamber's Edinburgh Journal*, Vol. XVIII (December 18, 1852), 395-7. M. D. Conway found "Modern Times" in 1859 an idyllic spot, and was so captivated by the "idea" and the atmosphere that he made one of the women whom he met there, the heroine in his novel *Pine and Palm*. The lively interest in the latest questions in science, literature, and general subjects, as well as the originality of opinion which he found there impressed Conway. Moncure D. Conway, *Autobiography,* Memories and Experiences of (2 vols., Boston and New York, 1905), I, 264-268. "Modern Times," *The Fortnightly Review*, Volume I (July, 1865), No. 4, 421-434.

[27] In 1844 he had first discovered this system and in that year printed a book on the subject by his newly perfected typography, a beautiful example of his stereotyping process and of his handwriting produced on delicate copper plate. The original is in the library of the New Harmony Working Men's Institute. Lockwood, *op. cit.,* 300.

[28] Dr. Paul Eltzbacher, *Anarchism* (New York, 1908), 182; Nettlau, *Der Vorfrühling,* 122.

[29] Max Nettlau, *Der Anarchismus, Von Proudhon Zu Kroptotkin Seine historische Entwicklung in den Jahren 1859-1880* (Berlin, 1927), 21.

acter of this denial and protest by considering Warren's philosophy as it was unsystematically set forth in his two best works *Practical Details in Equitable Commerce* (1852) and *True Civilization* (1863). We must not forget, however, that Josiah Warren's chief contribution rested in his practical experiments, not in his theoretical formulation of Individual Sovereignty.

Josiah Warren's basic assumptions are first, that men are the producers of their environment and second, that the law of self preservation is the basic law of the Universe. With the men of his Age, he believed that "the all pervading viciousness of society has originated not in our nature, as has been extensively taught, but in a subtle and undetected error in one of the starting points of our intercourse with each other, that this being corrected, the general cannibalism ceases, the demand for protection ceases along with it, and we begin to emerge from strife and confusion into order and harmony."[30] Human nature is perverted by improper environment. "I know that Krinklum Scraggs is an habitual villain, but he has been made a villain by his *conditions*; he does not deserve punishment but he must be restrained."[31] This is essentially the position of anarchists in general—that crime and perversions are not the result of *evil wills* but of environment, inheritance, and the struggle for "bread." To eliminate crime and the need for government is to reorganize the economic system and to use both doctor and hospital.

The law of self preservation rules the conduct of men. It has two corollaries. First, every individual protects his own life, property and progeny; second, from this follows that each individual restrains every other individual. This law is as absolute, amoral, impartial, and universal as the law of cause and effect. Warren, therefore, would resolve society, at least economically, to the primitive state where the law of cause and effect, of "natural consequence" would operate naturally. From these assumptions Warren builds up a philosophy of complete individualism. Every

[30] *Practical Details,* 39.
[31] *True Civilization* (Boston, 1863), 39. Is this not the modern attitude toward crime?

one has an equal right to his own life, his own property, and his own reputation, absolute freedom of action in so far as he does not invade another's equal right. Freedom is enjoyed at "his own cost." It is unlikeness that attracts him, not likeness. Diversity is a part of divinity and an habitual watchfulness is necessary to preserve the conditions necessary for this freedom.[32] Freedom requires tolerance of unlikeness as a primary condition. "Freedom for you to do (at your cost or within your own sphere) what I consider wrong, selfish or independent, is the vital principle of peace and all progress; for your experiments may prove that you are right."[33] The freedom to differ he found to be the basis of universal coöperation.[34] To invest any majority with the deciding power is fatal to the liberty of the individual. Liberty is "the vital principle of human happiness; and human nature seeks its liberty as the magnet seeks the north, or as water seeks its level."[35]

With John Stuart Mill Warren tried to discover the sphere within which an individual could harmlessly be sovereign. The "individual is the great cornerstone of order."[36] But he differs from Mill when he declares that liberty can never be defined, to define it is to limit it and then it ceases to be liberty. "Each one is alone the proper and legitimate authority to define it for himself."[37] Everything is relative to the individual—morality, religion, truth. He goes beyond Montaigne's skepticism "Que sais—je?" to Descarte's credo "Je pense donc que je suis" when he says "True religion is my religion, true morality is my particular morality."[38] The only limits to freedom are set by the individual himself. With a high degree of culture in the individual and a high degree of civilization in society a proper balance is maintained. Two conditions are necessary, one that the individual be free, second that he take the consequences of his acts. Society

[32] *Ibid.,* 116.
[33] *Ibid.,* 144.
[34] *Ibid.,* 145.
[35] *Ibid.,* 82.
[36] *Ibid.,* 182.
[37] *Practical Details,* 70. Mill did not publish *On Liberty* until 1859.
[38] *Ibid.,* 82.

"can never know peace until its members know liberty; but it can never be realized under any organization of society known to us."[39]   And, therefore, he denounces the state, law and government and demands the abolition of all governments as unnecessary and harmful: "There should be no such thing as the body politic— no member of any body but that of the human family.   Every man should be his own government, his own law, his own church, a system within himself."[40]

Warren then proposed a system which was to take the place of modern government of force and authority.   It was essentially government by experts.   In some degree his idea was prophetic.[41] A Deliberative Council made up of experts would discuss the problems which could not be settled by individuals themselves. These experts became members of the Council only by virtue of their knowledge and skill and not of political astuteness.   They were paid after, not before they rendered their services.   They convened for the discussion of one question only and when they had come to a decision, they published it with their reasons, allowing anyone to dissent from it for sufficient reason.   One of its duties as a Council was to set "prices" for coal dealers as well as for manufacturers, doctors and lawyers.[42]   This society would know no coercive taxation, army or navy, only a voluntary citizen militia.   Large-scale warfare would disappear when there were no governments.   Although Warren disbelieved in government he did not attack it.   He worked to create some institution or put into practice some principle which would eventually make government unnecessary.   It is apparent that Warren did not appreciate the complexity of the business of government even in his own times. The system which he proposed would not only be entirely insufficient, but would be a means of reëstablishing those abuses which it was designed to eliminate.   His scheme is interesting, however, because he hit upon the principle which today we hope to realize

[39] *Ibid.,* 82.

[40] *Ibid.,* 75.

[41] *True Civilization,* 26, 33.   This positive program has been overlooked by critics of his work.

[42] *Ibid.,* 110.   This might easily amount to a tyranny, however.

in government by experts and in national planning by economists divorced from politics.

This one principle he demonstrated to his own satisfaction in his "Time Store," which we have already said was established in 1827. The principle which he incorporated in this general store was essentially that of Proudhon's Bank of Exchange on a much smaller scale. It is important because it was an anticipation of Proudhon and because it was used as an early attempt to solve the labor problem. The theoretical basis of this labor exchange store was that "property is the whole produce or result of a man's own labor."[42a] Labor is manual, mental, and managerial. To this property every man has an unalienable right.[43] The only true basis of wealth or currency is labor. Labor is evaluated on the basis of "time" and "repugnance." Time and "repugnance" (that is the disagreeableness of any work) are represented by labor notes. The price of any article then in Warren's store was the cost price plus the cost of his labor in selling the article, measured by a clock, hence the name "Time Store."[44] "Cost, not value, the limit of price," was his motto. The labor notes with which each customer paid for the article he purchased was his promise to render a certain number of hours of work. The value of his own work he himself set. In his efforts to make labor the basis of currency, Warren gave to the menial and most "disagreeable" work the highest reward. A street-cleaner's hour of labor was worth more than that of a college professor. "The most disagreeable labor is entitled to the highest compensation." As an economic experiment it was an attempt to break the monopoly power of the merchant-capitalist who, by virtually controlling the media of exchange, prevented the exchange of commodities according to

[42a] *Practical Details*, 13.

[43] *True Civilization*, 62.

[44] The "Cash and Carry" and "Help Yourself" Groceries are today operated on virtually this same principle. The price of an article there is the cost price plus a small charge for "upkeep," transportation of goods, etc. The buyer is "paid" for his labor of selection, "self-service," by the reduction from the usual sale price at other stores. Warren's aim, however, could not be realized without a complete and universal adoption of this principle.

labor cost.[45]    On the basis of the labor-cost principle Warren
opposed high rates of interest.  The amount of interest collected
on a loan of money should be determined by the length of time
which the negotiation of the loan took, not by need of the borrower.[46]

Josiah Warren's methods were crude and almost primitive, but
his principles were those of Proudhon's Bank of Exchange.  His
knowledge of currency and credit was certainly not as profound
as that of Proudhon.  In these essentials, Warren anticipated
Proudhon: first, the labor-cost theory of value (indirectly from
Adam Smith); second, labor exchange in the distribution of goods,
not in the production of it; third, the mutual banking system
whereby the borrower could secure capital, that is, capital goods
(raw materials, machines, tools, and the like) directly from the
person who possessed them, without interest except for a small
charge for the cost of the negotiation to the bank.  Both Josiah
Warren and Pierre Proudhon attempted to destroy the undesirable
features of the industrial system—"the middle man," large unearned profits, the unequal distribution of wealth, and the tendency
to submerge the independent artisan.[47]

We have said that Warren anticipated Henry George.  He did
so by one act—the relinquishment of eight valuable blocks of
property in Cincinnati.  With Warren to think was to act.  On the
principle that a man is entitled *solely* to the product of his own
labor and not to wealth acquired by the work of others, or by
"situation," he gave up a large area of property.  The property,
which was in the business district of Cincinnati, was rapidly increasing in value by virtue of its location, to such an extent, in

[45] Warren's solution applied to the independent proprietors or artisan
stage of production but Tucker tried many years later to apply it to the
factory system.

[46] *Practical Details,* 37-39.

[47] Warren had in mind the destruction of the capitalistic system.  By his
system he aimed to eliminate rapacious competition, needless fluctuations in
business, wars over markets for trade, industrial rivalry, insecurity, and the
distinctions between rich and poor.  He aimed also to reduce the working
day to three hours. *True Civilization,* 82.

fact, that Warren would have amassed a large fortune had he held it.[48] Instead he returned the lease to the man from whom he had secured it because he condemned unearned increment in land as much as he did profit in industry. Henry George specifically declared in 1879 that "that which a man makes or produces is his own, as against all the world—to enjoy or to destroy, to use, to exchange, or to give."[49] The right of exclusive ownership sanctioned by natural law applies *only* to the product of a man's labor, however. "Nature acknowledges no ownership or control in man save as the result of exertion. . . . *She recognizes no claim but that of labor.*" This right "excludes the possibility of any other right of ownership." And to the specific point with which we are concerned, no men can legitimately accumulate profit from *land* which was the result of social advance. Such profit is the product of social effort, not of individual labor. Although he went farther than Josiah Warren in declaring that that surplus should be taken over by the State by means of a "single Tax," he nevertheless agreed with Warren in principle.

Before we consider the influence of Warren's doctrines on his contemporaries, however, it is necessary to survey the life and the writings of the man who made them known to the general public. It has been said that Stephen Pearl Andrew's *Science of Society* has "probably done more toward calling the attention of the independent thinkers and reformers to Warren's philosophy than anything ever put forth by himself, and is by far the ablest statement of the Principles which has yet appeared."[50] Andrews systematized the doctrine of Individual Sovereignty in the following works: *The Science of Society* (published in 1852 from the lec-

[48] *Bailie, op. cit.,* 23-24.

[49] Citations from Henry George's *Progress and Poverty, An Inquiry into the Cause of Industrial Depressions and of Increase of Want with Increase of Wealth* (New York, 1919), 332-334.

[50] Bailie, *op. cit.,* 57. Warren "converted" Stephen Pearl Andrews in 1850 at one of his "conversazione" in Boston. (*Ibid,* 58-59). Warren had at that time adopted private parlor discussions as a method of propaganda. Is this not reminiscent of Anne Hutchinson's "gossipings?" In general, Warren's method of propaganda included discussion, publication of books, and practical demonstration.

tures given before the Mechanics Institute of New York in 1851),
*Love, Marriage, and Divorce, A Discussion between Henry James,
Horace Greeley, and Stephen Pearl Andrews,* 1852 (published
1889), and *The Labor Dollar* (1877).

The life of Stephen Pearl Andrews is characteristic of an
"Individual Sovereign." Because it is typical and because it gives
us a more intimate understanding of Individualist Anarchism
itself, we shall consider it in its essential details.[51] Andrews was
born in Templeton, Massachusetts, on March 22, 1812, of a family
with characteristically "strong moral energy."[52] He was early
interested in practical social reform, particularly Abolitionism, and
had worked out a plan of manumission whereby the slaves would
be set free by government purchase. From 1839 until 1843 he
practiced law at Houston, Texas, where he rose to an outstanding
position in the community, but eventually made himself exceedingly unpopular by his fearless opposition to slavery. Excitement
rose to such a pitch that in 1843 his house was mobbed; he and
his wife and infant son managed to escape only by a dangerous
twenty mile drive across flooded prairies. He immediately went
to England to raise money for the purchase of the slaves in the
form of a loan from Great Britain to Texas. Lord Aberdeen and
Lord Palmerston were at first favorably inclined toward his project
but dropped it when Andrews was repudiated by Ashbel Smith,
Texan Chargé d'affaires. Andrews' participation in the cause of
abolition is a striking contrast to that of the group which we have
already considered—Garrison, Ballou, Thoreau, and Noyes. Andrews' attitude toward slavery was typical of that of the Individualists—Josiah Warren and Lysander Spooner. Both Andrews
and Garrison suffered from the violence of the mob, both realized
that the government was identified with slavery. Garrison assailed
the government and demanded its destruction; Andrews appealed

[51] Biographical sketch in: *Dictionary of American Biography,* edited by
Allen Johnson (New York, 1928), I, 298-299; J. T. Trowbridge, "A Rem-
iniscence of the Pantarch," *The Independent,* Volume 55 (February 26,
1903), 497-501. Trowbridge describes Andrews as "a man of pure intellect
of the logical order," p. 499.

[52] Elisha Benjamin Andrews (1844-1914), famous president of Brown
University, was his nephew.

to the government to emancipate the slaves and himself attempted to liberate them. No other situation brings out so clearly the contrast between the temperament and the method of the Individualist Anarchists and the Christian Anarchists.[53]

Immediately after the failure of his attempt to liberate the slaves, Andrews became interested in the short-hand system of Isaac Pitman and determined to introduce it into the United States, he opened up a school of phonography in Boston. Phonography, philology, a new international language "Alwato," Pantarchy (new system of "universology"), labor reform, and radical causes of many varieties continued to occupy his restless, fertile mind until his death in 1886.[54] His meeting with Josiah Warren in 1850, however, is most important for this study.

Stephen Pearl Andrews was the first to attempt to dignify individualist economic anarchism into a social philosophy. He attempted to apply to social science the same inductive method as that which was used in natural science and to do for anarchism what Fourier and Lasalle had done for socialism. The first words of his *Science of Society* are a plea for the use of the scientific method in the study of society:[55]

[53] The same contrast is apparent between the later Individualists, represented by Benjamin Tucker, and the Anarchist Communists of the late nineteenth and early twentieth centuries.

[54] (1) In 1847 he printed in phonetic type *The Anglo Saxon* and *Propagandist,* and in collaboration with Augustus F. Boyle compiled and published *The Comprehensive Phonographic Class Book,* 1845, and *The Phonographic Reader,* 1845. Each ran to sixteen editions within ten years and was largely responsible for the introduction of the short-hand system into the United States. (2) A linguist of amazing ability, reputed master of thirty-two languages, including Hebrew, Sanskrit, and Chinese, he stimulated interest in foreign languages at a time when little progress had been made by American schools in that direction. He devised an international language which he called Alwato—a forerunner of Esperanto and Volapuk. (1877, *Primary Grammar of Alwato.*) (3) His system of Pantarchy is found in the book, *The Basic Outline of Universology,* 1872, "a vast chaotic volume which remains one of the curiosities of philosophic literature," only a few copies of which were printed. *Dictionary of American Biography,* 298-299; Trowbridge, *op. cit.,* 499; Laura Stedman and George M. Gould, *Life and Letters of Edmund Clarence Stedman* (2 vols., New York, 1910), I, 176.

[55] Auguste Comte, "the father of sociology," published his great book in 1837, but his philosophy was first introduced to America in 1853 by Henry Edger, one of his disciples, formerly a follower of Josiah Warren, and resident at "Modern Times" at least until 1869. Nettlau, *Der Vorfrühling,* 120.

"The propriety of the use of the term Science, in such a connection, may be questioned by some whom habit has accustomed to apply that term to a much lower range of investigations. If researches into the habits of beetles and tadpoles, and their localities and conditions of existence, are entitled to the dignified appellation of Science, certainly similar researches into the Nature, the wants, the adaptations, and so to speak, into the true or requisite *moral and social habitat* of the spiritual animal called man, must be, if conducted *according to the rigid methods of scientific induction from observed facts, equally entitled to that distinction.*"[56]

His plan is scientific; therefore, it is true. If applied to society it will be an "adequate solution of the social problem." His solution is the same as Warren's. He tells us more clearly, however, what Warren meant by Individuality. "It pervades universal nature. Individuality is positively the most *fundamental* and *universal* principle which the finite mind seems capable of discovering." And by Individuality he means that "There are no two objects in the universe which are precisely alike. . . . *Infinite diversity is the universal law.*" This is true of persons, things, and events. "This indestructible and all-pervading Individuality furnishes itself the law, and the only true law, of order and harmony." Government does not and can not preserve order. Individuality is the essential law of order throughout the universe. Just as harmony of the universe is maintained by the single atom obeying its own law, so is it maintained in society by the single atom, the individual, obeying its own law.[57] This law of individuality must, therefore, be obeyed. It is infinite and cannot be measured or prescribed (to limit it is to destroy it), an inherent, and essential element of order, and cannot be disobeyed "without engendering infinite confusion."[58] This is the exact opposite of the ordinary conception which is that such a principle brings chaos and "anarchy." The only law is the Sovereignty of the Individual which gives *every* man absolute control over himself *limited only* "by the onerous consequences of his action."

[56] *The Science of Society* (Boston, 1888), 5-6.
[57] *Ibid.*, 13-15.
[58] *Idem.*

The present government, Andrews finds, violates this principle by slavery, commercial restrictions, limitation of free soil, treatment of crime, and finally by the restrictions it places on the marriage and parental relationships of its citizens. Hence he approves free trade, free land, and disapproves of capital punishment, taxation, the army and navy, and nationalism.[59] The proper care of the criminal he emphasizes particularly—*crime prevention not cure* is an urgent need. A criminal should be treated as a diseased person. He, therefore, considers the best government that which does not govern at all. This, he believes, will come about *gradually* with the proper development and cultivation of the individual. "The true constitution of government, therefore, is self government."[60] Furthermore, he finds nothing more foreign to true *Democracy* than the rule of majorities. True Democracy—and here he takes the pronouncement of the Declaration of Independence and the extreme individualism of Rousseau's doctrine as his justification—declares that all men are *born free and equal,* that *every* man is free from the governing control of every other man. *"Genuine Democracy is identical with the no-government doctrine."*[61] And for this reason Andrews finds the no-government men (meaning the Non-Resistants and Perfectionists, and others whom we have discussed in the preceding chapter), although *"practically not so wise,"* theoretically consistent. It is they who are "unterrified Democrats" because they take this doctrine to its logical conclusions. They insist that no government be higher than the individual *but* they do not destroy the causes which make government necessary.[62] For this reason, the Individualists are more *practical* than the ethical no-government men. They aim to prepare for no-government by destroying the basic evils which are, as Andrews sees them, mainly economic. He believes, therefore, that at some time in the future all government

---

[59] *Ibid.,* 17-19; 28-29.
[60] *Ibid.,* 30.
[61] *Ibid.,* 23.
[62] *Ibid.,* 24. Andrews, therefore, accuses the Non-Resistants of attempting to destroy the government without offering something to take its place. Tucker later accused the Anarchist-Communists of the same fault.

or restraint on the individual will cease to exist. The application of this principle—"that I should sedulously and religiously respect your Individuality, while I vindicate my own"—to all economic and social activity would completely dispense with all force and government.[63]

Corporations, according to Andrews, should take the place of political government.[64] Most of the business of governments could be handled more efficiently by private individuals, self-selected and self-authorized. It is apparent that Andrews did not conceive the vast development which a country as extensive as the United States would reach industrially and financially. His very principle was realized in the development of trusts and combines which were and are a menace to the sovereignty of *every* individual. It was, in fact, the trust which Benjamin Tucker assailed most violently. Government, therefore, was to be dissolved in the economic organism. The first step in the realization of a scientific economic order was currency and labor reform. The aim of reform was to bring the individual who "wants" together with the person who has. He, therefore, proposes a system of mutual coöperation which would be possible in large factories as well as in small shops.[65] Simple equity is to be the basis of co-operation, that is "so much of *your* labor as I take and apply to my benefit, so much of my labor ought I to give you to be applied to your benefit."[66] Labor has three bases of evaluation—intensity ("amount of repugnance overcome"), time, and skill. Fixed capital will be exchanged on this basis. But since exchange in kind is not always possible, a labor note will be made out which will give evidence of an obligation to be met at some future time. A new circulating medium would thus be introduced based solely upon individual responsibility, thus eliminating government mints and bankers. "It makes every man his own banker."[67] What money every individual had, therefore, would represent exactly what he

[63] *Ibid.*, 26.
[64] *Ibid.*, 33-34.
[65] *Ibid.*, 64-65.
[66] *Ibid.*, 67.
[67] *Ibid.*, 71.

could produce. Large fortunes could not be accumulated and wealth would be more evenly distributed. Land, which is part of natural wealth, belongs to all individuals equally. All wild unimproved land should cost nothing. But whatever improvements are added by *human labor* so much should be paid for by a purchaser.[68] Nor did Andrews find any objection to the wage system or the relationship of employer and employed. "It is right that one man employ another, it is right that he pay him wages, and it is right that he direct him absolutely, arbitrarily in the performance of his labor."[69]

How then would Andrews and Warren prevent a super-intelligent yet ruthless individual from usurping all the rights of another individual? Their answer is no answer at all. It is that he *ought* not use his superior skill and intelligence. He must deal with his inferiors as if they had the same amount of strength and mental powers as he has himself.[70] The critics of individualist anarchism have found this its weakest point and about which the whole beautifully constructed system collapsed. The very end which it hoped to realize, the equitable distribution of wealth, was at once defeated.

As a complete system, both economic and social, "Individual Sovereigntyism" was never accepted—by the laborers or by the intellectuals. Certain of the labor principles were tried as practical experiments, as we shall see, and failed, either because they were only partially applied or because they were impractical. The fact remains that they were not accepted completely. It is possible, however, that certain of these ideas, such as those of labor exchange and of currency, had an influence on the other proposals of the day which were put forward and accepted more generally, as for example, Greenbackism.[71] The close affinity of these two

[68] *Ibid.*, 76.
[69] *Ibid.*, 149. Stephen Pearl Andrews still held most of these ideas in 1877, although he had lost his optimistic faith that they would ever be accepted. See his "Labor Dollar," *Radical Review*, August, 1877, 168 ff.; also 287, 292-3.
[70] *Ibid.*, 82.
[71] At an Industrial Congress of Workingmen in New York on January 7, 1851, to which Stephen Pearl Andrews was sent by the Fifth Ward Re-

programs we shall consider subsequently, as well as the reasons why Individualism as a systematic philosophy never won a wide acceptance.

Both Josiah Warren and Stephen Pearl Andrews admitted that they had failed to get their programs accepted. Warren declares in his *Practical Details* that he found people willing to profit by cheap prices but that "there was a general lack of capacity to appreciate the subject, and an incapacity to overcome old habits of action."[72]   Andrews wrote more than twenty years later that he had never been satisfied with the moderate degree of success which he had achieved and that he had always felt he had partially failed.[73]   Nevertheless certain isolated individuals and labor groups had accepted their ideas.[74]

As early as 1839 Warren's currency and labor suggestions were recognized and taken up by William Beck of Cincinnati. His book, *Money and Banking, or their Nature and Effects considered together with a Plan for the Universal Diffusion of the Legitimate Benefits Without their Evils* (1839), showed unmistakably the influence of Warren.[75]   Beck proposed a ticket of

formers, Edward Kellogg's *Labor and Other Capital* (the philosophy of Greenbackism) was carefully considered by a committee and reported to have "ably exposed the evils that attend our present bank usury, and commercial laws and customs." At this same Congress each time Andrews set forth his "Declaration of Fundamental Truths" the meeting was adjourned or discussion postponed. His persistence won the appointment of a committee to investigate his "platform" but the committee never reported to the Congress. Fifteen years later Kellogg's ideas were proclaimed under the name of Greenbackism and were then to America what the coöperative anarchism of Proudhon was to France. Commons, *History of Labour*, I, 556; *Documentary History*, IX, 33.

[72] *Practical Details*, 43.

[73] *Radical Review*, August, 1877, p. 293.

[74] One of Andrew's contemporaries declared that he had a large personal following and was the leader among the radical groups in New York City. Trowbridge, *op. cit.*, 499. Consider his active participation in the *New Democracy* and the Manhattan Liberal Club. He founded the "Order of Recreation" in 1858, a group of intellectual radicals. See Stedman's description of the Unitary Home established through Andrews' influence on principles of "Individual Sovereignty" and "Cost the Limit of Price." Writers, lawyers, artists, made up his small coterie. Stedman, *op. cit.*, I, 161-176; Noyes, *American Socialism*, 94.

[75] Commons, *History of Labour*, I, note p. 511. William B. Greene had read this book but not Warren's. See below, note 139.

exchange and recognized that money was simply "an intermediate article moving between claim and claim, floating between commodity and commodity, taken in as the receipt for one and forming the title for another."[76] He suggested on this basis, therefore, that a system of account-keeping be substituted for money in the circle of creditors and debtors. Each piece of property was to be represented by a ticket of equivalent value—the aggregate value of tickets being the aggregate value of all property. But Beck would maintain the government for the purpose of regulating this system.

Retail stores based on Warren's Labor Exchange principle were established in Cincinnati, Philadelphia, and Boston.[77] In 1855 a Mr. Keith was won over to Warren's ideas and in that year opened up a "Boston House of Equity," where he sold all merchandise at cost price.[78] At the same time Keith adopted an educational program which included weekly lectures and the publication of a paper, *The People's Paper,* to propagate "Individual Sovereignty." The destruction of the establishment by fire and the severe financial reverses which Mr. Keith suffered in South American investments brought this experiment to an end.[79]

We have already seen that Warren's "Individual Sovereignty" was closely related to the Agrarian Individualism, particularly of George Henry Evans and Lewis Masquerier of this same period. The existence of this relationship is borne out by the recognition of Lewis Masquerier, who later broke away from Evans and

[76] Commons, *History of Labour,* I, 511. Beck's book was unfortunately not available to the writer.

[77] Commons, *Documentary History,* IX, 79. The Constitution of the Philadelphia *Labor for Labor Association* was printed in the *Mechanics Free Press* on May 24, 1828, and must have familiarized at least a few of the workers with Warren's ideas. Warren also wrote articles for this paper. *Ibid.,* V, 129-133.

[78] Bailie, *op. cit.,* 92-94.

[79] Keith later applied Warren's ideas to the sale of land—that is, the sale of land at cost price. But this is only one superficial aspect of the exchange idea. Certainly a scheme which requires a generous capitalist to endow it is an impractical solution of the labor problem. Bailie, *op. cit.,* 94. The *Boston Transcript,* commenting on the closing of the store, declared that the principle in that store was one which "a thousand failures could not effect." *Idem.*

veered into anarchism.[80]  In *Young America* (1846) he declared
that the principles of individual sovereignty and voluntary association which Josiah Warren and his associates were setting forth,
were the same as those of the *National Reform and Inalienable
Homestead and Township Organization,* of which he was a member.  He, therefore, wished them the success which he hoped for
and expected from such a true system.[81]

Warren's ideas seem to have had a significant influence on
certain so-called "intellectuals" both in England and in the United
States.  The philosophy of Frances Wright, one of the first advocates of women's rights, birth control, companionate marriage,
and abolitionism, was influenced by Warren, whom she had met
at New Harmony in 1827.[82]  Although her philosophy was the
"product" of her own mind, she had drawn appreciably upon the
socialism of Robert Owen and also upon the anarchism of her
friend, Josiah Warren.[83]  On October 23, 1830, she definitely
showed her acceptance of certain of Warren's ideas when she
wrote in the *Free Enquirer* that Warren's principles were "capable of opening up to every human being the path of honest
independence and removing the load of oppression which now
weighs upon youthful as upon female labor, of encouraging the
outcast and the vagrant to engage in virtuous exertions . . . , and
of restoring the human race that first best birthright held in virtue
of existence—individual, entire, and equal liberty."[84]  In a series
of articles which she published in the *Free Enquirer* (March 18-
April 22, 1829), on "The Causes of Existing Evils," Frances
Wright found the causes of existing evils not in changing economic
conditions, but in the unfortunate character of present governments
and in the organization of existing society.  One of the causes of
the evils rested in government itself—"the pressure of constraining

[80] Commons, *History of Labour,* I, 523.

[81] Nettlau, *Der Vorfrühling,* 110.

[82] Waterman, *op. cit.,* note 251.  In 1830 Warren had gone to New York
at the suggestion of Miss Wright and Robert Dale Owen to discuss the
possibility of establishing industrial colonies.  Bailie, *op. cit.,* 28.

[83] Waterman, *op. cit.,* note 251.

[84] Bailie, *op. cit.,* 28.

power, whether administered in the form of despotic executive authority, coercive law, or terrifying superstition."[85] "Government by violence" she found one of the greatest evils of society— "its motive principles are fear and coercion; its proposed objects —obedience, restraint, and constraint." The basic assumption of government was that man "is a vicious animal, in need of control." To improve the condition she proposed that labor be rewarded for its usefulness.[86]

Later, in 1835, Frances Wright propagated similar ideas on her lecture tours. In her lectures on "The Nature and History of Human Civilization, considered in the Past, the Present, and the Future," she found the great obstacle to freedom of action and of mind the *Banking* and *Funding* system, and Christianity. Both held the people in servitude.[87] With Warren she believed that the Declaration of Independence had laid the foundation of a new epoch in which justice and freedom for every one was guaranteed —particularly to the product of their own labor. Frances Wright's ideas of marriage were also "anarchistic," that is, she believed that moral obligation should be substituted for legal obligation.[88] The mutual voluntary obligation which she would make binding in marriage only, Warren and Andrews would extend generally throughout all social organization. In her recognition of the needs of the individual, and in her insistence on the change of the Banking system, the squaring of government administration with the Declaration of Independence, as well as in her ideas on marital relationship, Frances Wright was one with Josiah Warren.[89]

[85] Waterman, *op. cit.*, 191.

[86] *Ibid.*, 191-192.

[87] *Ibid.*, 250. President Andrew Jackson crusaded against the United States Bank and actually succeeded in destroying its Charter in 1833. Charles A. Beard and Mary R. Beard: *History of the United States* (New York, 1931), 291-2.

[88] Dr. Thomas L. Nichols, resident at "Modern Times," had written *Esoteric Anthropology* in 1853 under the influence of Warren's ideas on love and marriage. Noyes, *American Socialism*, 93. Nettlau, *Der Vorfrühling*, note, 119. Frances Wright lectured extensively throughout the East and Midwest from 1828 to 1830 and acquainted the public with her "radical" ideas in philosophy and sociology.

[89] With Owen, however, she advocated a kind of State Socialism to attain these ends.

As we have already seen, an independent school of Individualism had grown up in England, from which the early American anarchists had indirectly received inspiration—chiefly from their belief in the minimum function of the State. William Godwin, one of the "repentant" fathers of modern anarchism, had published his *Enquiry Concerning Political Justice* in 1793; John Gray his *Lecture on Human Happiness* in 1825 and his *Social System, A Treatise on the Principles of Exchange* in 1831, and in 1848 *Lectures on the Natural Use of Money,* advocating a type of Mutualism. Adam Smith and Jeremy Bentham had both fostered a philosophy of individualism which pointed out the dangers of state interference with economic activity and the right of the minority. William Thompson reflected this same tendency of free coöperation combined with individualism in his many works —*An Appeal of One-Half of the Human Race, Women, against the Pretentions of the Other Half, Men,* in 1825, *Labour Rewarded,* in 1827, and *Practical Directions for the Speedy and Economical Establishment of Communities on the Principle of Mutual Coöperation* in 1830. The finest expression of this philosophy came from the pen of John Stuart Mill in 1859 in his book, *On Liberty.*[90] In 1843 William Maccall had written *The Doctrine of Individuality,* in 1844 *The Individuality of the Individual,* and in 1847, *The Elements of Individualism.* It was pointed out in *Chamber's Edinburgh Journal,* December 18, 1852, that Warren's and Andrews' ideas were an extension of Maccall's applied to political economy. In this same article "Trialville" and "Modern Times" were described. It declared that Warren was right in looking for the clue to social order in the individual, in discarding benevolence, and accepting selfishness as motive powers of social progress. It further declared that the economization of selfhood and individuality was a basic principle. "Benevolence shows well on one of the Christian graces, but it cuts a poor figure as a prime social force."[91] "Selfish interest" was taken as

[90] John Stuart Mill must have known of Warren because he referred to Warren as "a remarkable American." Lockwood, *op. cit.,* 294.

[91] "Trialville and Modern Times," *Chamber's Edinburgh Journal,* Volume XVIII (Dec. 18, 1852), 396.

the basic element of Warren's philosophy.[92]   In England Warren's system was known chiefly through his letters which were occasionally published in the Owenist magazines.[93]   Warren's writings in themselves did not stimulate any curiosity until after 1853, when Proudhon's ideas had already come to England. Through Henry Edger's letters from America the readers of the *Leader* were acquainted with the idea of Warren and Andrews.[94] From this source in August, 1853, the first English anarchist group was founded, called the *London Confederation of Political Reformers*.  Their ideas are directly traceable to Warren in their publication, *A Contribution Towards the Elucidation of the Science of Society*.[95]   Ambrose Caston Cuddon was the most outstanding convert to Warren's philosophy in England.  Active in publishing Individualist magazines and in propagating ideas for industrial villages (after his visit to "Modern Times" 1857-1858), Cuddon forms one connecting link between the European individualists and the Bakunin revolutionary anarchists.  In 1862 Cuddon led an English deputation of the publishers of the *Working Man* to greet Bakunin, the Russian anarchist, directly after he had returned from Siberia and the United States, where he had been entertained by Henry Wadsworth Longfellow![96]

On the basis of this evidence we cannot say that the anarchism of Warren and Andrews met any more than a mild reception.

[92] Germany did not receive a translation of Andrew's *Science of Society* until 1904.  Mathilde Kriege translated it under the title, *Die Wissenschaft von der Gesellschaft*.  Nettlau, *Der Vorfrühling*, 111.

[93] Nettlau, *Der Vorfrühling*, 125.

[94] Henry Edger (1820-1885) was at first a follower of Warren and lived at "Modern Times" (1851-1860).  In 1853 he became one of August Comte's chosen disciples, with whom Edger carried on an extensive correspondence (1854-57).  At "Modern Times" Edger published Tracts and Expositions of Positivism.  See *Lettres d'Auguste Comte . . . à Henry Edger et à M. John Metcalf, 1854-1857*, and Noyes, *American Socialism*, 94.  Also Nettlau, *Der Vorfrühling*, note 120.

[95] Nettlau, *Der Vorfrühling*, 127-128.

[96] For account of Cuddon's activity see Nettlau, *op. cit.*, 128-130.  Nettlau remarks on this incident: "So kreutzen sich zum einzigen Male, soviel ich weiss, die Wege Bakunins und die eines individualistischen Anarchisten, ohne dass sich jedenfalls einer der beiden der sie der verbindenden Ideen bewusst war. *Ibid.*, 129.

But, although as a complete program it was not widely accepted, it seems to have had considerably more of an indirect influence than we have generally supposed both in England and in the United States, more in fact than we can determine because of insufficient material. For this reason its sphere of influence can only be suggested.[97]

### B. The Anarchism of Pierre Proudhon in the United States

The end of the forties and the beginning of the fifties of the nineteenth century finds two independent strains of pure individualistic and mutualistic anarchism in economic philosophy, one native in origin, the other foreign. The first of these elements we have considered in the philosophies of Josiah Warren and Stephen Pearl Andrews. The second element, which is that of Proudhonian Mutualism, was brought to the United States by the "Forty-Eighters" from Germany, by French radicals living in the United States, by newspaper reports, and by Americans who had visited in France, particularly in the year 1848. We shall now briefly consider, so far as it is possible to determine, how and when this philosophy was imported into the United States and what its form was before it was fused with American Individualism by Benjamin Tucker. It is, therefore, pertinent to consider briefly the life and philosophy of the man whose ideas were brought to America.

Pierre Joseph Proudhon was born at Besançon on January 15,

---

[97] Even reformers who might be expected to have been sympathetic to "Individual Sovereignty," since their ideas were so similar, were not. Adin Ballou, the "Christian Anarchist," whom we have already considered, found Individual Sovereignty a "selfish," "irreligious," immoral, licentious doctrine tending "to promote anarchy and war among human beings." Is it not ironical that this is the very accusation which the "fundamentalists" levelled against Ballou's Hopedale Community? Adin Ballou, *Practical Christian Socialism, A Conversational Exposition of the True System of Human Society* (New York, 1854), 601-639. Individual Sovereignty was cooly received by the prominent reformers of the day who sponsored Associationism, namely, George Ripley, Horace Greeley, and Albert Brisbane. See review in *New York Tribune* (1852) by Ripley—*The Science of Society*, Appendix, 153-160; and for philosophy of Associationism, Horace Greeley, *Hints Toward Reforms*, (New York, 1853), 167-198; Octavius B. Frothingham, *George Ripley* (Boston, 1888), 161-165.

1809, and died on January 19, 1865.[98] His father was a cooper
and his mother a servant. Brilliant, but poor, the story is told of
him that one day returning from school with a prize he had won
he found nothing in the house to eat. Of necessity he left school
to earn a living as a proof-reader in a printing office. In 1838 he
received a stipend from the Academy of Besançon, by means of
which he engaged in scientific studies at Paris. In 1843 he held a
mercantile position at Lyons, but gave it up in 1847 in order to
move to Paris. From 1848 to 1850 he published several periodicals. He was a member of the National Assembly in 1848. In
1849 he founded the Bank of the People, but sentenced to three
years' imprisonment for an offense against the press law, his success, if it may be called that, was of short duration. Imprisonment, however, did not interrupt his activity as an author. From
1852 until 1858 he remained in Paris when he was again sentenced to three years' imprisonment. This time he fled to Brussels. In 1860 he was pardoned, returned to France, and lived
thereafter at Passy, where he died in 1865.

Proudhon's masters, "those who have caused fertile ideas to
spring up in my mind, are three in number: first, the Bible; next
Adam Smith; and last, Hegel."[99] His ideas are to be found in
his three memoirs on *What is Property* (1840), *A System of
Economical Contradictions or the Philosophy of Misery* (1846),
*The General Idea of the Revolution of the Nineteenth Century*
(1851), *Justice in the Revolution and the Church* (1858), and
*War and Peace* (1861).

Proudhon holds that the supreme law is justice. Justice, as
he conceived it, is found in the adage, "Do unto others that which
you would that others should do unto you; do not unto others that
which you would not that others should do unto you."[100] His

---

[98] Biographical sketches: Introduction by J. A. Langlois to *What Is
Property?* translated by Benjamin R. Tucker (London, 1885), 127; *Proudhon's Solution of the Social Problem*, Commentary and Exposition by
Charles A. Dana and William B. Greene, ed. by Henry Cohen (New York,
1927), 5-12.
[99] *What is Property?* 11.
[100] *Ibid.*, 50.

treatises are concerned with the elaboration of this moral formula into a scientific one.  As a social philosopher he applies it to all life—political, social, and economic.  "Justice," he says, "is the central star which governs societies."  Justice is the "recognition of the equality between another's personality and our own."[101] It maintains the social equilibrium.  Justice requires first that every man has the right to the products of his own labor; second, that he share with society what he secures from it.  Property, therefore, that is the product of mental, managerial, and skillful labor is subject to individual "possession" but not ownership.[102] The right to the product of one's labor is natural and universal. Exchange of labor for labor will recognize these two principles. It must, therefore, be equal and voluntary.[103]  But justice, therefore, rejects almost all individual legal norms, and the State laws in particular.  Justice requires that only one legal norm be in force: the norm that contracts must be lived up to.

These principles are particularly applicable to the sad condition of labor where "the labourer who bakes a loaf that he may eat a slice of bread, who builds a palace that he may sleep in a stable, who weaves rich fabrics that he may dress in rags, who produces everything that he may dispense with everything."[104] The absolute value of labour—its value in exchange—is only what has been added to the *natural* product by human labour.  "Cost is the Limit of Price."  "The absolute value of a thing . . . is its cost in time and expense."[105]  With Adam Smith he agrees that,

"Le prix réel de chaque chose, ce que chaque chose conte réellement à celui qui vent se la procurer, *c'est le travail* et la peine qu'll faut s'imposer pour l'obtenir."[106]

[101] *Ibid.*, 225.
[102] When Proudhon says, "Property is robbery," he means property which earns interest, "unearned profit" from the operation of laws of supply and demand.
[103] *Ibid.*, 141.
[104] *Ibid.*, 142.
[105] *Ibid.*, 145.
[106] *Système des Contradictions Économiques ou Philosophe de la Misère* (2 Tomes, troisième Edition, Paris, 1867), I, 401.

or, as Warren called it, "Time and amount of repugnance over-come." Price, therefore, equals cost in time and outlay. Exchange is necessary because "the isolated man can supply but a very small portion of his wants; all *his power lies in association.*" Proudhon's emphasis is upon association. The labourer cannot say, "I produce, by my own effort, all that I consume." He insists upon the solidarity of *all society*.[107] Rent, therefore, cannot be taken from land—*except* for what improvements are added by individual effort.[108] Interest is impossible, for interest is what capital is *worth to you,* not, as it should be, what you have produced.

Individual sovereignty and voluntary coöperation are achieved in his system. He insists first, on the division of labor, and second, on communality—"division du travail" which ends in "communauté,"[109] or what resolves itself into *mutuality* or mutuum, as Proudhon himself says:

"Mutuum, c'est-à-dire de l'échange en nature, dont la forme la plus simple est le prêt de consommation, est, au point de vue de l'être collectif, la synthèse des deux idées de propriété et de communauté; synthèse aussi ancienne que les éléments qui la constituent puisqu'elle n'est autre chose qué le retour de la société à sa pratique primitive à travers un dédale d'invention et de systèmes, le résultat d'une méditation de six mille ans sur cette proposition fondamentale A égale A."[110]

Mutuality is efficient, just, destroys servitude to machines, creates a real solidarity among nations without destroying individual initiative, and restores to society the wealth which is diverted.

In summary, equal opportunity is to be guaranteed to all—*equal opportunity* to attain the comforts, but not equal comforts. Individual *independence,* or autonomy of the private reason, originating in the difference in talents and capacities, can exist within the limits of the Law (Justice) without danger. Liberty, or the

---

[107] *Ibid.,* 154-156. Proudhon uses brilliant mathematical demonstrations to establish his points.
[108] *Ibid.,* 154.
[109] *Contradictions Économiques,* I, 185.
[110] *Ibid.,* II, 414.

"balance of rights and duties," is a synthesis of "communism" and "property." It is an organizing force. It is the "Mother of Order." *Therefore,* the only true order of society is *anarchy.* Anarchy is "absence of a master, of a sovereign."[111] It is free association, liberty. This is the only just, the only true form of society. The government of man by man (under whatever name it be disguised) is oppression. Society finds its highest perfection in the union of order with anarchy.[112] "The ideal republic is a positive anarchy. It is liberty free from all its shackles, superstitions, prejudices, sophistries, usury, authority; it is reciprocal liberty and not limited liberty; liberty not the daughter but the Mother of Order."[113] Proudhon rejects the State, Law, and Government unconditionally—it offends against justice to an unusual degree.

The political order must be dissolved in the economic order. This dissolution he would effect by convincing other men to accept his practical schemes. To accomplish this, Proudhon constructs a Bank of Exchange—the Bank of the People which he actually established in 1849.[114] The bank was to be an association for Mutual Credit. Its medium was the labor value of its members represented by labor notes. The labor note is the promissory note inverted—it is not a promise to render service; it represents a real service actually rendered in merchandise delivered. All the merchants, manufacturers, and laborers would *unite* in this bank to exchange their labor—"products exchanged for products." Loans were to be made without interest, except for a small charge to pay the expenses of the bank. Loans were to be obtained with the labor of the individual as security. The administration of the bank was to be in the hands of its principal founders (not the government) elected for a five year term by the General Assembly, which comprises the total membership of the bank. The object of the bank was *exchange,* not production. It would, therefore, regulate wages. Each person would secure at the

[111] *What is Property?* 264.
[112] *Ibid.,* 272.
[113] *The Solution of the Social Problem,* 45.
[114] *Ibid.,* 60 and ff.

bank fixed capital, that is, products, tools, machines, etc. The products of its members would be stored in warehouses, but only those products which were in demand. In this manner, the bank would completely "absorb" the State. The dissolution of the government in the economic organism would be realized. This briefly is Proudhon's solution of the social problem.

Both in a modified form and in a pure form Proudhon's solution was offered to American labor by the Forty-Eighters, by Americans who had travelled in France, and by Frenchmen who travelled and settled for a time in the United States. Before 1848, however, it was scarcely known in the United States, if at all. Wilhelm Weitling of the first group; William B. Greene, Charles A. Dana, and Albert Brisbane[115] of the second, and Élisée Reclus and Joseph Déjacques of the third, are of outstanding importance.

America from the time of its discovery had stood for personal liberty.[116] In the nineteenth century particularly it was a haven where the individual was supposed to be untrammeled, where plans and theories could be put into effect which in Europe were outlawed. After the French and German Revolutions of 1830 and 1848, many of the enthusiastic young reformers came to the United States.[117] Finding that the America which they met did not square with the America which they had idealized, they assailed American institutions and set to work to reform them. "Staatsbekämpfende Kritik war in der Luft."[118] They were for the most part indoctrinated with the ideas of Lasalle, Cabet, Four-

[115] Charles A. Dana, as we shall see, was a Fourierist, but wrote from France a series of very sympathetic articles for an American newspaper syndicate in 1848 in exposition of Proudhon's philosophy. Albert Brisbane was also a Fourierist, but seems to have been influenced by Proudhon's ideas of credit and currency. See below, note 136.

[116] Thomas Stockham Baker, *Lenau and Young Germany in America* (Philadelphia, 1897), 46.

[117] There was a perfect furor for emigration from Germany in 1848. Large emigration societies, such as the Giessen Society under the direction of Frederick Muench, were organized to bring the discontented and the idealistic to America—doctors, lawyers, farmers, and mechanics. *Memoirs of Gustave Koerner 1809-1896, Life Sketches at the Suggestion of his Children.* Edited by Thomas J. McCormack (Iowa, 1909. 2 vols.), I, 306-7.

[118] Nettlau, *Der Vorfrühling*, p. 166.

ier, and Proudhon. In France new social theories were being discussed and social utopias invented; in Germany, political emancipation from feudal conditions was the one united aim of the discontented classes between 1830 and 1848. In both countries secret clubs and unions were formed for the propagation of the new ideas. The revolution in 1830 in France had brought more freedom, in Germany less. The repression of agitation in Germany strengthened revolutionism there and out of this grew the first unions of German refugees on foreign soil—der Deutscher Bund der Geröchteten in Paris, and Das junge Deutschland in Switzerland.[119] The Paris union came to be composed mostly of laborers. The schemes of Fourier and Baboeuf were eagerly read. Repression in Paris followed. But the laborers moved on through Lamenais' philosophy, with his religious emphasis, in *Les Parales d'un Croyant,* to Fourier and Cabet with his *Voyage en Ecarie* (1840), and finally to Proudhon with his *What is Property?* (1840), in the same year capturing many of the German reformers and French proletariat and converting no less a mind than Karl Marx. From this environment came many of the German Forty-Eighters to the United States.[120]

One of the more or less typical extremely radical Forty-Eighters whose enthusiasm for reform brought him to a kind of anarchism, was Carl Heinzen "a man of high intellect and of extensive information."[121] In 1848 he had fled to America to

---

[119] Das Junge Deutschland was influenced by Proudhon through one of his disciples, Wilhelm Marr (1819-1904). F. C. Clark, *A Neglected Socialist* (Philadelphia, 1895), 719; Nettlau, *op. cit.,* 155, 161.

[120] Clark, *op. cit.,* 66-68.

[121] Koerner, *Memoirs,* I, 547; Nettlau, *Der Vorfrühling,* note 118. The Revolutionists were at first welcomed by the American people. Frederick Hecker, leader of the Baden Revolution, was enthusiastically received in New York, Cincinnati, and St. Louis. Speeches were made to encourage the Revolutionists and even money was sent to them. Koerner, *Memoirs,* I, 528, 538, 539. They soon made themselves unpopular, however. The Know Nothing Movement rose to such a pitch in Louisville, Kentucky, in 1855, that Germans were driven away from the polls with stones and clubs, were beaten by crowds, and sometimes killed. *Ibid.,* I, 547; Baker, *op. cit.,* 53, 70 ff; Koerner, *Das deutsche Element,* 354-356. Compare this reaction with the banishment of Anne Hutchinson in 1636, and with the deportation of two hundred thirty-five anarchists in 1919. Has not opposition to alien critics become more general and repression more ruthless?

escape arrest in Germany for some articles he had written attacking the Prussian monarchy and bureaucratic system. In New York he published the *New Yorker Schnellpost* for a short time.[122] At the outbreak of the March revolution, he returned to Germany. Arrested and banished successively from Baden (where even the Liberal provincial government found him too radical), from Switzerland, and from France, he returned to New York in 1850. After several unsuccessful attempts, he succeeded in establishing a propagandistic newspaper in Boston, *The Pioneer.* His program provided for the complete emancipation of women, the immediate abolition of slavery, positive religion, the Presidency, the Senate, and for the immediate establishment of a government directly responsible to the people.[123] In a "hard, dry, scholastic style," he attacked the constitution, and won for himself a considerable following.[124]

Of all the reformers with whom the writer is acquainted, Wilhelm Weitling was most distinctly indebted to Proudhon. Born in Magdeburg in 1808, "the hot-bed of Liberalism," apprenticed to a tailor, and reared in abject poverty, "he acquired by inheritance a hostile spirit towards all masters."[125] From 1830 until 1837 he wandered from Leipzig to Vienna, and then to Paris, where he arrived in September, 1837. There he became an active member and leader of the Bund der Gerechten. In 1838 he published *Die Menschheit, wie sie ist und wie sie sein sollte.* Two thousand copies of the first edition were printed and in two years it had been translated into Hungarian and spread over Switzerland, Germany, France and Scandinavia. From 1840 to 1844 he organized the workers in Bern and Zurich and established there a revolutionary paper. There he came in contact with Proudhonian anarchism as it was advocated by Moses Hess and Wilhelm

---

[122] Koerner, *Das deutsche Element,* 122.

[123] Koerner, *Memoirs,* I, 547.

[124] *Idem.* Other radical Forty-Eighters were Hassaurek, Henry Bernstein, Louis Bernay, but their tendency was more toward socialism and communism. *Ibid.,* I, 548-549.

[125] Clark, *op. cit.,* 69.

Marr.[126] Arrested, imprisoned, and finally banished from Switzerland, he went to Hamburg, where he met Heine; to London, where he was hailed as a martyr; to Brussels, where he met Karl Marx and Friedrich Engels; and to the United States in December, 1847, where he almost immediately founded a Befreiungsbund.[127] Returning to Germany during the March days, he came back again to the United States, where he remained from 1849 until his death in 1871. From January, 1850, until 1855 he published the *Republik der Arbeiter* as a monthly to spread his ideas among the German laborers.[128]

Although Wietling's philosophy was authoritarian in tone, it held many important elements of Proudhon's Mutualism. His tone is softened by such statements as, "Eine vollkommene Gesellschaft hat keine Regierung, sondern eine Verwaltung; keine Gesetze, sondern Pflichten; keine Strafen, sondern Heilmittel."[129] His motto was "Frei wollen wir werden wie die Vögel des Himmels."[130] With Proudhon he found the most vicious evils in the private *ownership* of property and the present system of currency, and offered, as did Proudhon, "private possession" of property and Banks of Exchange to correct them.[131] On the assumption that the worker has the right to possess the product of his own labor and that the unequal distribution of capital results from a violation of this principle, he proposed a scheme whereby all material products and intellectual labor were to be estimated according to their value in labor hours. He proposed the establishment of

[126] Nettlau, *op. cit.*, 155, 161. Clark, *op. cit.*, 74. At the same time he is supposed to have influenced Bakunin to a belief in communism of property; *idem*. In America he dropped his idea of communal ownership. Revolutionary in Europe, he became conciliatory in America.

[127] Clark, *op. cit.*, 77.

[128] From 1851-1853 he attempted to establish a colony, "Communia" on his principles in Wisconsin, but the attempt was unsuccessful. *Ibid.*, 78-79. After 1855 Weitling took no more active part in labor or socialistic agitation.

[129] Nettlau, *op. cit.*, 154. Weitling's philosophy is to be found chiefly in his works: *Guarantien der Harmonie und Freiheit* (1842) and *Das Evangelium eines armen Sunders* (1845). His monthly *Republik der Arbeiter* shows the change of his belief from communal ownership to individual "possession" of property.

[130] Clark, *op. cit.*, 86.

[131] Commons, *History of Labour*, I, 515.

warehouses where the worker would bring his finished product and would receive what he needed according to the value of his products. His group of Triumvirs, which was to function as a government, was startlingly similar to Warren's Deliberative Council of Experts. As with Warren's experts, Weitling's Triumvirate was made up of teachers, doctors, etc., whose appointment depended upon their abilities.[132] It is significant as a commentary on the industrial conditions of the fifties, that Weitling gave up his earlier communistic faith in common ownership of property and centralized management of both production and exchange for Proudhon's anarchistic plan in which exchange alone was centralized.[133]

During the years 1850 and 1851 Weitling was a leading figure in the German Movement in the United States, and must certainly have contributed to the dissemination of Proudhonian ideas, even if they were not so labelled.[134] It was the year 1850 that William B. Greene published his book *Mutual Banking*. In 1848 Charles A. Dana had written from Paris a series of six magazine articles for the *New York Tribune,* which were revised in 1849 and published by the Reverend William H. Channing in *The Spirit of the Age* (1849), under the title, Proudhon's *Solution of the Social Problem*. In the same year, 1848, Albert Brisbane, one of the first to introduce the ideas of Fourier into the United States, sought out Proudhon, who was then in "enforced residence" at Mazas (the political prison), and talked with him "by the hour" on the money and credit question.[135] Later Brisbane wrote, "I was glad to find that Proudhon and I agreed perfectly as to (credit) principles which in our opinion could be applied prac-

---

[132] Clark, *op. cit.*, 83.

[133] Commons, *History of Labour,* I, 514-515.

[134] *Ibid.,* I, 515. Koerner, *Memoirs,* I, 548. Franz Arnold, a native of Germany was until July, 1851, a devoted disciple of Weitling, and throughout 1850 he campaigned in Philadelphia, Pittsburgh, St. Louis, and other western cities for the establishment of Banks of Exchange. But meeting with failure, he abandoned Weitling for Greeley's "coöperation" plan. Commons, *op. cit.*, note I, 515.

[135] *Albert Brisbane, A Mental Biography* with a character study by his wife, Redelia Brisbane (Boston, 1893), 292-293.

tically in various ways even in the present state of society."[136] Although finally developing into an anarchist communist, Joseph Déjacque published in the United States *Les Lazareenes* (1857), *Libertaire* (a magazine, 1858-1861) and *L'Humanisphère Utopie Anarchique* (1858-1859), all of which were strongly under the influence of Proudhon.[137]  Élisée Réclus, who along with Peter Kropotkin was called the father of Anarchist-Communism, lived in New Orleans and travelled about the Midwest and East in about the same period (1853-1856).  At this time he also was strongly "Proudhonian."[138]  It is apparent, therefore, that Proudhonian Anarchism was to be found in the United States at least as early as 1848 and that it was not conscious of its affinity to the Individualist Anarchism of Josiah Warren and Stephen Pearl Andrews.[139]

William B. Greene presented this Proudhonian Mutualism in its purest and most systematic form.  We shall consider his philosophy, therefore, before Benjamin Tucker united the two strains after 1872 in his scientific anarchism.  Greene was born at Haverhill, Massachusetts on April 4, 1819.  He was successively soldier, minister, and Proudhonian anarchist writer.[140]  Educated at West

---

[136] *Ibid.*, 293.  Brisbane expressed deep admiration for Proudhon as a man. *Ibid.*, 295.  For his program, strikingly similar to Proudhon's,—labor exchange for farmers, labor notes, warehouses, currency reform, interest, etc., and his influence on Greenback movement, see *ibid.*, 201-203.

[137] Déjacque and Ernest Coeurderoy have been called "die ersten vollständigen Anarchisten."  Déjacque was one of the Frenchmen who "propagated" anarchism in the United States from 1854-1861.  While Déjacque was in the States he wrote to Proudhon urging him to destroy *all* authority by abandoning "property" completely.  Nettlau, *op. cit.*, 208, 213, 216-218; E. V. Zenker, *Anarchism: A Criticism and History of the Anarchist Theory* (New York, 1897), 241.

[138] Max Nettlau, *Elisée Réclus: Anarchist und Gelehrter* (Berlin, 1928), 58-69.  Anselm Bellegarique, later a French anarchist communist, but in 1847 a confirmed *monarchist*, was travelling in the United States during this year.  On a Mississippi steam-boat President Polk converted him to a belief in a republic, during the course of an argument in which the two engaged! Nettlau, *Der Vorfrühling*, 186.

[139] Greene, in his *Mutual Banking*, acknowledged William Beck, but seemed to know nothing of Warren.  Some time after 1852 and before 1855, however, Weitling must have read *The Science of Society* because he referred his readers to it in his *Republik der Arbeiter*.  Nettlau, *Der Vorfrühling*, note 117.

[140] Biographical sketch from *Lamb's Biographical Dictionary of the United States*, edited by John H. Brown (Boston, 1900), III, 399.

Point, he participated both in the Florida and Civil Wars. In the interval between these two wars, however, his interests were diverted to reform. About the year 1842 he entered the Harvard Divinity School. Colonel T. W. Higginson, poet, reformer, and college acquaintance of Greene, describes Greene at this period:

"A young man who seemed to me the very handsomest and most distinguished looking person I had ever seen; nor could any one ever separate this picturesque aspect from his personality. He was more than six feet high, slender, and somewhat high-shouldered, but with an erectness brought from West Point. . . . His whole bearing was military and defiantly self-assertive. He had a mass of jet black hair and eyes that transfixed you with their blackness and penetration."[141]

Higginson had found Greene one of the two most interesting men at the Divinity School.[142]

After his graduation in 1845 (?) Greene was called to West Brookfield, Massachusetts to be the minister of the Unitarian Church.[143] Living in virtual retirement, he gave much of his time to writing. In 1849 he published *Remarks on the Science of History followed by an a priori Autobiography* and a pamphlet, *Equality*. In the year after Dana's commentary on Proudhon appeared, Greene brought out his exposition *Mutual Banking* (1850). After 1850 he became active in labor reform. In 1850-1851 he circulated petitions for a Bank of Exchange, which he submitted to the Massachusetts State Legislature. Nothing came of his efforts.[144] Greene seems to have been prominent enough to get himself elected as a delegate to the Massachusetts Constitutional Convention of 1853, which met to revise and amend the Constitu-

---

[141] *Proudhon's Solution of the Social Problem,* Introduction by the editor, 171.

[142] Thomas Wentworth Higginson, *Cheerful Yesterdays* (Boston and New York, 1898), 106.

[143] Greene seems to have had a good reputation as a speaker, for in 1850 he gave one of the four monthly addresses to the Town and Country Club of Boston, of which Higginson, the Channings, Emerson, Hawthorne, Longfellow and Lowell were members. No less than Theodore Parker, Henry James the elder, and Henry Giles, gave the other three addresses. Higginson, *op. cit.,* 175.

[144] *Mutual Banking* (West Brookfield, Mass., 1850), 94. *Socialistic, Communistic, Mutualistic and Financial Fragments* (Boston, 1875), 50.

tion. Proudhon had sat in the National Assembly at Paris as a delegate in Paris in 1848. Was this not indicative both of the aim and method of the Proudhonian anarchist—economic reform as a means to the abolition of government? In this respect they did not differ much from the socialists, except, of course, in their outspoken *demand* for the abolition of government. At this Convention Greene made an admirable defense of women's rights. The petitions which he presented from Mrs. Abbey Alcott, Wendell Phillips, and others, requesting that women be permitted to vote for the constitutional changes, and his eloquent address on July 12th in support of these petitions were influential in bringing the Convention to accept the favorable report of the committee and to act upon its suggestions.[145] In order to appreciate his advanced position, it must be remembered that Massachusetts saw its first Women's Rights Convention in 1851, and that as late as 1853 women were excluded from a World's Temperance Convention called under clerical auspices in New York City.[146] At this same convention and in the course of the discussion of women's rights, Greene defended the sanctity of Individualism, opposed majority rule, and championed the right of peaceful revolution.

After 1853 and until the outbreak of the Civil War, Greene lived in Paris, where his father, Nathaniel Greene, editor of the *Boston Statesman*, lived also from 1849-1861.[147] Assuming a commission, but resigning on October 11, 1862, Greene gave up his time to labor reform along the lines proposed by Proudhon. He was elected vice-president of the New England Labor Reform League, the majority of the members holding to Proudhon's scheme of mutual banking, and in 1869 president of the Massachusetts Labor Union.[148] He was also active in the French-speaking Working-People's International Association and, in fact,

[145] *Official Report of the Debates and Proceedings in the State Convention Assembled May 4, 1853 to Revise and Amend the Constitution of the Commonwealth of Massachusetts* (3 vols., Boston, 1853), I, 216-217, 359, 493, 613, 796, 842; II, 99, 287.

[146] Garrison, *op. cit.*, III, 312, 388. The *first* Women's Rights Convention in the United States was held at Genesee Falls, N. Y., in 1848. *Ibid.*, III, 262.

[147] *Lamb's Biographical Dictionary*, III, 397.

[148] Commons, *History of Labour*, II, 138, 142.

wrote the address of this section which was sent to the International in 1872. It was this International which excluded the Bakunin anarchists. Some time afterwards Greene went to England, where he lived until his death on May 30, 1878, at Weston-super-Mare.

The two books which he wrote under the influence of Proudhon are *Mutual Banking* (1850) and *Socialistic, Mutualistic, and Financial Fragments* (1875).

Greene's reading in the works of Proudhon, Pierre Leroux, Swedenborg, John Stuart Mill, Lamartine, De Maistre, Adam, Smith, Malthus, William Beck, and Edward Kellogg, led him to the conclusion which Proudhon had reached—that currency reform should be the basis of all social reform. He proposed to reform society on the principle of Mutualism, which implied a federal government, economic, however, not political. He aimed to realize his ideal by establishing a Bank of Exchange on lines similar to Proudhon's Bank of the People. To do this he presented petitions to the Senate and House of Representatives of Massachusetts, requesting the formation of such a bank, in 1850-1851, and in 1873, with other members of the New England Labor Reform League, the removal of all laws prohibiting the manufacture of "money" by any one but the government.[149] The character of this economic order would be *federative* and *non-authoritarian,* an order in which the individual would be sovereign in his own sphere, but at the same time responsible to society. Although his system is essentially the same as the native American anarchists, his emphasis is on Mutualism—Warren's on Individual Sovereignty. Coöperation, which was a secondary point in Warren's scheme (which he believed would follow naturally), appeared in Green's theories as the main theme, but was based essentially upon individualism. They were mutually independent. The difference, therefore, was chiefly a matter of emphasis.[150]

Mutualism is the philosophical basis of Greene's anarchism.

[149] *Fragments,* 227.
[150] Warren's philosophy, it must be remembered, was, first, a *reaction against* Owenism (socialism), and second, a product of mid-Western pioneer independence. Greene's philosophy was a direct offspring of Proudhonian Mutualism and an outgrowth of Eastern labour conditions.

His starting point, as with Proudhon, was the Golden Rule and the Sermon on the Mount as "enunciated by Christ in his ethical discourses."[151] "Mutualism," he declares, "is the synthesis of liberty and order." It is not extreme individualism. His position is most clearly stated in these words:

"The subjective divinity of the human soul seems to have been overdone by the existing generation. Individualism is good in its place, as qualified and balanced by socialism; but the experience of the world shows clearly that individualism unbalanced by socialism, and socialism unbalanced by individualism, lead always to disastrous social and political crises. . . . We are all mutually dependent, morally, intellectually, and physically upon each other. What we possess, we owe partly to our own faculties, but mainly to the educational and material aid received by us from our parents, friends, neighbors, and other members of society."[152]

But if this is associationism, it is checked by individualism, expressed in these words, "Mind your own business," "Judge not that ye be not judged." Over matters which are purely personal, as for example, moral conduct, the individual is sovereign, as well as over that which he himself produces. For this reason he demands "mutuality" in marriage—the equal right of a woman to her own personal freedom and property.[153] Proudhon, however, believed that the rights of woman were yet to be determined and was inclined to choose *excluding* her from society in preference to emancipating her.[154]

With Proudhon Greene believed that a mutualistic economic order, would eventually take the place of the political order.

"Mutualism operates, by its very nature, to render political government, founded on arbitrary force, superfluous, that is, it operates to the decentralization of the political power, and to the transformation of the State, by substituting self-government in the stead of government ab extra."[155]

With Jefferson and the early agrarians he approves the theory, the less government the better; with the Anti-Federalists, the sov-

[151] *Fragments*, 14, 26.
[152] *Ibid.*, 74.
[153] *Ibid.*, 14-16.
[154] *What is Property*, 237.
[155] *Fragments*, 76-77.

ereignty of state rights; and with Proudhon, the incorporation of his principle into the economic order to the destruction of the political organism.[156]  The Federal constitution must, therefore, be "repealed, revoked, or destroyed,"[157] and "every man . . . has a right to thwart the government if he can."[158]

Greene's economic individualism postulates the division of labor and voluntary coöperation. "It is identical with the principle of federation in politics."[159]  The general principle he describes in these words:

"Mutualism has unlimited individualism as the essential and necessary prior condition of its existence, and coördinates individuals without any sacrifice of individuality, into one collective whole, by spontaneous confederation or solidarity."[160]

Therefore, currency will be mutual—profit to all and misfortune shared by all.  Each will receive a just and exact pay for his work in the exchange of labor for labor without profit, the surplus of which in prosperity will be shared by the community.  The unity of labor—capitalist, merchant, factory worker, and farmer—is to be achieved in a new currency and hence, a new banking system. Labor becomes divided, money brings it together.  His economic philosophy is—non-wage conscious, non-class conscious.  The mutual bank is the great binding power, as with Proudhon.

Greene's system is characterized by a harmony of class interests —farmer, mechanic and capitalist.  It aimed to benefit all three— the capitalist and farmer directly, the mechanic indirectly.  Specifically, it would increase the amount of capital available to capitalists who owned real estate at negligible rates of interest, thereby reducing cost of operation and of products, and raising wages. Proudhon's bank he objects to on three grounds.  First, Proudhon provided no means of punishing or preventing "arbitrary conduct, partiality, favoritism, and self-sufficiency" on the part of the bank officers.[161]  Second, he provided no checks against certain mem-

[156] *Ibid.,* 143, 149, 158-163.
[157] *Ibid.,* 172-3.
[158] *Ibid.,* 159.
[159] *Ibid.,* 26.
[160] *Ibid.,* 25.
[161] *Ibid.,* 23.

bers assuming control over the bank. Third, in his system, the same property might be represented by different bills of exchange. He cannot claim, however, to have removed these same obstacles in his own system, which was essentially the same as Proudhon's. Property, real estate, machinery, or services, was to be the basis for currency. The bank was to be an association where each individual pledged his property as security, for which he would receive a bill of exchange, with only one per cent taken out for the running expenses of the bank. Bills would never be redeemable in specie but always in services and products, redeemable not at the counter of the Mutual Bank, "but always at the stores, mills, workshops, and other places of business."[162]

Greene's Mutual Bank is the "Bank of the People," but not as systematically or as masterfully constructed; his "mutual money" is the labor note of Proudhon. Of Josiah Warren and his philosophy, Greene was apparently ignorant. It may be said, therefore, that he was an independent disciple of Proudhon and attempted to inject into the labor movement the practical solutions of Proudhon.[163]  In this attempt he was later joined by Benjamin Tucker, who in 1872 met Josiah Warren and later declared that Warren's teachings were his "first source of light."[164]  Tucker and Greene united their efforts for a short time in labor reform on Warren-Proudhon principles. With them worked Lysander Spooner, Ezra Heywood, Joseph Labadie, and many others—but not in the nature of a united group. They were Individualists.

Scientific Anarchism, as it was called, was a fusion of the philosophy of Warren and Proudhon. As it was set forth by

[162] *Ibid.,* 27-28.

[163] Charles A. Dana *may* have been won over to an acceptance of Proudhon, but only his masterful commentary on Proudhon is extant.  Teacher at Brook Farm 1841-1847, newspaper correspondent in Europe in 1848, managing editor of *The Tribune* in 1849, later as editor of the *Sun* he became a distinct reactionary in politics.  In 1884 nevertheless the *Sun* supported the Greenback Labor and Anti-Monopolist candidate for the Presidency, but in 1896 Dana led the attack of the conservatives on William Jennings Bryan and his Free Silver Platform.  In that year Benjamin Tucker brought out Dana's commentary on Proudhon.  Dana became "the laughing-stock of the country."  *Proudhon's Solution,* etc., 3.  *Encyclopaedia Britannica,* VII, 11-12.  Swift, *op. cit.,* 145-152.

[164] Dedication of *Instead of a Book.*

Tucker, it won a wider recognition and respect than any other type of anarchism in the history of the United States. What it was we shall now consider.

C. "Scientific Anarchism"—the fusion of the philosophy of Josiah Warren and Pierre Proudhon.

In order to understand the problems for which the Individualist Anarchists, chiefly Benjamin R. Tucker and Lysander Spooner, were constructing a philosophy, it is necessary to consider briefly what the general economic condition was during the three decades after the Civil War. Within this description lies a partial explanation of why this type of anarchism failed of a general acceptance or fell short of a strong movement. The individual anarchist philosophers lost their way in a maze of economic problems, forgetting, as Proudhon never did, the aim of the emancipation of the masses. This is to be explained first, by the complicated meshwork of industrial activity, the lack of consolidation in the then young industrial system; second, by the lack of solidarity in labor itself; and third, by the unsystematic purely intellectual agitation of the anarchists themselves.

The period of the forties and fifties had seen an awakening in industrial life. Industry was exploring itself, as it were. As early as the thirties the artisans had begun agitation for improved working conditions. An anarchistic philosophy of the artisan had been formulated by Josiah Warren, an agrarian anarchistic philosophy by George Henry Evans, but more particularly by Lewis Masquerier. They supplied the basic demands which were taken up by the Proudhonian anarchists of the sixties and seventies for free currency, free exchange, free trade, free soil; by the Greenbackers[165] for the same freedom given and maintained by the

---

[165] Commons says: "What the socialism of Lasalle and Marx was to Germany, the coöperative anarchism of Proudhon to France, the revolutionary anarchism of Bakunin to Spain, Italy and Russia, what Fenianism was to Ireland and land nationalization to England, so was Greenbackism to America." In the sixties it was more than currency, it was industrial revolution. But the system proposed by Greenbackism was one which could and should be effected without disturbing government or the whole industrial system which was not possible with Proudhonian anarchism. Documentary History, IX, 33-39.

government, and in the sixties by the Single Taxers for "free land" or, as it happened, government owned land to all. It was they who won the relatively more general support which the anarchists failed to win.[166]

The conditions from which these philosophies originated were common.[167] The period after the Civil War was one of greater expansion of industry, one which saw a bigger scale of prosperity and depression in a program of nationalization than ever before. The period of the sixties saw the creation of a national market resulting from the consolidation of the principal railway lines into trunk lines, and the opening up of transcontinental railway communication. The period of the seventies was one of railway building, which operated both to bring the mechanics of the small towns into more direct competition, hence to the production of industrial centers, and to create for the latter an additional market in the new regions of the West. The eighties were years of marvellous industrial expansion which resulted mainly from the introduction of machinery on an unprecedented scale. For the first time the factory system became general. This led to a large increase in the class of unskilled and semi-skilled labor with inferior bargaining power. Population shifted from the country to the city. The wide distribution called for wholesale manufacturers. The individual manufacturer with insufficient capital contended with the wholesaler who attained a superior bargaining power. By playing off competing manufacturers he produced a cut-throat practice of competition. This made prices low, profits small, and caused pressure upon wages. Manufacturers sought to remedy the situation by combinations. This pooling system was an influence for instability and insecurity. There could be no fixed agreement where prices were fixed alternately by combination and by cut-

[166] Henry George acknowledged his indebtedness to Pierre Proudhon in the Preface to *Progress and Poverty* (New York, 1919), 187a, when he said that he "had sought to unite the truth perceived by the schools of Smith and Ricardo to the truth perceived by the schools of Proudhon and Lasalle," XV. The close relation of Anarchism and Single Tax is instanced by the easy passage of the members from one to the other, for example, Henry Bool of Ithaca, N. Y., Dyer D. Lum, and Joseph Labadie.

[167] Commons, *History of Labour, passim*.

throat competition. The cry was, therefore, for more capital, more money, and laissez faire in exploring enterprise. Combined with this situation was that caused by the unusually large immigration and the exhaustion of the public domain.[168] For the first time "American labor was now permanently shut up in the wage system."[169] The reduction of wages was considerable. A general depression prevailed from 1883 to 1885. The situation was further agitated, and chaotic conditions fostered by the suffering of the farmers who were effected by the exorbitant freight charges and low prices. Anti-monopoly, free coinage of silver, free trade, were the cries of reformers. Solutions were in general only partial solutions. It was in this milieu that the anarchism of Warren-Proudhon wandered and lost its way. It was in the fertile debris that Anarchist-Communism, which was largely foreign, flourished from 1882 until 1886, and struggled thereafter until 1919 to keep alive. The Individualist Anarchists were lost; they could not fasten themselves to the soil, because of their basic assumption of non-resistance; the Anarchist Communists fell down because their roots were fixed in a soil which was sandy and by no means cohesive—that is, there was no solidarity of labor. Not yet hopeless, not yet at the breaking point, labor recoiled from the violence of the Garrisonian type.

We shall, therefore, consider the Warren-Proudhon movement, if the desultory, unsystematic, and independent philosophies of this Individualist school may be thus termed. Just as the general romantic individualist atmosphere of the Humanitarian period was favorable to the growth of the extreme anarchism of John Humphrey Noyes, Henry David Thoreau, William Lloyd Garrison, and Adin Ballou, so was the industrial system to the anarchism of Benjamin Tucker. Tucker and his "school" were the spiritual successors of Thomas Jefferson and Josiah Warren in America, the spiritual relatives of Proudhon, Max Stirner, Herbert Spencer,

---

[168] Henry George's system of government ownership of land was directly related to the agrarianism of Masquerier and Evans, and even to that of Warren. He, too, demanded "free land," but ownership by the government, that it might be free for everyone, as the earlier agrarians demanded.

[169] Commons, *History of Labor,* II, 361.

and John Stuart Mill in Europe. They called themselves "unterrified Jeffersonian Democrats," believing that "the 'best government is that which governs least' and that that which governs least is no government at all." Their aim was voluntary coöperation without the sacrifice of the individual. Their cry was "mind your own business" more often than it was "coöperate." They declaimed the right of private possession but not ownership. Their method of realization and of propaganda was non-resistance. Converts they won in America and secured an intellectual recognition in Europe, which has been accorded to no other type of American anarchism.

Benjamin R. Tucker was the leading spirit of this movement. Like most of the other anarchists whom we have considered, he was born in Massachusetts, at South Dartmouth near New Bedford, in 1854.[170]  From 1870 until 1872 he studied technology in Boston, when he met Josiah Warren, his "teacher" and "first source of light."  In 1874 he traveled in England, France, and Italy, acquainting himself at the same time with the newest philosophical works.  In 1877 he became a temporary editor of the *World* but gave up his position to found his own paper, *The Radical Review,* "to publish what is not and is to be," "to *make* history, not to write it."[171]  He published only one volume, however, that is, four numbers, from May, 1877, to February, 1878, but long enough to translate and publish a large portion of Proudhon's *Contradictions Économiques.*  Stephen Pearl Andrews, Lysander Spooner, Ezra Heywood, Dyer D. Lum, Elie Reclus, were among the most outstanding contributors.  Their subjects covered a range from socialism, religion, science, labor, currency, "women," to poetry, reviews of the latest books, and "Chips from my Studio"—fragmentary comments by Tucker.

The development of Tucker's mild, tolerant individualism is easily traceable from the *Radical Review* to *Liberty.*[172]  In 1877 he wrote:

[170] Eltzbacher, *Anarchism* and the writer's interviews with his friends in New York City, November, 1930.  Biographic sketch.

[171] *Radical Review,* 203.

[172] Voltairine de Cleyre has described Benjamin Tucker's "style" very well—"cool, self-contained,—sending his fine hard shafts among foes and friends with icy impartiality, hitting swift and cutting keen, and ever ready

" 'The letter of the law killeth' . . . My own judgment would be that we should all be safer and happier without one (the constitution). With a disposition in the people to decide what is right rather than what is constitutional, liberty and justice would escape a vast deal of mystification."[173]

And again,

"Government is to be transferred from the State to the Individual. This is the new faith; faith no more in the gods over man, but in the God within him."

"The new order, however, will come slowly but certainly, for we have gained the ideas of law, order, and universal brotherhood, that these are not to be conserved by coercive systems of government but are to be found in the spontaneous action of the people."[174]

He optimistically perceives that day on the horizon when there will be no political power, when the purely social and economic problems confronting us will be solved by the scientific experts themselves. "In the place of legislative and executive officers, we shall welcome the teachers of equity and congresses of social science."[175] His individualism, however, is more marked than his mutualism. His faith is "love thy neighbor as thyself" but in himself he sees the universe. "Man sums up in his being all the universe contains. There within him, dwell the gods, the angels, and the kingdom of heaven."[176] Already the influence of Max Stirner is apparent.[177] The mutualism of Proudhon and "Cost the limit of Price" of Warren he already recognizes as the solution of poverty.[178]

The men whom he attracted by his philosophy or who had independently come to a philosophy of Individualism, became mem-

to nail a traitor. Holding to passive resistance as most effective, ready to change it whenever he deems it wise." *Selected Works,* "Anarchism," 115-116.

[173] *Radical Review,* 390-1.　　　[175] *Idem.*
[174] *Ibid.,* 606.　　　[176] *Ibid.,* 186-7.
[177] Max Stirner or Johann Kaspar Schmidt (1806-1856), is the author of *Der Einzige und sein Eigentum* (1845), which belongs in the same rank as Godwin's *Political Justice* and Proudhon's *Idée genérale de la Revolution au XIXe Siècle.* Compare this remark of Tucker's with Stirner's "Mir gehört die Welt," nicht "Allen gehört die Welt, alle sind ich," Nettlau, *Der Vorfrühling,* 169. Tucker acknowledged his indebtedness to Stirner. Benjamin R. Tucker, *Instead of a Book by a Man Too Busy to Write One. A Fragmentary Exposition on Philosophical Anarchism* (New York, 1893), 24.
[178] *Radical Review,* 201-203.

bers of the staff for his new magazine *Liberty*. A. P. Kelly became associate editor. The chief contributors were Henry Appleton, Lysander Spooner, Gertrude B. Kelley, "Phillip" (formerly of the *Irish World*), Dyer D. Lum, Sarah E. Holmes, M. E. Lazarus, J. William Lloyd, C. M. Hammond and Victor Yarros. While in the *Radical Review* he was "feeling his way" among anarchist ideas, in *Liberty* he found himself. It is significant, however, and almost characteristic of the Individualist Anarchists that they did not write systematic treatises on their philosophy.[179] The only partially systematic study Tucker wrote was a compilation of articles and editorials from *Liberty* entitled *Instead of a Book By a Man Too Busy to Write One*. *Liberty* he published as a semimonthly from August 6, 1881, until December, 1907, at first in Boston and after 1892 in New York.[180] The tone which Tucker adopted in *Liberty* was mild and extremely fair, aiming as he did to secure the eventual dissolution of government by a strong and rational conviction.

*Liberty* had for its purpose "to contribute to the solution of the social problem by carrying to a logical conclusion the battle against authority—to aid in what Proudhon had called 'the dissolution of government in the economic organism'."[181] Its program is best summarized in the program by which it was advertised:

"Liberty insists on the sovereignty of the individual and the just reward of labor; on the abolition of the State and the abolition of usury; on no more government of man by man, and no more exploitation of man by man; on Anarchy and Equity.'

"Liberty's war-cry is 'Down with authority,' and its chief battle with the State,—the State that corrupts children, the State that trammels law; the State that stifles thought; the State that monopolizes land, the State that limits credit; the State that restricts exchange; the State that gives idle capital the power of increase, and through interest, rent, profit, and taxes, robs industrious labor of its products."

---

[179] Lysander Spooner is an outstanding exception.

[180] Tucker was also editorial writer on the *Globe* for ten years.

[181] *Instead of a Book,* IX. There are no more than three or four complete files of *Liberty* in the United States. For this reason the writer has been able to consult only very incomplete files for this study.

The law which has supreme validity for every one of us is self-interest, and from this Tucker derives the law of equal liberty. He defines anarchism as "the doctrine that all the affairs of men should be managed by individuals or voluntary associations and that the State should be abolished."[182]  With Warren he makes individual sovereignty the supreme value. But he rejects entirely the theory of natural rights and natural equality. "I contend that men have no rights except those that they acquire by contract, and that the only equality which such a contract can aim to secure, if it would exempt itself from more or less speedy cancellation, is equality of liberty."[183]  Liberty is not a natural right but a necessity and an expedient—it is a law and universally applicable.[184] The only law which is equally binding on all men is that contracts must be lived up to.  This makes laissez faire laissez passer universal.  He finds difficulty, however, in setting the limits between invasion and non-invasion of liberty.  Between these two regions he finds a shadowy area.  The law of equal liberty makes the use of force *except in extreme* cases unlawful.  The greatest obstacle to the action of the law of liberty is political government. This he holds with Mill and Spencer.  He, therefore, proposes the removal of all political government but he does not attack present government.

His economics are identical with Proudhon's.  Instead of constructing his own system, he refers his readers to Proudhon's and William B. Greene's writings.[185]  The law of equal liberty demanded the destruction of all monopolies, the chief of which were: the money monopoly, land monopoly, the tariff-monopoly, and the patent monopoly.[186]  The fundamental basis was "the freedom of the individual, his right of sovereignty over himself, his products, and his affairs, and of rebellion against the dictation of external

[182] *Instead of a Book*, 9.
[183] *Liberty*, Vol. XIV (Sept. 1899), I :363.
[184] *Instead of a Book*, 132.
[185] His work, as he himself wrote, was to foster a growing discontent with and disgust for political government both among the people and among the liberal capitalists as a means to its dissolution.  He, therefore, reprinted Greene's, Spooner's, Andrew's, and Proudhon's chief works.
[186] "State Socialism and Anarchism" in *Instead of a Book*, 11-13.

authority."[187]   Labor, with Adams, Warren and Proudhon, therefore, was the only true measure of value.   Interest and unearned
capital, in general, are illegal and would be destroyed by mutual
banking.[188]   Property is legal property "which secures each in the
possession of his own products or the property of others, which
had not been attained by force or fraud."[189]   Titles based on actual
occupancy and use are also legitimate.   The individual alone or a
group joined in voluntary coöperation can enforce these titles or
contracts.   Political government is illegal.   On these principles he
denounces the "state ownership" conclusions of Henry George and
Single Taxers,[190] and at the same time he casts aside Greenbackism
because it approves profit and government control of currency.[191]
Opposing monopoly, he assails trusts and the government control
of letter-carrying.[192]   Prohibition by the government he found
particularly offensive.[193]   Compulsory taxation offended equally.
He, therefore, enjoined his followers to refuse and did himself
refuse to pay his poll tax.[194]   Although the great weight of his
opposition was thrown against political government, he extended
his principles to religion, education, and sex relations.   He was an
atheist because he could not sanction "class authority" in the
form of divine authority.[195]   A thorough-going individualist, however, he defended absolutely the right of any one else to believe in
religion.   The only moral code of an Individualist Anarchist was
"Mind your own business."[196]   Legal marriage and legal divorce
are "equal absurdities."   He defended the right of any man or
woman to love each other for as long or as short a time "as they

[187] *Ibid.*, 13.
[188] *Ibid.*, 190, 237.   He had practically abandoned the hope of establishing
a bank because the government had suppressed all their previous attempts,
*ibid.*, 243-244.
[189] *Ibid.*, 59-61.   The impracticability of this theory on modern industrial
conditions was later challenged by Johann Most and other anarchist communists.   Property and methods were their chief points of disagreement.
[190] *Ibid.*, 126, 206-8, 314-316, 319.
[191] *Ibid.*, 183, 284-6.
[192] *Ibid.*, 120-125.
[193] *Ibid.*, 154-156.
[194] *Ibid.*, 14, 43.
[195] *Ibid.*, 14.
[196] *Ibid.*, 15.

can, will, or may." He looked to a time in marital relations when both man and woman would be self-supporting, with perfect and equal freedom of movement, the mother having exclusive right to the children.[197] It must be said in concluding a sketch of his philosophy that he was a most consistent libertarian. Liberty he sustained *as both end and means*. The invasion of another's sovereignty by force, by anything except *moral force* was "illegal."[198] But he met the persistent dilemma which confronted the Antinomians, the Quakers, the Non-Resistants, the Perfectionists—to *resist* was to destroy.

As we have said, Benjamin Tucker did not himself formulate in writing a logical system of Individualist Philosophy. The finest and the most promising formulation was begun by Lysander Spooner but was never completed. For the most part these Individualist Anarchists worked and wrote independently. The writing of each one, although with much the same under-current of thought, appears distinctly different and unique. Lysander Spooner, a lawyer, gave to anarchism a legalistic interpretation, by means of which he verbally destroyed the constitution. His is the most devastating criticism of government which has yet been heard. He is, furthermore, the only Individualist Anarchist who indulged in verbal violence. From the ruins of government he built up a system based on natural law. Although he had from the earliest times postulated these laws as basic, he had not thought them inconsistent with government, or, as he said, "At that time, neither reason nor experience had demonstrated the utter incompatibility of all law-making whatsoever with men's natural rights."[199] Both his ideas and his eloquence and vehemence are reminiscent of Henry C. Wright. We read, however, not the "laws of God," but the "laws of Nature." What had been his position and importance before he came to these conclusions? Almost from his birth on January 19, 1808, at Athol, Massachu-

---

[197] *Idem.*

[198] "Legal" here refers to the law of equal liberty.

[199] Lysander Spooner, *A Letter to Grover Cleveland on His False Inaugural Address, the Usurpations and Crimes of Lawmakers and Judges, and the Consequent Poverty, Ignorance, and Servitude of the People* (Boston, 1886), 85.

setts, Spooner showed himself to be an individualist and anti-monopolist.[200]  He studied law in Worcester, Massachusetts, but on completing his reading course, he found that admission to the bar was permitted only to those who had studied for three years, except in the case of college graduates.  He considered the ruling obnoxious and worked to have it removed from the Statute books. It was removed.  In 1844 he opposed the government monopoly of letter-carrying.  The postal rate of 12½ cents from New York to Boston and 25 cents from Boston to Washington he considered exorbitant and the result of monopoly.  He himself started a postal service to prove that it could be carried for five cents.  His business grew rapidly, but the government so overwhelmed him with persecutions that he was compelled to retire but not until he had shown that the post-office department could be run on a lower rate of postage.  His efforts resulted in an act of Congress reducing the rates (and no doubt the general operating expense).

Spooner was an active abolitionist.  His book *The Unconstitutionality of Slavery*[201] was a masterful, brilliant analysis of the constitution, the Declaration of Independence, and of natural law.  Natural law he held supreme, but incorporated in government.  The constitution in accordance with natural justice made every man free—the sole owner of his own self.  Slavery, therefore, was unconstitutional.  The step is a short one to the establishment of natural law as the sole and necessary law, when it became apparent that government did not obey natural law. During the pre-Civil War period Spooner's book exercised a significant influence on Gerrit Smith, Elizur Wright, and William Goodell.[202]  Gerrit Smith, reformer, philanthropist, and politician who read very few books had read and re-read Spooner's *Unconstitutionality of Slavery*.  Spooner was his authority on the constitution of the United States.[203]  The governmentalist party of

---

[200] *Appleton's Cyclopaedia of American Biography,* edited by James G. Wilson and John Fiske (New York, 1894), V, 634-5.

[201] *The Unconstitutionality of Slavery* (Boston, 1845).

[202] William Goodell, abolitionist, cites Spooner's book as an authority on the subject.  Goodell, *Slavery and Anti-Slavery,* 22, 25.

[203] Octavius Brooks Frothingham, *Gerrit Smith, A Biography* (New York, 1879), 353.

Abolitionists, the Liberty Party, accepted in 1849 twenty-nine resolutions presented by Gerrit Smith, one of which adopted Spooner's book as conclusively proving the unconstitutionality of slavery:

"Whereas, Lysander Spooner, of Massachusetts, that man of honest heart and acute and profound intellect, has published a perfectly conclusive legal argument against the constitutionality of slavery: 22 Resolved, therefore, that we warmly recommend to the friends of freedom, in this and other States, to supply, within the coming six months, each lawyer in their respective counties with a copy of said argument."[204]

Garrison and the Non-Resistants, however, who had reached a point of development which Spooner did not come to until forty years later, declared slavery constitutional and the constitution "a covenant with death and an agreement with Hell." Garrison heartily disapproved of Spooner's book.[205]

The first work of importance which marked Spooner's conversion to no-government ideas was his unfinished treatise called *Natural Law or The Science of Justice,* published in 1882.[206] The major premises of his earlier philosophy he carried through to a no-government, no-law conclusion. He was then an Individualist Anarchist. But he was not content with stating only general principles. He proceeded to attack all law and all government. In the same year he published *A Letter to Thomas F. Bayard,*[207] Senator from Delaware, and four years later, in 1886, *A Letter to Grover*

[204] Frothingham, *op. cit.,* 190. Spooner, however, was not a member of the Liberty Party. *cf.* Goodell, *op. cit.,* 476.

[205] Garrison, *op. cit.,* III, 33. The reason for this reversal of the situation is by no means clear. May not difference in temperament be an important factor? Garrison was eager, impatient with compromise, devoted solely to abolition; Spooner was cool, rational, and a lawyer by profession.

[206] *Natural Law or The Science of Justice:* A Treatise on Natural Law, Natural Justice, Natural Rights, Natural Liberty, and Natural Society; Showing That All Legislation whatsoever is an absurdity, a usurpation, and a Crime. (Part First, Boston, 1882). In 1877 Spooner had already touched upon these principles as is apparent from his work "Our Financiers: Their Ignorance, Usurpations and Frauds," and "The Law of Prices," *Radical Review,* 141-157; 326-337.

[207] *A Letter to Thomas F. Bayard* challenging his right—and That of all the other So-called Senators and Representatives in Congress to Exercise any Legislative Power Whatever over the People of the United States (Boston, 1882).

*Cleveland.*[208]   Both attacks were daring, the latter particularly, directed as it was against the president of the United States.   Fearlessly he strode into the temple of government, and with his flail, natural justice, struck down one after the other the "Golden Cows"—the House of Representatives, the Senate, the Supreme Court, the Presidency, and finally the constitution.   As he left he pulled down the whole superstructure.   From the ruins he constructed his own building.

A true individualist, the basis of his ideal society is the individual.   For him it is not "the greatest good for the greatest number," but the "good of the individual is the good of the many."[209]   For him, as with Warren and Tucker, the individual "is" his mind, body, and labor.   These principles he supports by law—natural law.   "Natural law is the law of the universe as discerned by science"; it is a fixed, immutable, natural principle, unalterable.   It has all the validity of a scientific law—a law of gravity.   It is "amoral" and changeless.   It is a law which governs men as human beings.   The principle of justice (Tucker calls it "equity") is the only universal obligation "that men should live honestly towards each other."[210]   Justice is composed of legal duty and moral duty.   Legal duty is "to live honestly, to hurt no one, to give to every one his due."   It is obligatory and can be enforced, that is, one individual can compel another to live up to this duty, singly or *voluntarily* united with others.   This is what Warren calls the "law of natural consequences."   Moral duty is voluntary, individual, personal, "of which each man must be his own judge in each particular case, as to whether and how, and how far, he can, or will, perform them."[211]   It is "to feed the hungry, clothe the naked, shelter the homeless, care for the sick, protect the defenseless, assist the weak, and enlighten the ignorant."   The law of justice, therefore, is the only binding law.   It is sufficient to order

[208] *A Letter to Grover Cleveland,* on His False Inaugural Address, the Usurpations and Crimes of Lawmakers and Judges, and the Consequent Poverty, Ignorance and Servitude of the People, Boston (published by Benjamin Tucker, 1886).
[209] *Letter to Cleveland,* 8.
[210] *Natural Law,* 6.
[211] *Idem.*

the universe. It is what Proudhon says—"Liberty not the daughter but the Mother of Order."

The law of justice guarantees two rights—the rights of person and the rights of property, and to the protection thereof. The two corresponding duties are first, that contracts must be lived up to; second, that the equal rights of another individual be not trespassed.

"The only real 'sovereignty' . . . is that right of sovereignty which each and every human being has over his or her own person and property, so long as he or she obeys the one law of justice towards the person and property of every other human being. This is the only *natural* right of sovereignty, that was ever known among men. All other so-called rights of sovereignty are simply the usurpations of impostors, conspirators, robbers, tyrants and murderers. . . ."[212]

The rights of person are the right to one's own life and the protection thereof. The rights of property are "buying and selling, borrowing and lending, giving and receiving property."[213] Property consists of those things "which are indispensable to the maintenance of life"—natural resources and the products of labor. Labor which produces property is mental, physical, and managerial. Ownership of this property is arbitrary, irresponsible *except* that it not invade another's equal right. Spooner's emphasis here is even less on coöperation than Tucker's. Property is transferable by contract. Contracts are binding if made between parties mentally competent, and if they are made by *voluntary* mutual agreement.[214]

Independent action is desirable but *voluntary* association is sometimes useful. The purpose of association is mutual protection against wrongdoers and the maintenance of justice. Being voluntary, an individual is free to withdraw, or if not within, to resist if his natural right is invaded. Every individual is free to join or not to join. Every individual is free as long as he obeys the law of justice—of "mine and thine."[215]  Govern-

[212] *Letter to Cleveland*, 86.
[213] *Ibid.*, 60.
[214] *Idem.*
[215] *Natural Law*, 7-8.

ment and law as they have grown up are violations of the law of justice.[216]   They are the stronghold of the powerful few for the plunder of the many.   The enslavement of labor has resulted. Both must be abolished.   Justice alone should rule.

From the principles of natural justice Spooner demolishes existing government and constructs an ideal economic and social order.   His destructive attack is worthy of consideration because it is one of the most daring and logical of the latter part of the nineteenth century.   His program is important because, more unconditionally than that of any other anarchist we have considered thus far, it demands a *return* to *pre-industrial* society.   While other Individualist Anarchists propose to solve the social problem by introducing Labor Exchanges along with large scale industry, Spooner definitely proposes to solve it by a *return* to the period of the individual proprietor.   These words indicate that he aimed to destroy the complicated factory system:

"All the great establishments, of every kind, now in the hands of a few proprietors, but employing a great number of wage laborers, would be broken up; for few or no persons, who could hire capital and do business for themselves would consent to labor for wage for another."[217]

His was a revolt against the industrial system, a revolt against the interference and pressure of group action in the form of government, a revolt against corporateness and all that it means to the individual.   As that of the other Individualist Anarchists, but more distinctly and consistently was his philosophy a reaction against mass production, mass suggestion, and mental stereotypes. It was, as it were, the last living gasp of the older individualism.

Spooner calls upon Senator Bayard[218] and all the other legislators of the country "to burn all the existing statute books of the United States, and then to go home and content themselves with the exercise of only such rights and power as nature has given to

[216] *Ibid.,* 16-20.

[217] *Letter to Cleveland,* 41.

[218] Spooner directed this letter to Bayard merely as a specific point of attack.   It was immediately occasioned by a letter of Bayard to the Reverend Lyman Abbott in which he wrote that it was possible for a legislator to be an honest man. *Letter to Bayard,* 5.

them in common with the rest of mankind."[219]  The government
of the United States is a tyranny and a usurpation of power.
Government—legislative or executive, the laws, the courts, the
constitution have no authority because they are either a reiteration
of the rights guaranteed by natural law and are unnecessary, or
are a violation of the rights guaranteed by natural law and hence
are invalid.  The natural right of every individual to his own person and property are inalienable, cannot be transferred or delegated, for that would be equivalent to giving himself up as a
slave.[220]  Since this natural right cannot be delegated, and the
constitution and legislation based as they are upon the social contract or surrender of rights, neither the constitution, nor government has dominion over the individual.  They are a "falsehood"
and a "usurpation of power."[221]  Furthermore, the government
of the United States is a government by conspiracy, in which the
people have no rights.[222]  With calm irreverence he attacked the
constitution, declaring that it had never been accepted by even a
majority vote; that it had been used by "ambitious, rapacious men
to enslave the population."[223]

By far his most daring attack was levelled against the President of the United States.  It was occasioned by President Cleveland's Inaugural Address delivered on March 4, 1885.[224]  The
address expressed the usual democratic platitudes—that of a "general welfare," devotion to the constitution, the "submersion of
private interest and local advantage to the general welfare,"
"equal and exact justice" rendered to all men, and that the present
government was the best form of government ever vouchsafed to
man."  No, the present government of the United States was
everything but what Cleveland declared it to be.  "The government is a mere tool in the hands of a few rapacious and unprin-

---

[219] *Letter to Bayard,* 11.

[220] *Ibid.,* 3-4.

[221] Spooner's demolition of the "social contract theory" is very similar to
that of Proudhon—they proceed from similar premises.

[222] *Ibid.,* 6.

[223] *Ibid.,* 10.

[224] *A Compilation of the Messages and Papers of the Presidents* by James
D. Richardson, published by the Bureau of National Literature (1911), VII,
4884-4888.

cipled men . . . this injustice is the direct cause of all the widespread poverty, ignorance, and servitude among the great body of the people."[225]   All governments "whether called monarchies, aristocracies, republics, democracies . . . are all alike violations of men's natural and rightful liberty."[226]   The State and national governments are "criminal" and "rapacious." "There is nothing genuine, nothing real, nothing true, nothing honest to be found in any of them.   They all proceed upon the principle that governments have all the power, and the people no rights."[227]   No government has any right to live except on "purely voluntary support."   Specifically the American government violates all the natural rights of its citizens by conscription, by restrictions on industry, on the acquisition of "wilderness land," on trade, national and international.[228]   The government of the United States is no better than the tyrannical governments of the early eighteenth century.   "Our government, although a little different in form, stands on the same essential basis as theirs ("the tyrants of Europe") of a hundred years ago; that it is as absolute and irresponsible as theirs was then; that it will spend more money, and shed more blood, to maintain the power, than they have ever been able to do, that the people have no more rights here than there; and that the government is doing all it can to keep the producing classes as poor here as they are there."[229]

He calls upon President Cleveland to correct these evils.   "Unless you do that, is it not plain that the people have a right to consider you a tyrant, and the confederate and tool of tyrants, and *to get rid of you as unceremoniously as they would of any other tyrant?*"[230]   Is this not unusual violence for a non-resistant individualist?   Can Tucker legitimately say that the difference between his philosophy and that of the anarchist-communists is that he attacks "government," *not* the "present government,"

[225] *Letter to Cleveland,* 6.
[226] *Ibid.,* 28.
[227] *Ibid.,* 95.
[228] *Ibid.,* 31-32, 18, 33-34, 36, 42.
[229] *Ibid.,* 86.
[230] *Ibid.,* 6.

hence he is a true "an-archist" while the communists attack "present government" and are "archists?"

Spooner's ideal economic order, as that of Tucker, is based upon unrestricted competition (unrestricted except by the law that contracts must be lived up to and that the natural rights of *every* individual must be recognized), facilitated by a widespread currency reform in which land and labor would be an exact equivalent for money, and characterized by free trade, free labor, free land, and free banking—as well as a free conscience. His social ideal is based on the law that contracts must be lived up to and that the property and personal rights of each individual must be respected, and would be achieved by voluntary association, association in the form of a Mutual Insurance Company. The Mutual Insurance Company would take the place of government. It would be a voluntary, mutually protective association to which an individual might belong, might take his disputes to be settled, if he chose to do so. Disputes which could not be settled by mutual agreement would be presented to a tribunal in the association. Expenses would be borne by the parties concerned. Decisions would be kept by the judge in writing.[231] This would bring "justice to every man's door." The history of these privately organized institutions is a sad commentary on Spooner's idea. Except where supervised and restrained by the government, they have been mostly corrupt.

Spooner would destroy the factory system, wage labor, "crises," "panics," "stagnation of industry," and the "fall of prices," by making every individual a small capitalist, an independent producer. He would achieve this by representing all material property in the United States, land and its products, by promissory notes made payable in coin on demand. Every man who wanted to do business independently could borrow money at a low rate of interest from the bank. The wealth of the United States lying idle at that time he said was $50,000,000. It could be divided so that every person might secure $1,000 for private enterprise. Spooner, therefore, would turn the clock of time back-

[231] *Ibid.,* 104-106.

ward, not forward. His was no solution of a complex system of coöperative industry and a mass of "proletariat" workers. In spite of all its impracticabilities, Spooner's work remains an important contribution to the systematic literature of Individualist Anarchism.

Benjamin Tucker won the attention and sympathetic interest of the American public more than any other anarchist in the history of the United States. A small number were won over by his clear, unimpassioned, exposition of "philosophical anarchism." Those who could not accept his doctrines, listened, found something of truth in what he said, and went on their way, perhaps slightly more liberal. Nor was his influence limited to America alone. Although it has not been possible to determine the circulation of the *Liberty,* it is certain that copies of it circulated widely throughout the United States, England, France, and Germany, that it found converts, and that similar papers were started in various parts of the world.[232] Lothrop Withington, a young Englishman, an impassioned speaker and forceful writer, was at the beginning of his career a follower of Tucker. He helped publish in London *The Anarchist* from March, 1885, to August, 1889, with Henry Seymour, *The Revolutionary Review* from January to September, 1889, the Free Trade and Free Exchange in 1882.[233] John Henry Mackay, Scotch in origin, German by adoption, and resident of Switzerland, was influenced by Tucker.[234] Many of Tucker's works were translated in Germany from 1895 to 1911 under the general heading *Propaganda des individualistischen Anarchismus.* The chief pamphlets were *Staatsozialismus und Anarchismus,* Berlin, 1895, *Sind Anarchisten Mörder?* 1899, *Der Staat in seiner Beziehung zum Individuum,* 1899, *Was ist Sozialismus?* 1902, and *Die Stellung des Anarchismus zur*

---

[232] Tucker, *Instead of a Book,* IX. Controversies were carried on in *Liberty* between Tucker and some of his English readers. *Ibid.,* 99-103; 223-224; 227-244.

[233] Nettlau, *Der Vorfrühling,* 130.

[234] He published *Die Anarchistin* (Zurich, 1891), *Flugschriften für den individualistischen Anarchismus,* Berlin, 1894, and *Der Freiheitsucher. Psychologie einer Entwicklung* (Berlin, 1920). Nettlau, *Der Vorfrühling,* 131.

*Trustfrage,* 1911.[235]   Through E. Armand Tucker's philosophy was introduced into France.   Even in Australia can be found traces of his influence, where at Melbourne from April 1887-1889, *Honesty,* and at Hamilton, New South Wales about 1890, *The Australian Radical* were published.[236]   In 1908 in Copenhagen the *Individet* represented Individualistic Anarchism.[237]

Tucker won admiration and respect for his doctrine.[238]   Paul Ghio, a well-known French economist, who visited the United States in 1903, admired Tucker both for his ideas and for his method of propaganda.   Individualistic anarchism he regarded as a sign that democracy had failed in the United States.   He wrote that Tucker

"est un homme, solide de taille moyenne; sa figure, encadrée, d'une barbe epoisse, brune, mais déja grisonnante, respire la santé vigoureuse du travailleur; ses yeux luisants, au regard vif et penétrant, temaignent d'une intelligence prompte autant que d'une haute exquise.   La conversation de M. Tucker est, au plus haut degré instructive."

At the same time he testified to Tucker's extensive influence in the United States.[239]   The German anarchist, Rudolph Rocker, testified that Tucker "war ein glänzender und geistreicher Polemiker."[240]   Through addresses and conferences as well as through his magazine he propagated his ideas.   His philosophy met with

[235] *Ibid.,* 122.

[236] *Ibid.,* 130.

[237] Proudhon himself was read for certain in 1851 in England.   His works were much translated in Spain from 1860-1873, and widely circulated among Spanish-speaking people in America.   In Mexico also Proudhon was brought by an enthusiastic disciple, an Austrian, Plotino Rhodskanty, who translated Proudhon's *General Idea of a Revolution in the XIX Century* in 1877.   Nettlau, *Der Vorfrühling,* 125, 155, 161, 162-5, 181, 282.

[238] Professor H. L. Osgood wrote in 1889 a very sympathetic article on Tucker's anarchism for the *Political Science Quarterly,* IV (1889), 1-36.

[239] Paul Ghio: *L'Anarchisme aux États-Unis* (Paris, 1903), 86-91.   Emma Goldman who knew Tucker only through his writings in *Liberty* admitted that he wielded a forceful pen and that he had introduced his readers to some of the best German and French works on anarchism.   Emma Goldman, *op. cit.,* I, 232.

[240] Rudolf Rocker, *Johann Most, Das Leben eines Rebellen* (Berlin, 1924), 370.

considerable tolerance as is evidenced by the fact that along with President E. Benjamin Andrews of Brown University and the Reverend W. Bliss, Tucker addressed a Unitarian Ministers' Institute on October 14, 1890.[241]   In 1899 his address on anarchism at a Chicago Trust Conference under the Civic Federation, was well received.   Several Chicago newspapers praised his sound sense and good mind.[242]   Later in 1902 the well-known John R. Commons wrote in the *Chicago Tribune* that an address he had heard Benjamin Tucker deliver in Chicago was "the most brilliant piece of pure logic that has yet been heard."   The editor of *Free Society* commented that, "that the undiluted doctrines of anarchism should so transport a great gathering of all classes here in Chicago would not have been predicted."[243]   Hand-clapping and cheering followed his address.[244]

In the United States Tucker found converts.   Some of them multiplied books on economic subjects, others of them on sex subjects and the emancipation of women.   Still others of them organized discussion clubs and some engaged in the labor struggle.   Ezra Heywood, early a disciple of Josiah Warren, and subsequently a follower of Tucker, distinguished himself in his efforts to emancipate "labor and women."[245]   His *Uncivil Liberty, An Essay to Show the Injustice and Impolicy of Ruling Woman Without Her Consent,* in 1873, was an able defense of civil, pecuniary, and political equality for women.[246]   Heywood, along with Moses Harmon, was one of the pioneers of free love and birth con-

---

[241] Tucker, *Instead of a Book*, 21.

[242] *Liberty*, XIV (November 1899), 364.

[243] *Free Society*, IX, 344 (January 12, 1902).   Anarchist Communist Magazine.

[244] In a future study the reaction of the general public ought to be studied. The materials available to the writer were insufficient for this purpose.

[245] In 1869 he was active in the labor movement as president of the New England Labor Reform League. *Declaration of Sentiments and Constitution of the New England Reform League* (Boston, 1869).   As has been said, this group advocated Proudhon's mutual banking scheme as a solution of the labor problem.   Commons, *History of Labor*, II, 138.   See Heywood's "The Great Strike. Its Relation to Labor, Property, and Government," *Radical Review* (November 1877), 565.

[246] *Uncivil Liberty* (Princeton, Mass., 1873).

trol.[247]  Several times before 1890, Heywood was arrested for sending "obscene" publications through the mail, namely, *Sexual Physiology* and *Cupid's Yokes*.[248]  On May 13, 1890, he was convicted and put in jail for this same reason, under the Comstock Law.[249]

Joseph A. Labadie is among the most outstanding of the living Individualist Anarchists.  He was the first president of the Michigan Federation of Labor organized in 1888 and the first Detroit organizer of the Knights of Labor.[250]  To the Anarchist movement he has contributed a collection of forceful and colorful essays.[251]  But his most valuable contribution is the so-called "Labadie Collection," a collection which took more than fifty years to accumulate, and which he bequeathed to the University of Michigan in 1927.  It contains many kinds of materials on the labor movement and is particularly rich in sources for the Chicago Haymarket affair.  It composes a labor library of national importance.[252]

Many other devotees of Individualist Anarchism might be mentioned.  William Bailie expended much time and energy in collecting the material for and in writing the solitary biography of Josiah Warren.  Henry Bool, of Ithaca, New York, manufacturer and furniture dealer, was very active in advancing the cause of Individualist Anarchism.[253]  At first interested in the Single Tax Movement, he was won over to Tucker's anarchism.  The "brutal hanging" of the Chicago anarchists in 1886 had directed him to

[247] Moses Harmon, author of *Autonomy, Self Love*, but *not* a nominal anarchist, published with his daughter, Lillian Harmon, and E. C. Walker, the magazine *Lucifer*, in which he advocated sexual freedom.  Rocker, *op. cit.*, 371.

[248] *Radical Review*, I, 821-825.  Tucker regarded this a gross abridgement of the freedom of the press.

[249] Julian Hawthorne, "In Behalf of Personal Liberty," *Twentieth Century Library* (New York, 1891).

[250] *The Nation*, September 7, 1927.  Reprint of article, "A New Labor Library," from the University of Michigan Library.

[251] J. A. Labadie, *Essays* (Detroit, 1911).

[252] Information from University of Michigan.  Mr. Labadie is now eighty-one years old and still interested in the anarchist movement.

[253] J. A. Labadie dedicated his *Essays* to Henry Bool, "Lover of Justice, Equity, and Freedom."

the study of anarchist literature and through this study he became an anarchist in spirit.[254]     In Ithaca he established a Liberty Lending Library, which contained the works of Warren, Andrews, Spooner, Tucker, as well as of Tolstoy, Spencer, and Mill.[255]     At the same time he had private *"soirées"* where he discussed Individualist Anarchism.   Professors, doctors, lawyers were his "subjects."   Bool reports that one professor declared, "There is much truth in scientific anarchy."[256]     In the furor which arose in the United States in 1900 at the assassination of President McKinley by a supposed anarchist, Henry Bool ardently defended the peaceful anarchism of Benjamin Tucker, and for his defense was branded in the *Ithaca Journal News* as a "bloody anarchist."   He was threatened in the mails and in the papers.   At this same time, September 19, 1901, the President of Cornell University, President Schurman, afterwards Minister to China and later Ambassador to Germany, addressed a large audience, declaring that the State was rooted in human nature and divinely ordained.   And that "the ideal of the anarchist, the goal for the attainment of which he kills men as ruthlessly as summer flies, is the overturning of all political institutions and the adoption of the unrestrained and promiscuous life of brutish herds.   *With the anarchist, therefore, there can be nothing but war to the knife."*[257]     In the face of public criticism, violence and threat to boycott his products, Bool held to his principles of Individualist Anarchism.   In 1907, however, he left America to return to his old home in England, where he died in 1924.

Henry Bool left America in 1907, Benjamin Tucker in 1908—neither ever returned.   Anarchists who did remain, however, embraced either Anarchist-Communism as the result of governmental violence against the laborers and their cause, or abandoned the cause entirely.

[254] Henry Bool, "Liberty Without Invasion, Means and Ends of Progress," 1898. *Political Science Pamphlets,* 17.

[255] "Liberty Luminants."

[256] Henry Bool, "Apology for His Jeffersonian Anarchism," *Political Science Pamphlets,* No. 8, p. 6.

[257] Bool, *Liberty Without Invasion,* 15.

We have thus reached the maturity of native American Anarchism. It was conceived at the beginning of American history in the quest for the freedom of the individual. Its near-relative flourished in an agrarianism which demanded freedom from taxation, freedom of trade in a capitalistic laissez faire milieu, demanding the respect of minorities and freedom from government interference except for particular advantage; in a Greenbackism of artisan, pioneer, and farmer demanding free silver, free land, free trade. All of these particular elements united to produce Individualist or Scientific Anarchism. A discriminating individualism, discriminating in class and power, matured into a *universal* individualism. It could not, therefore, be expected to please all of its parents. Nor did it. Its demands to secure the just distribution of wealth did not please the capitalists. Its pacific, unclass conscious program left the proletariat cold. The capitalists wanted nothing of absolutely *unrestricted,* unprotected competition. Labor had had enough of what it thought was competition and individualism. What it wanted was class solidarity, coöperation and the distribution of the goods of this world irrespective of the accident of birth and inherited capacity. Its complete antigovernmentalism made them all tremble. But its lack of a definite means of destroying the present forms of inequalities made it impractical.[258] It is true that the early American Individualists aimed to return society to a Federalism, to an economic system where every one would be a small, independent proprietor. But Greene and Tucker, exceptions to this general rule, accepted the vast, complicated industrial system. They aimed to improve it, however, by basic reforms of currency which would eventually so change the economic system, so completely order it, that individual independence would be balanced with social welfare. Government would be completely absorbed in the economic organism. They agreed to build up in the present society a sound economic system

[258] The treatises which set forth Individualist Anarchism were too philosophical—and in other instances almost unreadable—to appeal in the first case to labor and in the second to the intellectual. The distinction between an "enlightened self interest" and "self interest," furthermore, was too fine and philosophical for the average laborer to understand.

as well as a strong opposition to all government which would over-throw government itself.

But if their program was rejected by both capitalist and la-borer, they themselves met such an obstacle, a dilemma in the practical realization of their ends, that the result of their failure was virtually predestined. The dilemma they met in "property" and in "method." If they remained within the government, they coöperated with and perpetuated it, even if they propagandized against it. If they withdrew from society to a colony, they had to compete economically with a completely different economic sys-tem—experiencing somewhat the same difficulty as that which Soviet Russia met with, although more disastrously. A prospec-tive anarchist would ask, "What shall I do if I would become an anarchist?" The answer was, "Educate! Educate!" If they re-jected private ownership of property, they destroyed their individ-ualism and "levelled" mankind. If they accepted it, they had the problem of offering a solution whereby the inequalities would not amount to a tyranny over the individual. They met the same dilemma in "method." If they were consistent libertarian indi-vidualists they could not force from "those who had" what they had acquired, justly or unjustly, but if they did not force it from them, they perpetuated inequalities. They met a stone wall. By 1908 the industrial system had fastened its claws into American soil. The Individualists found that in order to loosen the talons which caused injustice, they had to use a knife. Some of them used it. They became direct actionists—Voltairine de Cleyre and Dyer D. Lum. But they were no longer "scientific" anarchists. Benjamin Tucker and Henry Bool remained scientific anarchists; Benjamin Tucker went to France, Henry Bool to England. We can best understand this dilemma and disillusion by considering in conclusion its contrast with a type of anarchism—not native, but foreign in origin, an anarchism which leaped over this dilemma only to meet another on the other side.

## IV

## THE GREAT DISILLUSION

As we have seen, the native American Anarchism born of American tradition and perpetuated, among other philosophies, by an economic need, won no wide acceptance. Its exponents had consistently attacked government in general, but, for one exception, not existing government. They demanded an absolute and universal freedom which was saved from license by the scientific action of "check and balance" of individual interest, which for them was social interest. They concerned themselves for the most part with constructing and advocating a "true" economic program which was to be the basis of a new social order—centered chiefly in banking, currency, and labor exchange reform. The co-operation of capitalist and laborer they demanded as a primary condition to the realization of their ideal. This was at a time when the labor movement was advancing in the direction of the differentiation of interest and action but at the same time not with the rapidity which made it seize upon revolutionary Anarchism or Anarcho-Syndicalism as a solution.

This latter philosophy, as we shall see, required class solidarity and a strong class consciousness to win a large following. And in general, the increasing paternalism and repressive action of a government which attempted to regulate and in some cases to interfere with the private life of the individual by means of such laws as the Comstock, Volstead, Alien, Sedition, and Espionage Acts was no favorable environment for the peaceful philosophy of Individualist Anarchism. We may say, therefore, that the Individualist Anarchists had attempted to destroy monopoly, privilege, and inequality, originating in the lack of opportunity, in short the most offensive evils of the capitalistic system, to check the mad rush of the many for the benefit of the few, and to preserve the rapidly diminishing margin of individual freedom and autonomy. But by the superior force of the system which they opposed they were overwhelmed and as individuals they were completely disillusioned.

The same disenchantment was experienced by the Anarchist Communists in 1919. Although completely independent of each other in ideas and in action, unconscious, but for a few exceptions.[1] of the affinity which actually existed between them, the Individualist Anarchists and the Anarchist Communists assailed the same evils, but in a different manner, and aimed at the same theoretical objective, but proposed to arrive there by different routes. The important fact remains that, although independent, they both assailed the same conditions and on the ground that Authoritarianism, particularly as it appeared in its most vicious form in the existing industrial system, was inevitably destructive of the sacred principle of Individuality. For this reason they encountered the same superior force and with similar results, although for the Anarchist Communists more drastic chiefly because of their more uncompromising attack on the established authorities. They suffered the same disillusionment. A brief survey of the Anarchist Communist disillusion, therefore, will enable us to understand more clearly what the native American Anarchists opposed and visualized, and what significance the various shades of Anarchism could have had in American history as well as what it can have for the future.

The Anarchist Communists differed from the Individualists in origin, in manner of approach, and in specific interest. They were for the most part alien critics—German, Russian, Jewish, Italian. Their leaders were directly and personally interested in the proletariat, working very often with the laborers themselves in factory and sweatshop. Their philosophy differed from that of

[1] Voltairine de Cleyre and Dyer D. Lum, as we shall see. It is questionable, however, whether or not they had any actual influence in bringing the two groups together. Frequently they were personally antagonistic—for instance, Benjamin Tucker and Johann Most. Emma Goldman did not like Tucker personally—he did not impress her as "a large nature." Emma Goldman, op. cit., I, 232. In 1903, however, Tucker enrolled as a member of the Free Speech League which Emma Goldman had organized to protest against the deportation of the English Anarchist, John Turner. Ibid. I, 348.

Individualist Anarchism in that it was a class-conscious philosophy of the property-less wage-earner, a product of the Revolutionary movement in Russia, Italy, France, Spain, and Germany during the last quarter of the nineteenth century. While Individualist Anarchism had been strengthened by a philosophy of foreign origin, that of Proudhon, it was distinctly a product of the industrial conditions of the fifties, not of the late eighties or nineties. An essential difference, therefore, was one of origin in "time," as well as in "place." Anarchist Communism advocated communal ownership of the instruments of production and of the articles of consumption, the destruction of the wage system, and of the capitalistic system itself as we know it by means of the social revolution. Its motto was: "To each according to his needs, from each according to his ability." Michael Bakunin and Prince Peter Kropotkin were the "fathers" of Anarchist Communism in Europe. Bakunin (1814-1876), a Russian of the upper class, never worked out a systematic philosophy, but he fought throughout his life his arch enemies "Dieu et l'Etat."[2] Believing that "the desire for destruction is also a creative desire," he organized revolutionary labor groups and himself took part in uprisings in Russia, Germany, Switzerland, Austria, France, Italy, and Spain. Peter Kropotkin (1842-1921), Russian authority in geography and agriculture, a descendant of the Ruriks (he was said, in jest, to have had more right to the Russian throne than Czar Alexander II himself), gave to Anarchist Communism a systematic program.[3] He proposed the return of society to a federated state with the village commune, the "mir," as the unit. The laborer

[2] Biography of Bakunin: Michael Bakounine, *Oeuvres,* Tome II (Paris, 1907), Introduction by James Guillaume. Works: *Gesammelte. Werke,* 3 Bänder (Berlin, 1921). *God and the State,* Mother Earth Publishing Co. (New York, no date). Description of "battle" with Karl Marx, Robert Hunter, *Violence and the Labor Movement* (New York, 1914), 154-193.

[3] Autobiography: *Memoirs of a Revolutionist* (Boston and New York, 1899). Chief Works on anarchism consulted: *Freedom Pamphlets,* 1920 edition, "The Wage System," "The State: Its Historic Rôle," "Anarchist Communism," *Social Economic Papers:* "The Coming Anarchy," "The Breakdown of our Industrial System," "The Coming Reign of Plenty," "The Industrial Village of the Future," "Mutual Aid," "The Scientific Bases of Anarchy."

was in his system both farmer and worker, thus realizing the co-operation of agriculture and industry. Kropotkin also had intimate and painful experience with the prisons in Russia, Switzerland, and France.

From the extreme left wing of the revolutionary party came the Anarchist Communists during the last quarter of the nineteenth century. Their leaders, after the death of Bakunin, were Carlo Cafiero, Errico Malatesta, Paul Brousse, and Prince Kropotkin. Cafiero was an Italian of wealthy parents and a disciple of Bakunin. Malatesta had left the medical profession and his fortune for the sake of the revolution. Paul Brousse was of French parentage and had already distinguished himself in medicine, but cast it aside in his devotion to Anarchism.[4] The Jura Federation and then the International Working People's Party, the "Black International," organized in London in 1881 represented this faction.

From a milieu of Socialist and Anarchist Communist agitation and Nihilist activity come the immigrants to the United States. The German immigration from 1879-1890 rose 244% above the average level of the preceding four-year period as the result of Bismarck's "Exceptional Laws" (Ausnahmegesetze 1878) which put all labor unions under a ban alike with the political organizations of the Social Democracy.[5] A membership of fifty thousand was directly affected. The widespread discontent created by these repressive measures led many workingmen to seek liberty in the United States. Between 1881 and 1900 the Italian immigration had more than doubled. Its peak was reached between 1901 and 1910 when 2,045,877 were admitted.[6] Russian immigration in-

[4] Hunter, op. cit., 49-50. The repression of revolutionary activity in Europe during this period resulted in acts of violence, many of them by Anarchists: 1881 the assassination of Alexander II of Russia, 1892 of Carnot, President of France, 1897 the shooting of Prime Minister Canova del Costello, 1898 assassination of the Empress of Austria, 1900 of King Humbert of Italy. For description of violence see Robert Hunter, op. cit., 90-122.

[5] Isaac A. Hourwich, Immigration and Labor (New York, 1912), 191-3, 196.

[6] Statistical Abstract of the United States, U. S. Department of Commerce, Washington, 1930, 95.

creased from 1871-1880 more than twenty times what it had been in the previous nine-year period and from 1881-1890, one hundred times.[6a]. The industrial conditions which these immigrants met with in the United States during the last quarter of the nineteenth century were favorable to Socialist and Anarchist propaganda. The general depression, reduction of wages, especially of the unskilled and semi-skilled, unemployment, and the exhaustion of the public domain by 1884 had permanently shut up American labor in the wage system.[6b] In 1871 and 1872 sections of the Socialist International were established in the United States. In 1876 at Philadelphia, the International Workingmen's Association was formally organized. The Knights of Labor in 1878 and the Trade Unions in 1881 established national organizations. The general rush for organization bore all the aspects of a social war.[7] The Anarchist Communists, from 1882 until 1919, attempted to crystallize this tendency into a true social revolution. Their leaders were from 1882-1892, Johann Most, German Anarchist, from 1893-1919, Emma Goldman, Russian Jewess, joined by Alexander Berkman in 1906 (after his release from prison).[8]

Anarchist Communism was established as a distinct and independent movement by the formation of the International Working People's Association at Pittsburgh in October, 1883. The mani-

---

[6a] *Statistical Abstract of the United States,* U. S. Department of Commerce, Washington, 1930, 95.

[6b] Commons, *History of Labour,* II, 361.

[7] *Ibid.,* II, 374.

[8] Johann Most (1846-1906), Lasallean Socialist, then Anarchist through the influence of Victor Dave and August Reinsdorf, Bakuninists, member of German Reichstag 1874, leader of English Workingmen 1878-1881, came to the United States in 1882. In New York he established *Die Freiheit* (December 9, 1882-1910). He was the "teacher" of Emma Goldman and Alexander Berkman whom he met in New York in 1889. Emma Goldman, *Anarchism and Other Essays* (New York, 1910), 47 and Alexander Berkman, *Prison Memoirs of an Anarchist* (New York, 1912), 492. In 1892 he repudiated Berkman's attentat and thereafter opposed the use of violence (Berkman, *op. cit.,* 79, *Die Freiheit,* 1892) Autobiography (interesting material for psychological study of an Anarchist) John Most, *Memoiren Erlebtes, Erforschtes und Erdachtes* (4 parts, New York, 1903-1907); Emma Goldman, "Johann Most," *American Mercury,* Vol. 8 (June 1926), 158-166. The most detailed biography: Rudolf Rocker, *Johann Most, Das Leben Eines Rebellen* (Berlin, 1924).

festo was written by Johann Most and provided; first, "Destruction of the existing class rule, by all means, that is, by energetic, relentless, revolutionary, and international action." Second, "The establishment of a free society based upon coöperative organization of production." Third, "Free exchange of equivalent products by and between the productive organizations without commerce and profit-mongery." Fourth, "Organization of education on a secular, scientific, and equal basis for both sexes." Fifth, "Equal rights for all without distinction as to sex or race." Sixth, "Regulation of all public affairs by free contracts between the autonomous (independent) communes and associations, resting on a federalistic basis. . . ." And closes with the exhortation: "Proletarians of all countries, unite! You have nothing to lose but your chains, you have a world to win."[9] The centers of Anarchism were cities where the industrial conditions were particularly bad and in those cities were large foreign populations—Chicago, New York, Philadelphia, Pittsburgh, ·Paterson (New Jersey), and St. Louis. The immigrants were particularly receptive to Anarchist ideas. First, many of them came from countries oppressed by tyrannical governments and agitated by revolutionary movements.[10] Second, their ideal of economic opportunity and of freedom in America was destroyed by reality. Third, they were strangers—the evils of society stood out starkly and, unbound by American traditions or as they would say, not blinded by patriotism, they assailed what they thought were evil institutions and tried to make them square with their ideal. In some cases, however, their revolt was sheer desperation. At the same time they were encouraged in their revolt by European Anarchists and Syn-

[9] Pittsburgh Manifesto: Richard T. Ely, *The Labor Movement in America* (New York, 1886), Appendix V, 358-363, 363. This manifesto calls up the Declaration of Independence as a justification and exhortation to armed resistance, 358-359. Twenty-six cities were represented. Johann Most, August Spies, Albert R. Parsons, and Paul Grottkau were the most outstanding delegates. Rocker, *op. cit.*, 145.

[10] Alexander Berkman (1870-), Russian Jew of middle class, born in Kovno, Russia, came to New York in 1889. In his *Prison Memoirs* he describes the emotional motivation of his attempt to shoot Frick (see below, note, 20) and particularly the scenes of Cossack brutalities observed in his childhood.

dicalists. Charles Mowbray came to the United States for a lecture tour in 1894, John Turner in 1896 and 1903, and Tom Mann in 1913, Kropotkin in 1898 and 1901, and Errico Malatesta in 1899.[11] Rudolph Grossman (pen-name, Pierre Ramus), prominent Austrian Anarchist and Defeatist during the War of 1914, was one of the investigators of the Paterson strike in 1902.[12]

The climax of the revolutionary labor movement was reached in 1886 with the Chicago Haymarket riot. The details of this affair are too well known to call for an account at this point. The McCormick Reaper strike and subsequent lock-out in 1886 as part of the eight-hour movement, the brutality of police and Pinkerton detectives in attempting to break it, the parade of the English-speaking proletarians under Albert R. Parsons, and of the foreign workmen under Spies, Fielden, and Schwab, to inaugurate a General Strike on May first were antecedents to the events of May third. May third saw the shooting of four strikers, the subsequent Revenge Circular of August Spies in the *Vorbote* (Workingmen, arm yourselves and appear in full force!), the mass meeting at the Haymarket Square in the evening, addressed by August Spies, Albert R. Parsons, and Samuel Fielden, and the explosion of a bomb in the midst of one hundred and eighty policemen who had advanced on the assembly, although the Mayor, earlier in attendance, had informed the captain of police that the meeting was a peaceful one. Although the man who threw the bomb, which killed one police sergeant, was never discovered, Fielden and Schwab were sentenced to life imprisonment, Neebe to fifteen years, and on November 11, 1887, Parsons, Fischer, Engel, and Spies were hanged for the crime.[13] Six years later

[11] Rocker, *op. cit.*, 371-372; *Mother Earth*, volume X (1915), No. 6, 196-197; Jane Addams, *op. cit.*, 402; Max Nettlau, *Errico Malatesta. Das Leben Eines Anarchisten* (Berlin, 1922), 122-123. (Malatesta edited *La Questione Sociale* for a few months at Paterson, New Jersey in 1899); Paul Frederick Brissenden, *The I. W. W., A Study of American Syndicalism*, New York, 1920), 299-305.

[12] *Der Anarchiste*, edited by Rudolf Grossman (Vienna, Austria, 1927), Nos. 4 and 5.

[13] The writer has consulted the following materials for the Haymarket affair: General account: Commons, *History of Labour*, II, 386-394. Semi-official account: Dyer D. Lum, *A Concise History of the Chicago Anarch-*

on June 26, 1893, Governor Altgeld of Illinois reviewed the case and pardoned the three survivors on the grounds that the trial was illegal and that the State had never discovered who it was that threw the bomb.[14]

The Chicago Haymarket tragedy, as it is called, has had a manifold significance in the Anarchist Communist movement in the United States. In the first place, it gave to the cause four martyrs and an Anarchist shrine at Waldheim Cemetery. In the second place, however falsely, it permanently identified Anarchism with bomb throwing and violence and inspired a terror of Anarchism in the popular mind. In the third place, it completely turned labor as a whole away from Anarchism. Labor leaders hastened to deny any connection with the condemned men. Samuel Gompers afterwards testified that "the effect of that bomb was that it not only killed the policeman, but it killed our eight-hour movement, for that year and for a few years later, notwithstanding we had absolutely no connection with these people."[15] T. V. Powderly declared that "at Chicago the sound of a bomb did more injury to the good name of labor than all the strikes of that year."[16] But contrast with this the more disinterested and objective statement of Nathan Fine of the Rand School of Social Science, that the Haymarket bomb, far from ruining the labor movement, made the Chicago wage earners unite their forces and stiffen their resistance.[17] Jane Addams, Director of Hull House,

*ists in 1886.* Condensed from the official record (Chicago, no date). Waldo R. Browne, *Altgeld of Illinois* (New York, 1924), 74-115. Foreign account: Felix Dubois, *The Anarchist Peril* (translated by Ralph Derechef) (London, 1894), 38. *Presiding Judge's Account:* Joseph E. Gary, "The Chicago Anarchists of 1886. The Crime, the Trial, and the Punishment," *The Century Magazine,* XXIII (1892-1893), 803-837. Unreliable account of a policeman: M. J. Schaack, *Anarchy and Anarchists* (Chicago, 1889).

[14] Review of trial and reasons for pardon: John P. Altgeld, *Reasons for Pardoning Fielden, Neebe, and Schwab* (Springfield, Ill., 1893). Account by the man who made out the pardons and was present at their signing: Brand Whitlock, *Forty Years of It* (New York and London, 1914), 70-76.

[15] Commons, *History of Labour,* II, 386.

[16] T. V. Powderly, *Thirty Years of Labor, 1859 to 1889* (Columbus, Ohio, 1890), 543.

[17] As evidence he cites the fact that both the conservative and radical central bodies all got together for the first time on the political field in the

testified that from 1889-1890 Chicago indulged in freer discussion than it ever had before or since.[18]   Finally, the Chicago Haymarket conviction was one of the first of those state acts of violence which frequently converted agitators to Anarchism and which inspired reciprocal violence.

The Chicago Haymarket gave to the Anarchist movement two of its most outstanding women leaders, Emma Goldman and Voltairine de Cleyre.[19]   Against the account of Anarchist Communism must be laid Alexander Berkman's attack on Henry C. Frick in 1895 with intent to kill, as the only outstanding and admitted act of propaganda by deed.[20]   Other deeds attributed to them are the murder of a policeman by a bomb explosion at the Haymarket Square in 1886, the assassination of McKinley in 1901, the bomb plantings of 1919, and the murder of the paymaster at Braintree, Massachusetts, by Sacco and Vanzetti in 1920.   Some of these are declared to be only indirectly traceable to Anarchists, others not at all.   On the other side, are the execution of the Anarchist leaders in 1887, the attacks of the Pinkerton men on the Homestead Strikers in 1892, the arrests and denial of the right of assembly to Anarchist speakers from 1893 to 1919, the Anarchist raids in 1901 and 1907, the San Diego lynchings in

summer following the Haymarket affair and that the Knights of Labor doubled its membership, reaching 40,000 in the fall of 1886.   Nathan Fine, *Labour and Farmer Parties in the United States 1828-1928* (New York, 1928), 53.

[18] She described open-air meetings held every Sunday evening where every shade of opinion had a free voice and even Anarchists were allowed to talk.   The same was true of "The Working People's Social Science Club" organized in the spring of 1890.   She adds that "One cannot imagine such meetings being held in Chicago today."   Jane Addams, *op. cit.*, 177-179.

[19] Emma Goldman: *Essays*, 17; *Living My Life*, 1, 7-10; V. de Cleyre: "The Making of an Anarchist," *Selected Works*, 156.

[20] For dramatic account of how he expected this act to stir to revolution the workers who had been attacked, deceived, and brutally treated by the State Militia during the Homestead Strike at the Carnegie Steel Company, as well as of his prison experiences see his *Prison Memoirs*.   The effect of J. Most's repudiation, *ibid.*, 79, 492.   Some of the workers wanted to lynch Berkman.   *Letter to E. M. S. From Carl Nold*, February 14, 1931 (sentenced to five years for complicity).   Berkman today regards such acts as "harmful to the spread of their ideas."   *Now and After* (New York, 1929), 177.

1912, the deportations of 1919, and the execution of Sacco and Vanzetti in 1927.[21] Whether or not the use of violence is justified on either side, the fact remains that such action by the State has "made" Anarchists and has aroused the sympathies of libertarians for those who suffered from it.[22]

The leadership of the Anarchist Communist movement in 1893 was taken over by Emma Goldman.[23] This marks the beginning of its second period in the United States. Emma Goldman was born in Kovno, Russia, on June 27, 1869 of Russian Jewish parents, spent much of her childhood in Germany, and at the age of seventeen she and her sister came to the United States. From 1886 until 1889 she worked first in a clothing factory at Rochester, New York, and then at a corset factory at New Haven, Connecticut. In 1889 she met Johann Most and Alexander Berkman in New York City and from that time on she spoke at German and Yiddish Anarchist meetings, participated in strikes, and in 1891 split with Johann Most and his party over parliamentary action and propaganda by deed. She joined the group of younger radicals, "Autonomy" in which Joseph Peukert, Alexander Berkman,

[21] *Homestead Strike:* Commons, *History of Labour,* II, 495-497. *Use of Pinkertons:* Hunter, *op. cit.,* 281-326. Their function, Hunter declares, is (1) to break strikes, (2) to apprehend leaders, (3) to incite strikes. *Violations of Freedom of Speech, Press, and Assembly:* Whipple, *op. cit.,* 301-309. Whipple testifies "The development of the laws against Anarchists is an important chapter in the history of liberty. These extreme libertarians have had rather less liberty than anybody else. . . . They have suffered primarily for their opinions," 301, 302. *Sacco-Vanzetti Case.* Transcript of the trial of Nicola Sacco and Bartolomeo Vanzetti in the courts of Massachusetts and subsequent proceedings, 1920-1927 (six vols., New York, 1928-1929.

[22] Dyer D. Lum, descendant of the Tappan family, his grandfather a Revolutionist, himself, secretary to Samuel Gompers, an Individualist Anarchist (1839-1893), but by the Chicago affair was convinced of the necessity for direct action. Edited Parson's *Alarm,* 1892-1893. V. de Cleyre, *Selected Works,* 284-296. Lum was "the moving spirit of the American group" which worked for the commutation of Berkman's sentence. Goldman, *op. cit.,* I, 110. Tucker expressed sympathy for Chicago "Martyrs" but disapproved method. *Instead of a Book,* 386, 446-447, 448, 449.

[23] Biography to 1911. Introduction by Hippolyte Havel to Emma Goldman's *Anarchism and Other Essays,* 5-44. After 1906: *Mother Earth,* Anarchist monthly edited by Emma Goldman from March 1906-August 1917, 12 volumes. Russian experiences: *My Disillusionment in Russia* (New York, 1923); complete biography, *Living My Life,* 2 vols.

Otto Rinke, and Claus Timmerman took an active part. In 1892 she defended Berkman's act. In 1893 she addressed a large group of unemployed and of striking garment workers at Union Square closing her impassioned speech with her version of Cardinal Manning's words, "necessity knows no law, and a striving man has a natural right to his neighbor's bread" which was: "Ask for work; if they do not give you work, ask for bread; if they do not give you work or bread, then take bread."[24]  For this address she was arrested, tried in the criminal courts of New York and sentenced to one year in the penitentiary at Blackwell's Island. This experience confirmed her Anarchism.

The philosophy which Emma Goldman developed was very similar to that of Kropotkin—free communism, defined as: "Voluntary economic coöperation of all towards the needs of each. A social arrangement based on the principle 'to each according to his needs; from each according to his ability.' "[25] Anarchism she defined as, "The philosophy of the new social order based on liberty unrestricted by man-made law; the theory that all forms of government rest on violence, and are therefore wrong and harmful, as well as unnecessary."[26]  She advocated Direct Action "con-

---

[24] Voltairine de Cleyre, *In Defense of Emma Goldman and the Right of Expropriation* (Philadelphia, 1894). Voltairine de Cleyre while herself not approving of advising anyone to do anything "involving a risk to himself," declared "the spirit which animates Emma Goldman is the only one which will emancipate the slave from his slavery, the tyrant from his tyranny— the spirit which is willing to dare and suffer." *Ibid.,* 9-10. In 1911 Voltairine gave herself to Revolution as a kind of escape. Only her death prevented her from going to Mexico to take part in the Mexican Revolution. Biography of Voltairine by Hippolyte Havel. Introduction to her *Selected Works,* 5-14 and interviews by the writer with her friends in New York City, November 22-24, 1930. Emma Goldman's speech and its effect—Goldman, *op. cit.,* I, 122-123; arrest and life in prison, *ibid.,* I, 124-126; 132-148.

[25] *Mother Earth,* Volume VII (December, 1912), No. 10, 357.

[26] *Essays,* 56. Miss Goldman still believes in the Anarchist Communism of Kropotkin, but not in the "Moscow, Lenin, or Marxian school." The loss of individual freedom is her most serious objection to Communism as it is found in Russia today (Letter to writer, January 1, 1931). For Alexander Berkman's Russian reaction see *The Anti-Climax* (heretofore unpublished chapter of *The Bolshevik Myth*) (Berlin, 1925). For treatment of Anarchists in Russia see *Bulletin of the Relief Fund of the International Working Men's Association for Anarchists and Anarcho-Syndicalists Imprisoned or Exiled in Russia,* Berlin-Paris. Latest exposition of

scious individual or collective effort to protest against, or remedy, social conditions through the systematic assertion of the economic power of the workers."[27]    The Anarchist Communists in general justified Direct Action, not only by what they considered necessity, but also by precedent—Shay's Rebellion, the Boston Tea Party, the American Revolution itself, and John Brown's raid.[28] The chief organ of Anarchist Communism from 1906 until 1917 was *Mother Earth,* founded and edited by Emma Goldman with the assistance of Alexander Berkman.    In this periodical and in her lectures, Emma Goldman defended the cause of the proletariat and the social revolution in general.    She sponsored strikes, industrial education, the dissemination of birth control information, contests for freedom of speech, press and assembly, and consistently from 1898-1917 opposed all war except the social war.[29]

Anarchist Communism: Alexander Berkman, *Now and After, the ABC of Communist Anarchism* (New York, 1929).

[27] Emma Goldman in later years grew to doubt the value of violence, regarding it as "a tragic waste." It is interesting to note that the development of Voltairine de Cleyre was the reverse—first a non-resistant, finally an advocate of revolution. Goldman: *Living My Life,* I, 152; II, 536; *Mother Earth,* VII (February 1913), No. 12.

[28] *Mother Earth,* VII (August 1912), No. 6, 182-4; VII (June 1912), No. 4; I, 12 (February 1907), 34-37. Chafee points out the inconsistency of declaring the removal of evils by force, vicious and intolerable, in the light of American tradition, *Freedom of Speech,* 209-210.

[29] The Italians, French, Spanish, Bohemian, German, and Jewish Anarchist groups worked independently and published their own periodicals. Pietro Gori, Luigi Galleani, and Guiseppe Ciancabilla led the Italians who were very strong among the textile workers of Paterson, New Jersey. *Anarchico,* 1888, *Gridodigli Oppressi* (New York, 1892-1894), *La Questione Sociale* and *L'Era Nuova* (1895?, Paterson, New Jersey), *La Cronaca Souversiva,* June 6, 1903-1918 (1919?) were the chief Italian periodicals. The French Anarchists have propagated actively the General Strike and Revolutionary Syndicalism, 1899, *Germinal* (Paterson, New Jersey). Spanish Anarchists were strong among the long-shoremen and cigar makers in New York, Florida, and Texas. *El Desperatar,* 1891-?, *El Esclava,* 1894-? (Tampa, Florida). *Vorbote,* 1881-1887, *Chicagoer Arbeiterzeitung, Der Arme Teufel* (Detroit, Mich., 1884-1899), represented German elements; *Volne Listy* (New York, 1890), the Bohemians. The Jewish Anarchism was found in the *Wahrheit* (1889), and in the *Freie Arbeiterstimme* (New York, 1888-). Other English periodicals besides *Mother Earth* published for a relatively short time were *The Alarm,* 1884-1898, *The Firebrand* (Portland, Oregon, 1895), later *Free Society* (1897-November 30, 1914), at San Francisco, Chicago, and New York, *Discontent* (1898), changed to *Syndicalist* (Chicago, 1913). *Home Colony* (Washington). Rocker, *op. cit.,* 372-381 and letter from Max Nettlau, November 21, 1930; *Mother Earth,* I, 326-329.

Throughout her active career in the United States Emma Goldman established contacts with the leading European Anarchists and from them her anarchistic zeal and hope were often rekindled. Peter Kropotkin of Russia, Dr. Max Nettlau of Austria, Domela Nieuwenhuis of Holland, Victor Dave and Louise Michel of France were her greatest inspiration.

Education was an important part of the Anarchist Communist program. In 1897 Emma Goldman began her cross-continent lecture tours which she continued until 1917. From 1899-1900 (eight months) she visited sixty cities and lectured at two hundred and ten different meetings.[30] The modern drama was one of her frequent and favorite subjects. When George Bernard Shaw was scarcely known in the United States, Emma Goldman was lecturing to the workers on the social significance of his plays. The foundation of the Ferrer Modern School movement was largely initiated by Emma Goldman. The Ferrer Association was established on June 12, 1910 at Harlem in honor of Francisco Ferrer, Spanish Anarchist teacher, executed in 1909 for his alleged participation in a riot.[31] The association united Anarchists, Socialists, Single Taxers, and other radicals for a three-fold purpose: first, to start a school for children on the model of the schools Ferrer had established in Spain; second, to give evening lectures on the latest subjects in art, music, drama, economics, and philosophy; and third, to establish a center for radicals. On October 13, 1911, the first school was opened at 104 East 12th Street, New York City, where no less a person than Will Durant, now professor of Philosophy at Columbia University was Principal from 1911-1913.[32] In the summer of 1912 he had assisted in a

---

[30] Rocker, op. cit., 372.

[31] Joseph J. Cohen and Alexis C. Ferm, The Modern School of Stelton (Stelton, New Jersey, 1925), 17.

[32] Ibid., 19, 62. His relations came to a rather sudden close when he married one of the pupils of the school. Professor Bayard Boyesen, dismissed from Columbia University, was associated with the school, ibid., 61-120. The New York school interested many prominent people and was visited by such men as Clarence Darrow, Joseph McCabe of England, Edwin Markham, Hutchins Hapgood, and Theodore Schroeder. Cohen and Ferm, op. cit., 25.

Ferrer school in London where he had met Peter Kropotkin of whom he said in a letter to *Mother Earth* on September 16, 1912: "A gentle, fatherly old man whom I have learned to love."[33] Desiring to place the school in more suitable surroundings Harry Kelly suggested that it be moved outside of the city. Land was purchased and on March 15, 1915, the colonists, teachers, and pupils took formal possession of the Ferrer Modern School at Stelton, New Jersey.[34]

The present writer visited the school and found that today it has approximately sixty pupils and six teachers. Those who had continued their education in the public high schools had graduated with honors. Some of them had made distinguished records for themselves in Eastern Colleges.[35] The Ferrer School method, according to the principal, is a modification of the Pestalozzian and Froebel systems but at the same time aims to be thoroughly anarchistic. The purpose of the teacher as in all progressive schools is to call forth the powers of the child rather than to inject her own ideas into it.[36] It is surprising that with such scant and inadequate material, the children could have produced the strikingly original and artistic work which they have. They make their own regulations; they have no fixed schedule for work. Nevertheless their routine moves smoothly. There is no segregation of sex even in the dormitory, nor is the principal troubled with sex problems. The Ferrer School at Stelton is unique because it is a Progressive school for the children of the workers and directed by the workers themselves. Their teachers are, for the most part, graduates of the school. This institution is one of the few which has survived the general disillusionment in the Anarchist Communist movement.

[33] *Mother Earth*, VII (October, 1912), 245-247. In the same letter he described a statue of Ferrer holding a torch, which he had seen in Brussels saying, "Oh, to be a bearer of the torch even if only for a little while! Could one ask any more of whatever gods there be? . . . But as the world moves on one perceives that it is the crucified who live, and the persecutors who are dead."

[34] *Ibid.*, 33.

[35] *Ibid.*, 37. The writer visited the school and the colony on November 23, 1930. Mr. and Mrs. Dick are at present the principals of the school.

[36] Theory by one-time principal—Elizabeth B. Ferm, *The Spirit of Freedom in Education* (Stelton, New Jersey, 1919).

Emma Goldman was one of the earliest disseminators of birth control information among the proletariat, a matter which she considered relevant to economic emancipation.[37]  Her lectures on this subject were raided by the police and she was herself arrested, as was Margaret Sanger.  It was through *Mother Earth,* moreover, that Miss Goldman collected funds to assist Mr. and Mrs. Sanger in their occasional court trials.[38]  During the year 1916 she lectured frequently to large audiences throughout the United States on this subject, a task for which she felt particularly qualified since she had been trained as a nurse and her associate, Ben Reitman, as a medical doctor.  Despite this fact on April 20, 1916, Miss Goldman was arrested, tried, and sentenced to a one hundred dollar fine or a maximum of fifteen days in the workhouse for addressing a meeting on birth control.  She chose the workhouse declaring "If giving one's life for the purpose of awakening social consciousness in the masses which will compel them to bring quality not quantity into society, be a crime, I am glad to be such a criminal."[39]  The trial was attended by many New York doctors, literati, and radicals, arousing so much interest that a meeting was called by Max Eastman and Rose Pastor Stokes on May fifth at Carnegie Hall to welcome her back from prison.[40] The propaganda value of such incidents was appreciable, as we shall see.

The Anarchist Communists, at least their leaders, consistently opposed all war except the "social war," on the grounds that it was always for the advantage of the Capitalists and for the disadvantage of the workers.  It led, in fact, they said to the enslavement of the proletariat.  In 1898 Emma Goldman lectured throughout the United States against the Spanish-American War

[37] Instance also her fight for Free Speech in San Diego—for the I. W. W.'s, Ben Reitman was lynched and the letters I. W. W. burned on his back; organization of Workers' International Defence League to defend Mooney and Billings in 1916. *Mother Earth* VII (June, 1912), No. 4; *Literary Digest,* Vol. 44 (June 1, 1912), 1146; *Mother Earth,* XI (1916), pp. 597-603.

[38] *Mother Earth,* IX (November, 1914), X (February, 1915).

[39] *Mother Earth,* XI (April, 1916), 504.

[40] *Mother Earth,* XI (May and June, 1916); Emma Goldman, *Living My Life,* II, 570-571.

and collected money for the Cuban Revolutionists without once being arrested.[41] During her visit in England in 1899 she toured both England and Scotland lecturing against the Boer War.[42] *Mother Earth* denounced the War of 1914, the Mexican War of the same year, and acclaimed the Mexican Revolution.[43] But in 1917 she took her most forceful, and her last, stand against the participation of the United States in the War.[44] While the Socialists organized the Anti-Conscription League instructing labor to demand a referendum on the entrance of the United States into the War, Emma Goldman organized the No-Conscription League and urged labor to refuse to fight. Although she did not directly counsel men to evade the draft, she nevertheless pointed out the efficacy of refusing to register—in short a General Strike against fighting would be effected. On June 5, 1917 she addressed an audience of five thousand people at a meeting of the No-Conscription League. For this address and for articles in *Mother Earth,* both editors, Emma Goldman and Alexander Berkman, were arrested by Federal officials, tried, and, under the Espionage Act of 1917, sentenced to two years in the penitentiary, subject thereafter to deportation.[45] In 1898 Emma Goldman opposed the

[41] *Essays,* 30. Goldman, *Living My Life,* I, 226-227.

[42] *Ibid.,* I, 225-257.

[43] Such declarations as "No war is justified unless it be for the purpose of overthrowing the Capitalist system and establishing industrial control for the working class," "One thing is certain—war is *not* for the working class" are to be found in the 1914-1917 issues of *Mother Earth* (Volumes IX-XII).

[44] European Anarchists had been particularly anti-Militaristic. In 1904 Domela Nieuwenhuis, Dutch Anarchist, founded the International Anti-Militarist Union. At the 1907 congress of this union Emma Goldman represented American Anarchists. On July 27, 1924, she gave an impassioned address against war and against trusting in any political party. Pamphlets *War Against War* International Anti-Militarist Bureau, Hague, Holland, N. D. and *I. A. M. B.* February 1925. For activity of Anarchists against war and important work in the peace movement, A. Hamon: *Psychologie Du Militaire Professionel* (Nouvelle Edition, avec une Defense, Paris, 1895), 197.

[45] Socialists and Communists were arrested and imprisoned under this act. Rose Pastor Stokes, Eugene V. Debs, Victor Berger, Max Eastman are among those who were tried under the Espionage Act. Account of the trial: *Mother Earth,* XII (1917), No. 5, references to Chafee, *op. cit.,* 47, 126. Margaret C. Anderson, *My Thirty Years' War* (New York, 1930), 195-196. For activities of Emma Goldman against war, her arrest and trial see Goldman, *Living My Life,* II, 598-623.

Spanish-American War without arrest; in 1917 she opposed the Conscription Act and was sentenced to the penitentiary.

This marks the beginning of the end of a virtual Anarchist Communist movement in the United States. The years 1919 and 1920 were convulsed by a "deportations delirium." The first federal act to exclude Anarchists was passed in 1903 to forbid the entrance of alien Anarchists to the United States. Before this time in the years 1887, 1889, 1890-1893, 1894 investigations were made for the purpose of passing such a law. It was only after the assassination of President McKinley by a half-crazed youth, however, that such a law was passed. Its test came in the same year when John Turner, an English Tolstoyan Anarchist, came to the United States to lecture on trade unionism and Anarchism as he had freely done, six years before. The case was appealed to the Supreme Court but the constitutionality of the law was maintained, "Constructive Anarchy" defined, and Turner, although a "peaceful" Anarchist was deported. This act was followed by the New York State Criminal Anarchy law in 1906 defining Anarchism as the criminal doctrine "that organized government should be overthrown by force or violence, or by assassination of the executive head or any of the executive officials of government, or by any unlawful means." The advocacy of such a doctrine "either by word of mouth or writing is a felony." This law was used as a model for similar laws in thirty other different states. The Federal acts which provided specifically for the deportation of Alien Anarchists and which served as the basis of the 1919-1920 deportations were those of February 5, 1917 (the Burnett Act), October 16, 1918, and June 5, 1920. They provided for the deportation of Aliens who were Anarchists, that is, who advocated the overthrow of the government of the United States or all forms of law by force or violence. Aliens *who disbelieved* in or *opposed* all organized government or aliens who were members of organizations which advocated or believed in Anarchism as defined above.[46]

[46] Federal Anarchist Laws against Anarchists, *Communist and Anarchist Deportation Cases.* Hearings before a subcommittee on Immigration and Naturalization. House of Representatives, Sixty-Sixth Congress, Second

The prologue to the deportations was the discovery of bombs in the mails and in public buildings during May and June, 1919, which caused a wave of terror to sweep the country.[47] Although thousands of dollars were appropriated to the Department of Justice by Congress and the country "combed" with "fine-combs" by detectives, the origin of the bombs was never discovered.[48] Terroristic raids were instituted in all the large cities of the United States, 6,000 warrants of arrest issued by the Department of Labor, 4,000 arrests made, 3,000 cancelled after hearings chiefly by Mr. Louis F. Post, Assistant Secretary of Labor, and from December 29, 1919 to June 30, 1920, 556 aliens deported.[49] On December 21, 1919, fifty-one "Anarchists or persons who did not believe in any form of government" and one hundred eighty-four members of an organization that taught the overthrow of government by force (Federation of Unions of Russian Workers) sailed for Russia in the United States steamship, Buford (the "Soviet Ark").[50] Emma Goldman and Alexander Berkman were among the fifty-one.

By this wholesale deportation the United States completely reversed its traditional national policy. To the immigrant it had stood as an ideal of liberty. Those who tested this ideal more than any others were the Anarchist Communists. From the begin-

Session (Washington, D. C., 1920) ; *Exclusion and Expulsion of Aliens of Anarchistic and Similar Cases. Report of the Committee on Immigration and Naturalization,* House of Representatives, Sixty-Sixth Congress. Second Session (Washington, D. C., 1920) ; Whipple, *op. cit., passim.* State Anarchy laws: Lusk Investigating Committee Report: *Revolutionary, Radicalism, Its History, Purpose, and Tactics* (4 Vols., Albany, New York, 1920).

[47] Louis F. Post, *The Deportation Delirium of Nineteen-Twenty* (Chicago, 1923), 36-50.

[48] *Idem.*

[49] *Ibid.,* 167. "Tons of seditious and Anarchistic literature were seized." (Lusk reports I, 20-22). The conditions under which the prisoners were held pending investigation were declared shocking. Post, *op. cit.,* 91-153. The raids themselves were conducted in a terroristic fashion, *ibid.,* 28-35.

[50] Louis F. Post, *The Deportation Delirium of Nineteen-Twenty* (Chicago, 1923), 27, *Communist Anarchist Deportation Cases* and *Reports.* Post declares on intimate knowledge that the relatives of those deported were not notified of the time of their departure or of their destination. Most of the families were left in "abject want" by the deportation of the fathers. *Ibid.,* 6. Deportations and trip on *S. S. Buford.* Goldman, *Living My Life,* II, 711-725.

ning of their agitation in the United States in 1882 to the virtual end in 1919, the action used against them was a continuous violation of the Bill of Rights. If it is supposed, however, that all citizens were acquiescent or unconscious of this trend rapidly developing into a distinct policy, evidence shows quite the contrary. Instance the amnesty association founded in 1890 and the protests voiced by prominent people both in America and England against the extreme sentence imposed upon the Haymarket leaders.[51] The debate in the Senate over the passage of the Alien Anarchist law in 1903 brought forth a lingering defense of the tradition of political asylum. Senator Hoar even declared that there were in the world governments that he would overthrow by force and violence.[52] By still others the deportation of John Turner was regarded as a dangerous method of combating erroneous and pernicious ideas, as well as a dangerous precedent. Clarence Darrow and Edgar Lee Masters wrote the appeal of Turner's case to the Supreme Court.[53] To protest against the deportation of Turner the Free Speech League was organized by Emma Goldman with the help of such prominent libertarians as Theodore Schroeder, Benjamin Tucker, Ernest Crosby, Bolton Hall, and Charles B. Spahr.[54] The general effect of the government's action was to make the liberals more belligerent and to make Emma Goldman more acceptable to the liberals. Emma Goldman herself felt that it brought her nearer to the American Intellectuals.[55]

When in the first five months of the year 1909 Emma Goldman's meetings were broken up eleven times by the police, a group of periodicals demanded that the freedom of speech, press, and

[51] Browne, *Altgeld of Illinois*, 82, 86-87.

[52] *Congressional Record*, XXXVI, Part I, 44.

[53] Whipple, *op. cit.*, 304. For expression of liberal reaction see *The Independent*, Volume 55 (December 10, 1903) ; John Turner, "The Protest of an Anarchist," December 24, 1903, pp. 3052-4; *Current Literature*, Volume 37 (July, 1904), 17-18, 5; Volume 36 (April, 1904), 405-406.

[54] Emma Goldman, *Living My Life*, I, 348-9. See also articles by Theodore Schroeder, "Our Vanishing Liberty of Press," *The Arena*, Volume 36 (December 1906), 617-620; "The Lawless Suppression of the Freedom of Speech in New York," *The Arena*, Volume 39 (June 1908), 394-399.

[55] Emma Goldman, *op. cit.*, I, 335.

assembly be respected.[56]   In order to protest against the same
violations and to arouse the interest of liberals, a National Free
Speech Committee was formed on May 23 with Leonard D. Abbott of New York as chairman.   The meeting of two thousand
people at Cooper Union was addressed by all shades of radicals
and liberals.   John S. Crosby, Gilbert E. Roe, former law partner
of the late Senator LaFollette, the Honorable Robert Baker and
Mrs. Milton Rathbun were among the most prominent speakers,
while letters from Mr. J. Phelps Stokes and Eugene V. Debs
were read, the latter saying:

"Emma Goldman has been persecuted and outraged by the
police.   She has a right to be heard. . . . Cowardice deserves no
hearing, but only contempt, and we are certainly guilty of cowardice, if we do not fight for the preservation of free speech.   In
that kind of a fight count on me, if it is to give the devil a hearing."[57]   A similar demonstration was arranged in Philadelphia
where letters from Charles E. Russell, Rose Pastor Stokes, and
William Reedy of the St. Louis *Mirror* were read.[58]

The arrest and imprisonment of Emma Goldman and Alexander Berkman, as well as their deportation called forth protests
as late as 1917 and 1920.   Max Eastman called them "elemental
forces" and "friends of American freedom."

> "Like the water that climbs down the rocks;
> Like the wind in the leaves,
> Like the gentle night that holds us."[59]

And Helen Keller sent words of encouragement to Emma Goldman in prison saying, "Your work must go on, even though all
earthly powers combine against it," and asking, "How can there
be a democracy unless people think and speak their minds freely—

[56] *The New York Sun,* the *New Haven Union* and Louis F. Post were
the most outstanding critics.   Quotations in *Mother Earth,* IV (June, 1919),
No. 4.

[57] *Mother Earth,* IV (July, 1909), 146-150; protest and Society, Goldman,
*Living My Life,* I, 452-453.

[58] *Mother Earth,* IV (October, 1909), 244-245; Goldman: *Living My
Life,* I, 459.

[59] For this poem and certain cartoons his paper, *The Masses,* was excluded from the mails.   Chafee, *op. cit.,* 47.

unless the minority is treated with tolerance and justice."[60] Nor did the deportations escape censure from the liberal press.[61] The departure of the United States from its national policy may be explained in part by the nervous effect of the war, the shock of the Russian Revolution, the unpreparedness for wide, intellectual divergencies, and the dislike of the foreigners' presence originating in the consciousness of unlikeness.[62] The general significance of this departure, however, is to be found in an interpretation of the Anarchist movement itself from the point of view of its earliest development.

We have said that the central doctrine of Anarchism is "no authority." It is a philosophy and not a practical program, in spite of the attempts of some of its exponents to make it so. It is a negative doctrine in its opposition or revolt against authority wherever it appears most oppressive. It is positive in character in its insistence that human beings can and will live harmoniously, peacefully, more richly and fully, if they are unhampered by any kind of authority except that coming from within. They will respect each other's rights because, if men possess the necessities of life they will have no reason to injure anyone else. While other philosophies, as for instance, Socialism, Communism, and Syndicalism hope that freedom will be won after or as the result of the establishment of certain economic principles, Anarchism declares that *freedom* is a fundamental, basic *condition* about which all other adjustment must follow and from which all solutions of the social problem must come. Although the ideal may be impossible to realize, its importance and value lies in its being affirmed so positively and under all conditions. In short, what the modern school method would apply to the school period alone, Anarchism would apply to the whole of life. And as such a

[60] *Mother Earth Bulletin,* January 1918, No. 4, 9.
[61] "Deporting a Political Party," *New Republic,* Volume 21 (January 14, 1920), 186. Ernst Freund, "Burning Heretics." *Ibid.,* XXI, 226; "Deportations and the Law," *Nation,* Volume 110 (January 31, 1920), 131. The Lusk reports declared that "the exercise of free speech was intended for the perpetuation of a free government and not for the destruction thereof." III, 2025.
[62] Chafee, *op. cit.,* 289.

philosophy, we must interrogate it, and on the basis of the evidence which has already been presented, we may suggest what significance it may have had in American history.

The general philosophy as outlined above has been elaborated and experimented with during a course of three hundred years in the United States. The divergencies in interpretation and in the method of "making the ideal real" have been determined largely by the temperament of their exponents and by the conditions which they desired to correct. Their specific programs have been almost as varied as the personalities of the individuals who formulated them. This study has been concerned chiefly with native American Anarchism and by virtue of the general definition of it has included movements which are not generally conceived as Anarchistic. The milieus most favorable to the growth of Anarchism were found to have been first, those in which the individual was autocratically suppressed, that is, where his freedom of mental or physical development were most restrained and second, those where economic life was unadjusted, social life in the state of "unsettling itself" and intellectual life adventurous, many-sided, self-exploring and optimistic. In the latter condition, the exponents of Anarchism did not enjoy complete tolerance, for their extreme ideas have never won that, but they have been more tolerated than in the other condition. This applies mostly to the Romantic period—the first half of the nineteenth century. In the former condition fear of disagreement in the interest of self preservation has motivated drastic action—in the Commonwealth of Massachusetts, the Alien Act of 1637 and the banishment of Anne Hutchinson from the colony in 1638, in the latest period, the Alien Act of 1903 and the deportation of Emma Goldman from the States.

Religion was the source of the greatest Authoritarianism in the Commonwealth of Massachusetts in the days of its early foundation. Religion was one of the most vital interests in the Puritan colony, as is "business" in the present age. Religious observance and religious controversy was the source of pleasure and diversion; religious law the chief regulator of the colonists' lives and took precedence over Common Law. A revolt against the prescriptions of religious law was a revolt against the civil law, the government, society, and the State. Against the formalism and infallibility of the religious creed, William Wheelwright and Anne Hutchinson revolted and for this they were banished. Their revolt was Anarchistic because in their attempt to defend their own individual religion, they denounced *all* religious law (which we must remember comprised the main body of the legal code), and the authority of *any one* over their own lives. They were *above* law. They were "newer" immigrants, unbound by the tradition of the colony (although still very young it had already set down a rigid code), inspired by an ideal of religious freedom to be found in the new colony, and animated by the questioning spirit of Descartes. We find a similar situation in 1848 and 1878, but still more aggravated by a difference in "nationality," a consciousness of unlikeness. They failed of a complete Anarchism because they placed only the *Elect* above law. It was not until the Romantic Period that this principle was extended to all men, that is, in a sense *all* were Elect. From the point of view of the individual it was an assertion of freedom, of a right to spontaneous development. From the point of view of the society, that is, the Commonwealth, it revealed the danger of group solidarity, characterized by conformity and intolerance for the new. As an attempt to break up this solidarity, the revolt of Anne Hutchinson was a failure, the Commonwealth continued in the same manner for almost two centuries. But its influence may be sought in the traditional liberalism of the Rhode Island government. It is not unlikely that these early founders of Rhode Island, "refugees" from the Commonwealth, were a moderating influence.

A kind of Anarchism found expression in the Romantic period, the first half of the nineteenth century. Faith in the innate goodness of human nature and a reliance on that goodness was a favorable and even necessary condition for a "healthy" growth of Anarchism. It failed only in its division between the spiritual and the physical natures of man which even many of the reformers perpetuated. In the same period, however, a new faith in the goodness of ·the unity of man, both of his physical and moral self was proclaimed by a few reformers. Conduct with some of these reformers became amoral, "useful or useless," "practical or impractical," "scientific or unscientific." It was the influence of science which made possible the development of an Individualistic Anarchism. But first, as to the Anarchism which appeared in the moral and social spheres. As we have seen, the agitation for the abolition of slavery, of war, of intemperance, of the inequality of the sexes, and of "wickedness" in general developed in its extreme left wing a spiritual Anarchism. It was Anarchistic in philosophy —it asserted the supremacy of the individual to law, government, and the State. It was Anarchistic in practice—it lead its exponents to condemn present government and to resist it by a spiritual force —that is, it refused to vote, to hold office, and to pay taxes even to the point of going to jail. Many of its exponents were absolutely uncompromising—at least philosophically, but as we have seen they met a dilemma in attempting to make their philosophy square with their action. They could not remain in society without aiding and countenancing the government which they damned and which they held to be an agent inevitably destructive of their principles. William Lloyd Garrison declared that he would be as harsh as truth and as uncompromising as justice in his mission to liberate the black slaves. In utter defiance of and in disdain for the government he declared the Constitution a covenant with death and an agreement with Hell and publicly burned it to ashes. Nor was he arrested, although he did attack many vested interests. John Brown attempted to liberate the slave by force, by direct action. He failed. But the leading reformers eulogized him and some of them even contributed money to his act of violence. They were fired by no less passionate hatred for black slavery than were the Anarchist Communists Johann Most, Alexander Berkman, and Emma Goldman for the white "slave." But at the same time, they were blind to the fact that they had violated individual right in denying the principle of secession, of State Rights.

In philosophy they asserted the supremacy of the individual to government, to society. Some of them called this, submission to

God and Love. Adin Ballou convinced of the innate evil of government, because of its ultimate reliance on force, withdrew to a colony where he established rules of moral conduct which, if applied to a society as a whole would have amounted to a strict moral tyranny. John Humphrey Noyes, Christian Anarchist, withdrew to Oneida, New York, where he substituted mutual criticism and personal leadership for government. From an economic point of view his community was Anarchist Communist, but the chasm between one small community and the rest of a large country fast developing a complex system of industry made the practical application of such principles to the United States a complete impracticability. It remained "just another" community. Where might we look, therefore, either for a monument to its philosophical influence or its practical influence? For the success of method we may look to the emancipation of the slaves. For the influence of its ideas we look to the writings of Count Leo Tolstoy, who, although arriving at similar ideas independently, was directly inspired by the non-resistance of Adin Ballou and by the influence of non-resistance in the abolition of slavery.

But, as we have said, the Anarchism of this period was largely ethical. At the same time, however, but actually as harbingers of a new period, the Individualist Anarchists developed a type of Anarchism—applicable to moral, social, economic, and political life, and based on American tradition. The philosophy of Josiah Warren took from American tradition the rights of the individual which before had applied only to certain classes and made them equally applicable to all classes. It was a reaction against the associationism of the period of the forties and fifties but at the same time it pointed to a method of coöperation which would make possible the fullest development of the individual without sacrifice of the community interest. This is the first completely Anarchist economic philosophy which appeared in the United States. It is significant that the economics of Anarchism maintaining as it does the sovereignty of the individual, proposes a system whereby decentralization of production may be achieved. It is necessarily, therefore, a reaction against the capitalistic system of centralization

in industry.  Instead of being a retrogressive economic ideal, however, it might possibly be a goal toward which the industrial system
would progress after it had reached a maximum of centralization.
Because the Individualist Anarchists include the economic element
as well, we consider that native American Anarchism matures in
their philosophy.  It is a systematization of traditional American
individualism and lawlessness.  It failed of general acceptance because it applied equally to all classes, because it was not class conscious.  It did not appeal to the Capitalist because it demanded not
"rugged individualism" but universal individualism.  It did not
appeal to the worker because it did not offer a practical means of
increasing his bargaining power which he hoped to achieve by
association, by trade unions and national labor organizations.  It
was sponsored by intellectuals who had no direct personal contact
with the propertyless wage earner.  Nor was it a philosophy of
"get rich quick."  It did, however, successfully point out to intellectuals the need for recognizing the individual, for setting the
limits of state interference.  The Individualist Anarchists from
Josiah Warren down to Benjamin Tucker did for the United
States in their small way what John Stuart Mill and Herbert
Spencer did for England.  The leaders of the movement were discouraged and disillusioned—some of them left the United States,
others of them went over to a more active philosophy, Anarchist
Communism.  In the words of an authority on the Anarchist
movement, Individualist Anarchism in the United States was:

"A reflection of the sturdy independence which the pioneers in
the West could assert a century ago and its gradual waning when
Capitalism proceeds and Tucker tries to make an individualist
stand even against this superior force which gradually absorbs
him, amalgamates him."[63]

Anarchist Communism, however, which has been treated here
in only a very cursory manner, since, strictly speaking, it was not
native in origin, has also flourished in the United States.  It was
American only in the sense that it was nurtured by American
needs in its economic and social system.  Inspired by the Revolu-

[63] Letter from Max Nettlau, November 21, 1930.

tionary Anarchist Communism of Bakunin and Kropotkin, and adapted to the needs of the property-less wage earner, it denounced all political government, the wage system, the private ownership of property in favor of the communal ownership of the instruments of production and the articles of consumption. It endorsed Direct Action and aimed to prepare the proletariat for the social revolution. For its method of realizing these objectives it had precedent of long standing in American history. As to its economic program it was distinctly "ahead" of the development of the American labor movement. Insofar as the European Anarchist Communists emphasized the return to the village communal method of production, their program was a distinct protest against the existing industrial system. Such a system as they proposed would achieve a free Communism. Anarchist Communism as it was propagated in the United States by Emma Goldman and Alexander Berkman omitted instinctively this positive program because the United States had no such traditional economic unit. The omission is significant. They devoted themselves to "waking up" the American proletariat to its power, its potentialities, its rights. Their words were violent and bombastic as they intended them to be. In preparing for the social revolution they aimed to make American labor self-conscious and cognizant of the value of direct action, and thereby to emancipate the proletariat. The overthrow of the Capitalist system, as we know it today, was their ultimate objective.

They failed to win the united support of labor; it is questionable, however, whether they wished to do more than to spur labor on to assert itself. Their constructive work consisted in helping to cultivate a sentiment against war, in establishing a modern school for workers' children, in disseminating important hygienic information, and in calling the attention of libertarians to the need of defending the Bill of Rights. The deportations of 1919 and 1920 ended one phase of the Anarchist movement in the United States.[64]

[64] Although the Anarchist-communists have been silenced and their movement broken up, certain of their leaders still believe in Anarchism. Emma Goldman in a letter to the writer on November 18, 1931, reaffirmed her faith in these words: "I was never surer and more convinced of the justice and

Anarchism in its most mature form in the United States, has demanded freedom, not for one individual or one group, but for each and every individual.  Within the particular sphere where the Anarchist felt the greatest restraint or even denial of that freedom, he centered his attack.  In the early colonial period it was in religious life, in the latest period in economic life.  Nor was it for pure licentiousness that this condition was demanded. The free and spontaneous inner life of the individual the Anarchists have regarded as the source of greatest pleasure and also of progress itself, or as some would prefer to say, social change. They held that in a society where this freedom was denied the natural processes of change were held in check and that intellectual life became sterile, economic and social life stagnant.  In the earliest period this denial resulted in a corporateness, a group solidarity which was characterized by intolerance for the new and in a refusal to grant the right of asylum to the first critical immigrants who came to the shores of New England; in the later period by standardization and intolerance for the individual and his philosophy which challenged the status quo.

In a sense, therefore, our treatment of the immigrant has been a barometer of this much sought freedom.  With changing economic conditions the significance and seriousness of denying the traditional right of asylum has deepened.  In 1637 the "obstreperous" or maladjusted aliens could be and were retired to the outlying country.  In 1919 they had to be completely ejected.  The earlier banishment and later deportation, therefore, were motivated by similar causes but differed in intensity and extent.  In 1861 Longfellow entertained Bakunin, the "father of terrorism" and found his exploits of the greatest interest and the revolutionary himself "a giant of a man."[65]  In 1919 the individuals who approved and propagated the philosophy of this man were deported. If American labor in 1884 found itself shut up for the first time

logic of anarchism than since the world war and all the horrible things that have followed in its wake . . . Anarchism alone stands out as the only redeemer of humanity, the only promise of a sane and free world."

[65] Samuel Longfellow, *Life of Henry Wadsworth Longfellow with extracts from his Journals and Correspondence* (2 vols., Boston, 1886), II, 371 (recorded in his diary November 27, 1861).

in the wage system, so did the American people find themselves shut up for the first time in a strange social and economic system.

The question is, and the Anarchists from the earliest time have asked this, will the people of the United States allow any authority to destroy that vital principle of Individuality which finds the greatest personal happiness and the highest social good in the free and spontaneous development of a rich *individual* life, both in thought and in action? Viewed in perspective, therefore, the Anarchist movement both native and foreign suggests two things: first, that Democracy has failed to protect the critical minority, and second, that authority institutionalized, whether religious, social, moral, or economic strikes both the one who wields it and the one who suffers from it. These two things point out to us the necessity of constant vigilance for the freedom of the individual.

# BIBLIOGRAPHY

## Introduction

General Works:

Allport, Floyd H.: *The Group Fallacy in Relation to Social Science* (Hanover, New Hampshire, 1927).

Brissenden, Paul F.: *The I. W. W. A Study of American Syndicalism* (Second ed., New York, 1920).

Dewey, John: *Individualism Old and New* (New York, 1930).

Dubois, Félix: *The Anarchist Peril*. Translated by Ralph Derechef (London, 1894).

Eltzbacher, Dr. Paul: *Anarchism*. Translated by Steven T. Byington (New York, 1908).

Fite, Warren: *Individualism. Four Lectures on the Significance of Consciousness for Social Relations* (London, Bombay, and Calcutta, 1911).

Ghio, Paul: *L'Anarchisme aux États-Unis* (Paris, 1903).

Hillquit, Morris: *History of Socialism in the United States* (New York and London, 1906).

Hunter, Robert: *Violence and the Labor Movement* (New York, 1914).

Irwin, Will: *How Red is America* (New York, 1927).

Jászi, Oscar: "Anarchism." *Encyclopoedia of the Social Sciences*. Edited by Edwin R. A. Seligman and Alvin Johnson (New York, 1930-), Vol. II, 46-53.

Jordan, E.: *Forms of Individuality. An Inquiry into the Grounds of Order in Human Relations* (Indianapolis, 1927).

Kropotkin, Peter A.: "Anarchism." *Encyclopoedia Britannica* (New York and London, 1929), Vol. I, 873-878.

Laski, Harold J.: *The Dangers of Obedience and Other Essays* (New York and London, 1930).

Levine, Louis: *The Labor Movement in France: A Study in Revolutionary Syndicalism* (New York, 1912).

Martin, Everett Dean: *The Conflict of the Individual and the Mass in the Modern World* (New York, 1932).

Nettlau, Max: *Der Anarchismus von Proudhon zu Kropotkin. Seine historische Entwicklung in den Jahren 1859-1880* (Berlin, 1927).
*Der Vorfrühling der Anarchie. Ihre historische Entwicklung von den Anfängen bis zum Jahre 1846* (Berlin, 1925).

Russell, Bertrand: *Proposed Roads to Freedom. Socialism, Anarchism, Syndicalism* (London, 1919).

*The Socialism of Our Times. A Symposium*. Vanguard Press (New York, 1929).

Tridon, André: *The New Unionism* (New York, 1913).
Zenker, E. V.: *Anarchism. A Criticism and History of the Anarchist Theory* (New York, 1897).
Zimand, Savel: *Modern Social Movements* (New York, 1921).

## I

Primary Sources:
*Antinomianism in the Colony of Massachusetts Bay 1636-1638, Including the Short History and Other Documents.* Edited by Charles Francis Adams (Boston, 1894).
Barclay, Robert: *An Apology for the True Christian Divinity As the Same as Held Forth and Preached by the People in Scorn, Called Quakers, Being a Full Vindication of Their Principles and Doctrines* (Fourteenth ed., Glasgow, 1886).
Bell, Charles H.: *John Wheelwright. His Writings, Including His Fast-Day Sermon 1637 and His Mercurius Americanus 1645 with a Paper upon the Genuineness of the Indian Deed of 1629 and a Memoir* (Boston, 1876).
Mather, Cotton: *Magnalia Christi Americana, or the Ecclesiastical History of New England, 1620-1698.* Seven Books (First American ed., 2 vols., Hartford, Conn., 1820).
*Penn, William, Select Works of, to which is Prefixed a Journal of His Life* (London, 1771).
Winthrop, John: *The History of New England from 1630 to 1649.* Edited by James Savage (2 vols., Boston, 1825).

Secondary Sources:
Adams, Charles Francis: *Three Episodes of Massachusetts History* (2 vols., Boston and New York, 1893).
Adams, James Truslow: *The Founding of New England* (Boston, 1921).
Bancroft, George: *History of the United States, From the Discovery of the American Continent* (Second ed., Boston, 1838. 10 vols.). Quakers: II, 336-355.
Blankenship, Russell: *American Literature as an Expression of the National Mind* (New York, 1931).
Gooch, G. P. and H. J. Laski: *English Democratic Ideas in the Seventeenth Century* (Second ed., Cambridge, 1927).
Hutchinson, Thomas: *The History of Massachusetts From the First Settlement Thereof in 1628 until the year 1750* (Third ed., 2 vols., Boston, 1795).
Jones, Rufus M.: *The Quakers in the American Colonies* (London, 1911).
Merriam, C. Edward: *A History of American Political Theories* (New York, 1903).
Morison, Samuel Eliot: *Builders of the Bay Colony* (Boston and New York, 1930).

Richman, Irving Berdine: *Rhode Island. Its Making and Its Meaning 1636-1683* (Second ed., New York and London, 1908).

Riley, I. Woodbridge: *American Philosophy. The Early Schools* (New York, 1907).

Sparks, Jared: "The Life of Anne Hutchinson." *The Library of American Biography* (Boston, 1845), Vol. VI.

II

Primary Sources:

Addams, Jane: *Twenty-Five Years at Hull House* (New York, 1912).

*Ballou, Adin, Autobiography of, 1803-1890.* Edited by W. S. Heywood (Lowell, Mass., 1896).

*History of the Hopedale Community, From Its Inception to Its Virtual Submergence in the Hopedale Parish* (Lowell, Mass., 1897).

*Practical Christian Socialism. A Conversational Exposition of the True System of Human Society* (New York, 1854).

*Channing, Works of William Ellery.* New and complete edition, American Unitarian Association (Boston, 1875).

Darrow, Clarence S.: *Resist Not Evil* (Chicago, 1903).

*The Story of My Life* (New York, 1932).

Dodge, David Low: *War Inconsistent with the Religion of Jesus Christ.* Reprinted from 1812 edition (Boston, 1905).

Emerson, Ralph Waldo: *Essays.* First and third series. Everyman edition (London and New York, 1920).

*Journals of Ralph Waldo Emerson.* Edited by Edward W. Emerson and Waldo E. Forbes (10 vols., Boston and New York, 1909-1914).

Goodell, William: *Slavery and Anti-Slavery. A History of the Great Struggle in Both Hemispheres with a View of the Slavery Question in the United States* (Third ed., New York, 1855).

*Noyes, Religious Experiences of John Humphrey.* Compiled and edited by George Wallingford Noyes (New York, 1923).

Periodicals:

*The Arena.*
*The Century.*
*The Independent.*
*The Non-Resistant.* Boston. January 1839-June 29, 1842.
*Outlook.*

Rousseau, Jean-Jacques: *The Social Contract or the Principles of Political Rights* (New York and London, 1893).

Thoreau, *The Writings of Henry David* (20 vols., Boston and New York, 1906).

Tolstoi, Count L. N.: *My Religion*. Translated from the French by Huntingdon Smith (New York, 1885).

Secondary Sources:

Curti, Merle Eugene: *The American Peace Crusade 1815-1860* (Durham, North Carolina, 1929).

"Non-Resistance in New England," *The New England Quarterly*. Vol. II (January, 1929), No. 1, 34-57.

Frothingham, Octavius B.: *Gerrit Smith. A Biography* (Second ed., New York, 1879).

Garrison, W. P. and F. J.: *William Lloyd Garrison 1805-1879. The Story of His Life Told by His Children* (4 vols., New York, 1885).

Nordhoff, Charles: *Communistic Societies of the United States* (New York, 1875).

Noyes, John Humphrey: *History of American Socialisms* (Philadelphia, 1870).

Parrington, Vernon Louis: *An Interpretation of American Literature from the Beginnings to 1920* (New York, 1927-30).

Volume I. *The Colonial Mind. 1625-1800.*

Volume II. *The Romantic Revolution in America. 1800-60.*

Volume III. *The Beginnings of Critical Realism in America. 1860-1920.*

Schinz, Albert: *Vie et Oeuvres de J. J. Rousseau* (Boston, New York, and Chicago, 1921).

Sears, Clara Endicott: *Days of Delusion. A Strange Bit of History* (Boston and New York, 1924).

Seldes, Gilbert: *The Stammering Century* (New York, 1928).

Waterman, William Randall: "Frances Wright." *Columbia University Studies in History, Economics, and Public Law.* Vol. CXV, No. 1 (New York, 1924).

## III

Primary Sources:

Andrews, Stephen Pearl: *The Science of Society.*

No. 1. *The True Constitution of Government in the Sovereignty of the Individual as the Final Development of Protestantism, Democracy, and Socialism.*

No. 2. *Cost the Limit of Price—A Scientific Measure of Honesty in Trade as One of the Fundamental Principles in the Solution of the Social Problem* (Boston, 1888. First ed., 1852).

Ballou, Adin: *History of the Hopedale Community, From Its Inception to Its Virtual Submergence in the Hopedale Parish* (Lowell, Mass., 1897).
*Practical Christian Socialism. A Conversational Exposition of the True System of Human Society* (New York, 1854).

Bool, Henry: "Apology for His Jeffersonian Anarchism" (1901).
"Exposition of Socialism and Collectivism." (?)
"Liberty Luminants." Compilation. (?)
"Liberty Without Invasion, Means, and End of Progress" (1898). *Political Science Pamphlets*, Nos. 5 and 8.

*Brisbane, Albert. A Mental Biography with a Character Study by His Wife Redelia Brisbane* (Boston, 1893).

Conway, Moncure D.: *Autobiography. Memories and Experiences* (2 vols., Boston and New York, 1905).
"Modern Times," *Fortnightly Review*, Vol. I (July 1865), No. 4, 421-434.

Godwin, William: *Enquiry Concerning Political Justice and Its Influence on Morals and Happiness* (Fourth ed., 2 vols., London, 1842).

Greeley, Horace: *Hints Towards Reforms in Lectures, Addresses, and Other Writings* (New York, 1853).

Greene, William Batchelder: *Mutual Banking* (West Brookfield, Mass., 1850).
*Socialistic, Communistic, Mutualistic, and Financial Fragments* (Boston, 1875).

Heywood, Ezra H.: *Uncivil Liberty. An Essay to Show the Injustice and Impolicy of Ruling Woman Without Her Consent* (Princeton, Mass., 1873).

Higginson, Thomas Wentworth: *Cheerful Yesterdays* (Boston and New York, 1898).

Koerner, Gustav, *Memoirs of, 1809-1896, Life Sketches at the Suggestion of his Children.* Edited by Thomas J. McCormack (2 vols., Iowa, 1909).

Labadie, Jo: *Essays* (Detroit, Mich., 1911).

Mill, John Stuart: *On Liberty* (London and New York, 1892).

*Official Report of the Debates and Proceedings in the State Convention Assembled May 4, 1853 To Revise and Amend the Constitution of the Commonwealth of Massachusetts* (Boston, 1853).

Owen, Robert: *A New View of Society* (London, 1818).

Owen, Robert Dale: *Threading My Way. Twenty-Five Years of Autobiography* (London, 1874).

*Paine, The Writings of Thomas.* Collected and edited by Moncure D. Conway (4 vols., New York, 1894-1896).

Pare, William (?): "Trialville and Modern Times." *Chambers' Edinburgh Journal.* Vol. XVIII (December 18, 1852), 395-397.

Periodicals:

*Discontent.* Vol. IV, 17.

*Free Society.* Vol. IX, 2.

*Liberty.* Incomplete file, 1895-1903.

*Lucifer.* Vol. V, 49.

*The Radical Review.* New Bedford, Mass., May 1877-February 1878.

Proudhon, P.-J.: *What is Property. An Inquiry into the Principle of Right and of Government.* Translated by Benjamin R. Tucker (London, 1885).

*Systèm dees Contradictions Économiques ou Philosophe de la Misère* (Third ed., 2 vols., Paris, 1867).

*Proudhon's Solution of the Social Problem.* Commentary and Exposition by Charles A. Dana and William B. Greene. Edited by Henry Cohen (New York, 1927).

Richardson, James D.: *A Compilation of the Messages and Papers of the Presidents.* Vol. VII (11 vols., 1911).

Spooner, Lysander: *A Letter to Thomas F. Bayard Challenging His Right and that of All the Other So-called Senators and Representatives in Congress—To Exercise Any Legislative Power Whatever over the People of the United States* (Boston, 1882).

*A Letter to Grover Cleveland on His False Inaugural Address, the Usurpations and Crimes of Lawmakers and the Consequent Poverty, Ignorance, and Servitude of the People* (Boston, 1886).

*Natural Law or the Science of Justice. A Treatise on Natural Law, Natural Justice, Natural Rights, Natural Liberty, and Natural Society—Showing that all Legislation Whatever is an Absurdity, a Usurpation, and a Crime.* Part first. Unfinished. (Boston, 1882.)

*The Unconstitutionality of Slavery* (Boston, 1845).

Tucker, Benjamin R.: *Instead of a Book. By a Man Too Busy to Write One. A Fragmentary Exposition of Philosophical Anarchism* (New York, 1893).

Warren, Josiah: *Practical Details in Equitable Commerce* (New York, 1852).

*True Civilization. An Immediate Necessity and the Last Ground of Hope for Mankind* (Boston, 1863).

Secondary Sources:

*Appleton's Cyclopoedia of American Biography.* Edited by James G. Wilson and John Fiske (New York, 1894).

Bailie, William: *Josiah Warren. The First American Anarchist* (Boston, 1906).

Baker, Thomas Stockham: *Lenau and Young Germany in America* (Philadelphia, Penn., 1897).

Beard, Charles A.: *Economic Origins of Jeffersonian Democracy* (New York, 1915).

Becker, Carl L.: *The Declaration of Independence* (New York, 1922).

Clark, F. C.: *A Neglected Socialist* (Philadelphia, Penn., 1895).

Codman, John Thomas: *Brook Farm. Historic and Personal Memoirs* (Boston, 1894).

Commons, John R. and Associates: *A Documentary History of Industrial Society* (10 vols., Cleveland, Ohio, 1910). *History of Labour in the United States* (2 vols., New York, 1918).

*Dictionary of American Biography.* Edited by Allen Johnson (New York, 1928-).

Frothingham, Octavius B.: *George Ripley* (Boston, 1888).

Hillquit, Morris: *History of Socialism in the United States* (New York and London, 1906).

Hinds, William Alfred: *American Communities* (Revised ed., Chicago, 1902).

Koerner, Gustav: *Das deutsche Element in den Vereinigten Staaten von Nordamerika 1818-1848* (Cincinnati, Ohio, 1880).

*Lamb's Biographical Dictionary of the United States.* Edited by John H. Brown (Boston, 1900).

Lockwood, George B.: *The New Harmony Movement* (New York, 1905).

Martin, Everett Dean: *Liberty* (New York, 1930).

Merriam, C. Edward: *American Political Ideas* (New York, 1920). *A History of American Political Theories* (New York, 1903).

Osgood, H. L.: "Scientific Anarchism." *Political Science Quarterly.* Vol. IV (1889), No. 1, 1-36.

Stedman, Laura and George M. Gould: *Life and Letters of Edmund Clarence Stedman* (2 vols., New York, 1910).

Swift, Lindsay: *Brook Farm. Its Members, Scholars, and Visitors* (New York, 1908).

Waterman, William Randall: "Frances Wright." *Columbia University Studies in History, Economics, and Public Law.* Vol. CXV, No. 1 (New York, 1924).

Whipple, Leon: *The Story of Civil Liberty in the United States* (New York, 1927).

IV

Primary Sources:

Altgeld, John P.: *Reasons for Pardoning Fielden, Neebe, and Schwab* (Springfield, Ill., 1893).

Anderson, Margaret: *My Thirty Years' War* (New York, 1930).

Bakunin, Michael: *Gesammelte Werke* (3 Bänder, Berlin, 1921).

*God and the State* (New York, no date).

Berkman, Alexander: *The Anti-Climax.* Concluding chapter, published by the author of *The Bolshevik Myth* (Berlin, 1925).

*Now and After. The ABC of Communist Anarchism* (New York, 1929).

*Prison Memoirs of an Anarchist* (New York, 1912).

*Bulletin of the Relief Fund of the International Workingmen's Association for Anarchists and Anarcho-Syndicalists, Imprisoned or Exiled in Russia* (Berlin-Paris, November-December, 1930).

*Cleyre, Voltairine de, Selected Works of* (New York, 1914).

Pamphlets:

*How to End Panics* (1908).

*In the Defense of Emma Goldman and the Right of Expropriation* (Philadelphia, Penn., 1894).

Cohen, Joseph J. and Alexis C. Ferm: *The Modern School of Stelton* (Stelton, New Jersey, 1925).

*Communist and Anarchist Deportation Cases. Hearings before a Subcommittee of the Committee on Immigration and Naturalization. House of Representatives. Sixty-sixth Congress. Second session* (Washington, D. C., 1920).

*Exclusion and Expulsion of Aliens, of Anarchists and Similar Classes. House of Representatives. Sixty-sixth Congress. Second session.* Report No. 504. Committee on Immigration and Naturalization (1920).

Ferm, Elizabeth B.: *The Spirit of Freedom in Education* (Stelton, New Jersey, 1919).

Gary, Joseph E.: "The Chicago Anarchists of 1886. The Crime, the Trial, and the Punishment." *The Century Magazine*, Vol. XXIII (1892-93), 803-837.

Goldman, Emma: *Anarchism and Other Essays.* (Second revised ed., New York, 1911).

*Deportation: Its Meaning and Menace.* Joint authorship with Alexander Berkman (New York, 1919).

"Johann Most," *American Mercury,* Vol. VIII (1926), 158-166.

*Living my Life* (2 vols., New York, 1931).

*My Disillusionment in Russia* (New York, 1923).

*Voltairine de Cleyre.* Unpublished manuscript.

Kropotkin, Peter: *Freedom Pamphlets.* 1920 edition:
"The Wage System."
"The State. Its Historic Rôle."
"Anarchist Communism."
"Law and Authority."
*Memoirs of a Revolutionist* (Boston and New York, 1899),
*Social Economic Papers:*
"The Coming Anarchy."
"The Breakdown of Our Industrial System."
"The Coming Reign of Plenty."
"The Industrial Village of the Future."
"Mutual Aid."
"The Scientific Bases of Anarchy."

Lum, Dyer D.: *A Concise History of the Chicago Anarchists in 1886.* Condensed from official record (No date).

Lusk Investigating Committee Report: *Revolutionary Radicalism: Its History, Purpose, and Tactics* (4 vols., Albany, New York, 1920).

Most, John: *Memoiren, Erlebtes, Erforschtes und Erdachtes* (4 parts, New York, 1903-1907).

Periodicals:
*Der Anarchiste.* Edited by Rudolf Grossman (Vienna, Austria. Nos. 4 and 5, 1927).
*Mother Earth.* March 1906-August 1917. 12 vols.

Post, Louis F.: *The Deportations Delirium of Nineteen-Twenty* (Chicago, 1923).

Powderly, T. V.: *Thirty Years of Labor 1859 to 1889* (Columbus, Ohio, 1890).

Ramus, Pierre (Rudolf Grossman): *Friedenskrieger des Hinterlandes. Der Schicksalsroman eines Anarchistes im Weltkriege* (Mannheim, 1924).

*Steffens, The Autobiography of Lincoln* (New York, 1931).

Turner, John: "The Protest of an Anarchist," *The Independent,* vol. 55 (December 24, 1903), 3052-4.

Whitlock, Brand: *Forty Years of It* (New York and London, 1914).

*War Against War* and *I.A.M.B.* Pamphlets, International, Anti-Militarist Bureau (Hague, Holland, 1925?).

Secondary Sources:
Brissenden, Paul F.: *The I. W. W. A Study of American Syndicalism* (Second ed., New York, 1920).

Browne, Waldo R.: *Altgeld of Illinois* (New York, 1924).

Chafee, Zechariah: *Freedom of Speech* (New York, 1920).

Ely, Richard T.: *The Labor Movement in America* (New York, 1886).

Fine, Nathan: *Labor and Farmer Parties in the United States 1828-1928* (New York, 1928).

Ghio, Paul: "L'Anarchisme Insurrectionnel aux États-Unis." *Journal des Économistes.* Cinquième Serie. Tome LV (Juillet à Septembre, 1903) Paris, 1903.

Hamon, A.: *Psychologie Du Militaire Professionnel* (Paris, 1895).

Hourwich, Isaac A.: *Immigration and Labor* (New York, 1912).

Hunter, Robert: *Violence and the Labor Movement* (New York, 1914).

Longfellow, Samuel: *Life of Henry W. Longfellow* (2 vols., Boston, 1886).

Nettlau, Max: *Errico Malatesta. Das Leben Eines Anarchisten* (Berlin, 1922).

*Élisée Reclus. Anarchist und Gelehrter. 1830-1905* (Berlin, 1928).

Perlman, Selig: *A History of Trade Unionism in the United States* (New York, 1922).

Rocker, Rudolf: *Johann Most. Das Leben Eines Rebellen* (Berlin, 1924).

Schaack, M. J.: *Anarchy and Anarchists* (Chicago, 1889).

# INDEX

## DATE DUE

| | | | |
|---|---|---|---|
| | | | |
| | | | |
| | | | |
| | | | |
| | | | |
| | | | |
| | | | |
| | | | |
| | | | |
| | | | |
| | | | |
| | | | |
| | | | |
| | | | |
| | | | |
| | | | |
| | | | |
| | | | |
| | | | |